The Kingship-Cross Interplay in the Gospel of John

The Kingship-Cross Interplay in the Gospel of John

Jesus' Death as Corroboration of His Royal Messiahship

Mavis M. Leung

With a Foreword by I. Howard Marshall

WIPF & STOCK · Eugene, Oregon

THE KINGSHIP-CROSS INTERPLAY IN THE GOSPEL OF JOHN
Jesus' Death as Corroboration of His Royal Messiahship

Wipf & Stock
An Imprint of Wipf and Stock Publishers
199 W. 8th Ave., Suite 3
Eugene, OR 97401

www.wipfandstock.com

ISBN 13: 978-1-61097-242-0

Manufactured in the U.S.A.

Contents

Foreword

IN A RECENT LECTURE at the meeting of the Institute for Biblical Research held at Atlanta, GA, the British New Testament scholar N. T. (Tom) Wright lamented the way in which scholars tend to separate off Jesus' message and activity with respect to the Kingdom of God from the material regarding his crucifixion in the Gospels and went on to propose that future scholarship must integrate these two themes in a way that does justice to the unified presentation of his life and mission in the Gospels. He was not to know at that time that a treatment of one important aspect of this general topic had already been undertaken by Dr. Mavis Leung in her doctoral work supervised by Professor Donald A. Carson at Trinity International University, Deerfield. She has thus unconsciously anticipated his call for a new direction in scholarship and written a thesis that is at one of what Tom would regard as the cutting edges of Gospel research. The topic is indeed an important one in that in my experience evangelical preaching expounding the message of the Gospels tends to ignore Jesus' central message of the coming of the Kingdom, and liberal preaching conversely tends to ignore the cross, both groups thus leaving us with the uneasy feeling that the two themes cannot be integrated. This kind of approach likewise governs much exposition of the significance of the death of Jesus in the Gospel of John, following the tendency developed by Rudolf Bultmann to see little or no saving efficacy in that event as depicted in this Gospel and to regard Jesus as a revealer rather than as a redeemer.

By contrast Dr. Leung's thesis shows in an impressive way how Jesus is presented in the Gospel of John as the Messiah, and specifically as a Davidic, kingly messiah (rather than as simply a prophetic leader of the people) and how his death is understood in close relationship to his messiahship. She achieves this goal by considering how John uses Old

Testament material concerning the Messiah, and as a result she throws fresh light on a number of Johannine texts, arguing for a greater degree of scriptural allusiveness than has previously been recognised in the Gospel. Here she profits from the methods of study developed by Richard Hays in his work on Paul.

This is thus a significant contribution to Johannine studies both in terms of the methodology employed and of the results achieved by it. At the same time it has another kind of significance. Scholarly biblical research is only just beginning to flourish in Chinese Christianity, and Dr Leung's work is a fine example of this new trend, standing alongside such other contributions as E. Y. L. Ng, *Reconstructing Christian Origins: The Feminist Theology of Elisabeth Schlüsser Fiorenza: An Evaluation* (Carlisle: Paternoster, 2002), D. W. Pao, *Acts and the Isaianic New Exodus* (Tübingen: Mohr Siebeck, 2000), and M. W. Yeung, *Faith in Jesus and Paul* (Tübingen: Mohr Siebeck, 2002). This fresh input into Biblical Studies made by these and a growing number of other scholars is much to be welcomed and encouraged, and those of us who work in Europe and North America can only rejoice that so many scholars who have done their doctoral studies in our geographical areas are now active in research and teaching in Asia and more widely.

I therefore most warmly welcome this book and commend it to students of the Gospels.

I. Howard Marshall
Professor Emeritus of New Testament,
University of Aberdeen, England
and
Adjunct Professor,
Evangel Seminary, Hong Kong

Preface

THIS BOOK IS A revised version of my PhD dissertation that was defended in 2009 at Trinity Evangelical Divinity School, Deerfield, Illinois.

Many people contributed to the completion of this work. I would like to express my gratitude to Dr. D. A. Carson, who patiently directed my research and served as mentor of my dissertation. I have benefited greatly from his incisive insights and rigorous supervision, which made my dissertation far better than it would have been otherwise. It is a privilege to have studied under Dr. Carson. I am also thankful to the other two members of my dissertation committee, Dr. Robert W. Yarbrough and Dr. Willem A. VanGemeren. Dr. Yarbrough served as second reader and Dr. VanGemeren was the director of the doctoral program. I am grateful for their counsel and continuing support during my time at Trinity. I thank Trinity's Faculty of New Testament for being excellent examples of dedicated teachers and providing me with a rewarding learning experience.

I want to express my appreciation to Professor I. Howard Marshall, who gave the manuscript a critical reading, offered helpful comments on each chapter, and contributed a foreword to this book. Thanks are also due to Dr. Maureen W. S. Yeung, President of Evangel Seminary, Hong Kong. She introduced me to Professor Marshall and has been supportive of my work in many ways.

Last but not least, I am very grateful for the patience, care, and love of my husband, Reverend Felix Lam, and our son, Ryan. They have been a constant source of joy and encouragement to me. It is my delight to dedicate this work to them.

Mavis M. Leung
May 2011

Abbreviations

ABD	*The Anchor Bible Dictionary*
APOT	*The Apocrypha and Pseudepigrapha of the Old Testament in English*
BDAG	*A Greek-English Lexicon of the New Testament and Other Early Christian Literature*
BDF	*A Greek Grammar of the New Testament and Other Early Christian Literature*
DJG	*Dictionary of Jesus and the Gospels*
DNTB	*Dictionary of New Testament Background*
LCL	*The Loeb Classical Library*
LXX	Septuagint
MT	Masoretic Text
NA27	*Novum Testamentum Graece*, 27th revised edition
NIDOTTE	*New International Dictionary of Old Testament Theology and Exegesis*
NT	New Testament
OT	Old Testament
OTP	*The Old Testament Pseudepigrapha*
TDNT	*Theological Dictionary of the New Testament*

1

Introduction

R ECENT STUDIES OF THE Christology of John's Gospel have agreed in recognizing the centrality of the concept of messianism, but differ markedly in their interpretation of its character. Alongside the traditional understanding of messiahship in terms of a kingly role related to that of David, there is a newer understanding which is related to the role of Moses and has little or no Davidic background.

Most scholars would agree that there are strong conceptual links between messiahship and the death of Jesus. For example, Köstenberger states: "John's theology of the cross may be particularly designed to illumine for his readers the notion of a crucified Messiah."[1] More sharply Koester says: "The cross was the proper place to proclaim the Messiah's reign."[2] But while there is a broad consensus regarding the Johannine connection between crucifixion and messianism, little attention has been paid to the role of crucifixion in relation to the nature of messiahship and in particular to the possibility that this may shed light on whether or not John's messianism is decisively shaped by the kingly or *royal* background (as is apparently assumed by Koester). It is our contention in this monograph that the cross motif plays a major role in authenticating the *royal* character of messiahship in John over against views that deny or play down this element. An initial pointer in this direction is provided by the way in which the passion narrative gives a prominent place to the kingship of Jesus (John 18:33, 36 [3x], 37 [2x], 39; 19:3, 12, 14, 15 [2x];

1. Köstenberger, *A Theology of John's Gospel and Letters*, 538.
2. Koester, *The Word of Life*, 109.

I

19:19, 21 [2x]). The present study will attempt to take this pointer further and so to fill a notable lacuna in Johannine scholarship.

We propose, therefore, to advance into new territory by examining the intricate interplay between the motifs of Jesus' messianic kingship and death (the kingship-cross interplay) in the Gospel of John against the background of Jewish royal-messianic expectations. The specific interest of this study will lie in the significance and apologetic function of the cross as a corroboration of the Johannine assertion that the crucified Jesus is Israel's Messiah-King. While much research has been conducted to investigate the Johannine conceptualization of Jesus' kingship or death, discussion of the kingship-cross connection is often limited to the materials in the trial and crucifixion accounts. Outside the passion narrative, the complex interplay of Jesus' messianic kingship and death has very rarely been the object of systematic analysis.

The working definition of the "Messiah" adopted in our study is along the lines of the basic ideas posited by Andrew Chester and shared by John Collins, Adela Yarbro Collins, Gerbern Oegema, and some other scholars: "A messiah is a figure who acts as the agent of the final divine deliverance, whether or not he is specifically designated as 'messiah' or 'anointed.'"[3] This study does not follow the view that a text must contain the term משח or χριστός to be designated messianic.[4] According to the definition above, the term "messianism" in a broad sense refers to the complex of ideas, concepts, and beliefs with respect to the Jewish hopes for the Messiah.[5] The term "royal messianism" denotes that particular aspect of messianism that revolves around the expectation for a figure with a kingly role. In this monograph, we will use the term "royal" and "kingly" as synonyms.

Despite the provocative proposal of Ernst Käsemann to dismiss the Johannine passion narrative as a superfluous addendum lacking an organic connection with the Gospel story,[6] there is a growing scholarly consensus that the crucifixion account not only fits in the storyline but

---

3. Chester, *Messiah and Exaltation*, 201; Collins and Collins, *King and Messiah as Son of God*, 2; Longman, "The Messiah," 14; Oegema, *The Anointed and His People*, 26–27.

4. E.g., Fitzmyer, *The One Who Is to Come*; Charlesworth, "From Messianology to Christology," 3–35; Jonge, "Messiah," in *ABD* 4:777–88.

5. This study makes a distinction between "messianism" and "eschatology," as Jewish beliefs that express Israel's end-time hopes do not necessarily pertain to a specific expectation concerning the Messiah.

6. Käsemann, *The Testament of Jesus according to John 17*, 7.

also represents the climax of the plot. "The Passion Narrative," as Senior aptly puts it, "stands as the culmination of major themes of the Gospel."[7] Frey is correct when he comments that the scene of Jesus' crucifixion (esp. John 19:28–30) marks "der innere Zielpunkt der johanneischen Jesuerzählung."[8] In view of the passion narrative's pivotal importance in the Johannine story of Jesus, its notion of Jesus' death as the Messiah-King is doubtless one of the theological foci of John's Gospel. Outside the passion narrative, we shall demonstrate that subtle royal connotations are present in various places of the Gospel story and are bound up with the cross motif within their immediate context. In fact, these subtle royal connotations combine with the passion narrative's explicit presentation of the crucified Jesus to provide a holistic portrait of the Messiah-King's death in John's Gospel as a whole.

Given the numerous publications on the Johannine passion account, textual analysis in the following chapters will focus on the kingship-cross interactions (both explicit and implicit) in the narrative prior to this account. We will endeavor to collate and incorporate these interactions together into an integral conception of the crucified Messiah-King. In the course of our discussions, we will examine how the Johannine kingship-cross interactions evoke and resonate with the biblical and extra-biblical Jewish traditions in order to reinterpret the traditional entailments of royal messianism and to demonstrate the royal messiahship of Jesus accordingly.[9] It is expected that this study will help us gain a better understanding of not only the entailments of his royal messiahship and death but also the paradoxical relationship of these two notions in Johannine thinking.

7. Senior, *The Passion of Jesus in the Gospel of John*, 144.

8. Frey, "Edler Tod–wirksamer Tod–stellvertrender Tod–heilschaffender Tod," 66.

9. Although our interest lies mainly in the relationship and interplay of the cross motif with the kingship theme, the notion of Jesus' resurrection will be addressed alongside the notion of Jesus' death when necessary in order to analyze fully the selected Johannine passages (e.g., John 2:19–22). Scholars in general concur that crucifixion and resurrection in John's Gospel have collapsed into a unified event in which the cross takes on the notions of exaltation and glorification that other early Christian traditions give to resurrection (e.g., Phil 2:1–11). As Nielsen notes, "we can say that Good Friday and Easter fall together in John, and that this is reflected in the passages on Jesus' death. But there is nevertheless both a Good Friday and an Easter Day." See Nielsen, "John's Understanding of the Death of Jesus," 254. For Jesus' resurrection in Johannine thought, see Koester and Bieringer, *The Resurrection of Jesus in the Gospel of John*; Hays, *The Art of Reading Scripture*, 216–38 (esp. 221–24); Lincoln, "'I am the Resurrection and the Life,'" 122–44.

Survey of Previous Studies

This section will provide a survey of previous works on the topics of Jesus' kingship and death in the Gospel of John. The primary aim of this survey is to underline the main issues raised in previous treatments of these two topics. We will first discuss studies that deal with the kingship theme, focusing on those that tend to downplay this theme's connection with Jesus' messiahship. Next we will look at studies that attempt to explicate the Johannine construal of Jesus' death.

The Kingship of Jesus as Lacking (Davidic) Messianism

Research centering specifically on Jesus' messianic kingship in the Fourth Gospel is scant. One of the reasons for the meager amount of literature is the dearth of explicit Davidic references in this Gospel, in which David is mentioned by name only twice in one verse (John 7:42). Even in this verse, nothing intimates the Johannine interest in claiming Jesus' Davidic descent. John Ashton says that the lack of the title "Son of David" in the Gospel is one of the "two negative facts" that caution the interpreter not to presume "king of Israel" (John 1:49; 12:13) as a messianic epithet.[10] Several scholars even opine that the parameters of John's royal Christology are virtually non-Davidic or even anti-Davidic in nature. Furthermore, these scholars often not only relegate the Davidic notion to an inconsequential role in the Johannine portrait of Jesus but they also tend to play down the importance of the royal-messianic facet of this portrait.

Christoph Burger explores the tradition-historical background and the development of Jesus' Davidic messianic status in early Christianity. In his chapter on John's Gospel, Burger claims that its silence on Jesus' Davidic pedigree and his birth in Bethlehem raises doubts about the evangelist's commitment to the belief of Jesus' association with this great king of Israel.[11] However, the scope of analysis in this chapter is rather narrow. Burger devotes exclusive attention to the single pericope John 7:40–44, which recounts the Jewish controversy over the Messiah's origin. It is Burger's opinion that this pericope serves a polemical purpose by implicitly censuring or even rejecting an inadequate Christology in John's time, which exalted Jesus' Davidic ties. For Burger, so minimal is David's role in Johannine Christology that "im ganzen 4. Evangelium gilt Jesus

---

10. Ashton, *Understanding the Fourth Gospel*, 262.

11. Burger, *Jesus als Davidssohn*, 153–58.

nicht als Davidide."[12] While Burger's study remains a valuable resource for understanding the subject of Jesus' Davidic identity in the NT documents, his treatment of John's Gospel addresses only the text John 7:40–44 and gives no attention to other relevant passages that evoke the Davidic tradition in the OT. These passages include the shepherd discourse in John 10:1–21 and the references to several Davidic psalms in the passion account (e.g., Ps 22:18 [21:19 LXX] in John 19:24; Ps 69:21 [68:22 LXX] in John 19:28; Ps 34:20 [33:21 LXX] in John 19:36). In short, Burger's analysis of the Johannine view of Jesus' Davidic status is very limited.

Wayne Meeks argues, on the basis of the thematic link between "prophet" and "king" in John 6:14–15, that "the two terms 'prophet' and 'king' in the Fourth Gospel not only are interrelated, but interpret each other."[13] Meeks emphasizes that Moses, not David, provides the best biblical precedent of the Johannine combination of kingly and prophetic qualities in one individual. In Meeks's view, a neglect of titular nuances among "king," "Messiah" and "Son of David" has led some scholars to mistakenly assume that these titles are interchangeable. Moreover, he notes that little evidence in the Gospel suggests that Davidic status is of any importance to its messianic portrait of Jesus. In Meeks's words, "the only occurrence of the Son of David notion in John is in a polemic which denies Jesus' Davidic legitimation."[14] According to Meeks, the Johannine allusions to the Jewish tradition of the prophet like Moses (Deut 18:15) in the shepherd discourse and in the court scene indicate clearly that "the function of the king is absorbed almost completely into the mission of the prophet."[15]

In agreement with Meeks's contention, John Lierman has recently written an essay to argue for a Mosaic interpretation of Johannine Christology.[16] Lierman's essay levels criticism against Richard Bauckham's assertion that John conceives of Jesus as the "Davidic royal Messiah," an assertion made by Bauckham in an article included with Lierman's essay in the same book. On account of the titular distinction between

---

12. Ibid., 158.

13. Meeks, *The Prophet-King*, 1.

14. Ibid., 21.

15. Ibid., 67.

16. Lierman, "The Mosaic Pattern of John's Christology," 210–34.

"prophet" and "Messiah" in John 1:20–21 and 7:40–41, Bauckham insists on a clear border between the notions of "prophet" and "king" in John 6:15.[17] Bauckham builds up further arguments for a strong Davidic flavor in John's messianic portrayal of Jesus. From Lierman's perspective, Bauckham's treatment is fundamentally flawed because it assumes the unproven thesis that the Messiah was most likely a Davidic royal figure in first-century CE Judaism. By contrast to Bauckham's view, Lierman declares that "nothing in the Fourth Gospel itself indicates that John had the slightest interest in advancing a Davidic appraisal of Messiah Jesus."[18] Instead of David, Moses is the figure standing "at the center of the total Christological portrait laid out by John."[19]

Andrew Brunson, in his intertextual investigation on John's use of Psalm 118, contends that the kingship of Jesus is identified with the kingship of Yahweh within the Johannine new exodus framework.[20] In Brunson's view, the royal acclamation at Jesus' entrance into Jerusalem does not serve to highlight his status as the Davidic Messiah (John 12:12–15). Rather, the title "king of Israel" in this passage invokes Israel's new exodus hope for Yahweh's eschatological coming to save his people. Holding fast to the belief that "the New Exodus agenda must be carried out by Yahweh," Brunson asserts that "Jesus is identified both ontologically and functionally with the Father."[21] Moreover, he claims that although "the stated intent of the Gospel is that people might believe that Jesus is the Christ (John 20:31)," the evangelist lays "relatively little emphasis on the fulfillment of 'messianic' expectations."[22]

In response to the scholarly works summarized above, it is true that the kingship of Jesus in John's Gospel entails prophetic and divine notions. The presence of these notions is evident in particular in the king's task of testifying to the truth (John 18:37) and the high Christology of this Gospel. It is unlikely, however, that a literary work whose stated aim is demonstration of Jesus' messiahship (John 20:30–31) would have perceived and portrayed his kingship as lacking strong messianic overtones.

17. Bauckham, "Messianism according to the Gospel of John," 34–68.

18. Lierman, "The Mosaic Pattern of John's Christology," 233.

19. Ibid., 234.

20. Brunson, *Psalm 118 in the Gospel of John*, esp. 223–34.

21. Ibid., 388.

22. Ibid., 387.

As Köstenberger rightly notes, "John's narrative focuses on Jesus and his messianic mission."[23] Meeks and Lierman are right in calling attention to the importance of the Mosaic tradition in the Johannine articulation of Christology. Yet it is dubious that this tradition is so important that Moses is *the* model of this articulation. It is noteworthy that the term "prophet" is missing from the Johannine passion narrative, where a redefinition of kingship is evidently underway.[24] After a thorough analysis of Jesus' prophetic status, Cho concludes that "Jesus' kingship is not radically redefined in terms of the mission of the prophet."[25] As regards Brunson's work, his statement that John pays little attention to "the fulfillment of messianic expectations" merits criticism because this statement implies that the evangelist has failed to do what he claimed and aimed to do (cf. John 20:31). It also seems that Brunson has incorrectly toned down Jesus' messianic status as the Father's agent in order to underline "the complete identification of Jesus with Yahweh."[26]

For the present purpose it is crucial to observe that these scholarly treatments share in common a tendency (albeit in various degrees) of divorcing Jesus' kingship from his messiahship. This tendency has the corollary of marginalizing the place of Jesus' messianic status in the construction of John's royal Christology. Our approach will diverge from these treatments in that it will argue that the notions of Jesus' kingship and messiahship are woven tightly together in the Christology of the Fourth Gospel. In support of this approach, we will show that John is concerned to present the identity of Jesus as the royal Messiah. The question of whether the evangelist really portrays Jesus as a royal-messianic figure is tied to the broader subjects regarding the compositional purpose of the Gospel, its treatment of individual royal or messianic ideas, and the interrelations of these ideas in Johannine theology. To a certain degree this question also hinges on the character of Jewish messianism during the late Second Temple period. To put the matter negatively: if the messianic

---

23. Köstenberger, *John*, 13.

24. Jonge, *Jesus*, 51–52; Appold, *The Oneness Motif in the Fourth Gospel*, 74–78.

25. Cho, *Jesus as Prophet in the Fourth Gospel*, 266.

26. Brunson, *Psalm 118 in the Gospel of John*, 388. While Appold asserts that the "king of Israel" title is subordinate to John's Christology of oneness, he rightly comments that "although the Father and Son are one, John never speaks of the relation in terms of mergence" (Appold, *The Oneness Motif*, 282). For Appold's view of Jesus' kingship, see pp. 74–78.

hopes were negligible within the milieu of first-century CE Judaism, and if the particular hope for a royal Messiah was inconsequential within the diverse Jewish messianic phenomena, it would be less likely that John is interested in the royal-messianic status of Jesus. For the purpose of laying the research foundation, chapter two will establish the conceptual linkage between Jesus' kingship and messiahship within the Christological scheme of John's Gospel.

The Death of Jesus without Special Reference to Jewish Eschatology

This survey of the state of scholarship begins with the works of Bultmann and Käsemann, whose views on the role and meaning of Jesus' death in Johannine theology have largely set the tone for subsequent research on the subject matter. Bultmann considers "the Word became flesh" (John 1:14a) in the prologue as the statement that steers the theological orientation of the entire Gospel of John. In Bultmann's words, "John has subsumed the death of Jesus under his idea of Revelation"[27] and the cross "has no preeminent importance for salvation."[28] Unlike Bultmann's view that the Revealer's incarnation is central to Johannine theology, Käsemann finds in the announcement "We beheld his glory" (John 1:14c) the defining motif that has shaped the Gospel's theological outlook.[29] Departure to the heavenly abode is, for Käsemann, the principal thrust of the death of Jesus in John's Gospel.[30] Moreover, Käsemann regards the death of Jesus as so incongruous with John's theology of glory that the passion narrative is a "mere postscript" of his Gospel.[31] This allegation must be challenged because it implies that the snapshot of Jesus' death as the Messiah-King in the passion account lacks an organic unity—thematically and theologically—with other formulations of the motif of Jesus' death (or his kingship) elsewhere in the Gospel. As will be seen, our research on the subtle kingship-cross interactions outside the passion narrative affirms its integral connection with the rest of the Johannine story and thus undermines this problematic allegation of Käsemann.

27. Bultmann, *Theology of the New Testament*, 2:53.

28. Ibid., 2:52; cf. 2:53–55.

29. Käsemann, *The Testament of Jesus*, 6.

30. Ibid., 17–18.

31. Ibid., 7.

A number of scholars have reacted, consciously or unconsciously, to Bultmann's and Käsemann's challenging proposals which assign the cross to a peripheral place on the fringes of Johannine theology. Most scholars place greater weight on Jesus' death than do Bultmann and Käsemann. Nevertheless, some interpreters have taken stances essentially consistent with that of Bultmann/Käsemann in that they uphold the notion of revelation/departure as central to John's construction of the cross. J. Terence Forestell argues that "the properly Johannine theology of salvation does not consider the death of Jesus to be a vicarious and expiatory sacrifice for sin," but rather it conceives of salvation as revelation.[32] Ignace de la Potterie praises Bultmann for his observation that "Jesus the Revealer" is the thematic synopsis of the Gospel of John.[33] For la Potterie, "[t]he cross is regarded not so much as the sacrifice of Jesus, but rather as a revelation, even as the high point of the revelation of Christ."[34] John Painter claims that the sacrificial notion is wanting in the Johannine articulation of the cross, which is constructed as "an act of revelation through which the love of God for the world is revealed in such a way as to draw all people."[35]

In line with Käsemann's understanding, Ulrich Müller, Mark Appold, and Godfrey Nicholson assert that the thrust of John's presentation of Jesus' death is departure. According to Müller, the crucifixion primarily denotes the Son's return to the Father and the endpoint of his mission on earth.[36] However, moving away from Käsemann, Müller believes that the cross is not insignificant in Johannine thinking because it is the "Durchgang" via which the Son receives glorification.[37] Appold follows in the footsteps of his teacher Käsemann and approaches the cross from the vantage point of John's Christology of oneness. In Appold's view, the evangelist's treatment of the death of Jesus "reflects throughout the victorious action of a sovereign Jesus who returns to the heavenly world of glory from which he had come."[38] For Nicholson, "the dominant Christology

---

32. Forestell, *The Word of the Cross*, 2. The influence of Forestell's view can be seen in a recent article written by Scrutton. "'The Truth Will Set You Free,'" 36.

33. La Potterie, *The Hour of Jesus*, 53.

34. Ibid., 54.

35. Painter, "Sacrifice and Atonement in the Gospel of John," 311.

36. Müller, "Zur Eigentümlichkeit des Johannesevangeliums," 24–55; idem, "Der Bedeutung des Kreuzestodes Jesu im Johannesevangelium," 49–71.

37. Müller, "Der Bedeutung des Kreuzestodes Jesu," 68.

38. Appold, *The Oneness Motif in the Fourth Gospel*, 136.

of the Gospel is framed in terms of descent and ascent, and . . . the death of Jesus takes its place within the movement of Jesus back to the Father."[39] The crucifixion is not articulated in terms of "an ignominious death but a return to glory."[40]

One of the controversial issues raised by Käsemann that has attracted much attention is whether one can justifiably speak of a theology of the cross in Johannine thinking.[41] Müller supports Käsemann's view which sees Johannine theology as one that is a thorough *theologia gloriae*. From Müller's perspective, scholars' attempts to derive a theology of the cross from John's Gospel are unwarranted and anachronistic because the term *theologia crucis* is not present in this Gospel but was coined by Martin Luther, the harbinger of the Reformation.[42] On the affirmative side of the debate stand Marianne Thompson, Pierre Bühler, Thomas Knöppler, and Jörg Frey, to name a few representatives. From Thompson's point of view, observable traits of Jesus' humanity are present in the Johannine treatment of Jesus' death. Although John's articulation of the cross may not be characterized in terms of the paradox "glorification in humiliation," it can justifiably be denoted in terms of "glorification in death."[43] While addressing the glory motif linked to Jesus' death, Bühler propounds a view that sees "theologia crucis als theologia gloriae per crucem."[44] Knöppler attempts to assemble all the explicit and implicit denotations regarding the cross into a coherent perspective.[45] In his judgment, "die theologia crucis ein wesentliches Moment der Theologie des vierten Evangeliums ist."[46] Frey criticizes the sharp antithesis posed by Käsemann between *theologia crucis* and *theologia gloriae* as being a false alternative. For Frey, persistent significance of the signs of crucifixion in the Thomas episode (John 20:24–29) reveals that the Johannine focus of the cross centers upon "der Gekreuzigte," who is the locus of God's eschatological revelation.[47] In

---

39. Nicholson, *Death as Departure*, 164.

40. Ibid., 163.

41. Käsemann, *The Testament of Jesus*, 51–52.

42. Müller, "Die Bedeutung des Kreuzestodes Jesu," 50–51, 68–71 (esp. 69).

43. Thompson, *The Humanity of Jesus in the Fourth Gospel*, 112.

44. Bühler, "Ist Johannes ein Kreuzestheologie?" 207.

45. Knöppler, *Die theologia crucis des Johannesevangeliums*.

46. Ibid., 277.

47. Frey, "Die ‚theologia crucifixi' des Johannesevangeliums," 169–238. Frey says that "insofern läßt sich die johanneische Verkündigung zu Recht als theologia crucifixi beschreiben" (p. 235).

a more recent analysis of Jesus' death under four headings ("edler Tod," "wirksamer Tod," "stellvertretender Tod," and "heilschaffender Tod"), Frey further asserts that overtones of vicarious sacrifice are operative in the Johannine construction of Jesus' death.[48]

Lastly, there are some other works that devote specific attention to sundry features—source-critical, redaction-critical, literary, historical, or theological—of Jesus' death or the passion narrative in the Gospel of John.[49] However, this survey will not look at these works because they are not directly relevant to the goal of our investigation. The subsequent scrutiny of the selected Gospel passages will touch upon them as necessary. In short, recent scholarship has generally moved away from Bultmann and Käsemann in affirming that the Johannine construal of the cross entails a salvific significance—albeit with different interpretations. *Pace* Käsemann, scholars on virtually all sides of the debate agree that Jesus' death is an essential part of his vocation on earth; in fact, it is the zenith of his saving mission. As far as our purpose is concerned, it must be noted that many studies on the cross in the post-Bultmann-Käsemann era do not center on the Jewish background of Jesus' death. This phenomenon is partly due to the fact that many interpreters have written (consciously or unconsciously) in reaction to the allegations and challenges posited by Bultmann and Käsemann. While scholars broadly agree on the prominence of the kingship theme in the passion account, they have not adequately related the royal-messianic depiction of the crucified Jesus to the cross motif seen elsewhere in the Fourth Gospel. It is hoped that our investigation on the kingship-cross interplay outside the passion narrative will contribute to the subject matter by helping to fill this lacuna.

The Death of Jesus with Special Reference to Jewish Eschatology

Several recent studies explore the significance of Jesus' death against the background of Jewish eschatological beliefs. To varying degrees, these studies bear on the subject of our investigation. The ensuing paragraphs

48. Idem, "Edler Tod–Wirksamer Tod–Stellvertrender Tod–Heilschaffender Tod," 65–94.

49. Some of the studies are Dauer, *Die Passionsgeschichte im Johannesevangelium*; Moo, *The Old Testament in the Gospel Passion Narratives*; Green, *The Death of Jesus*; Brown, *The Death of the Messiah: From Gethsemane to the Grave*; Heil, *Blood and Water*; Lang, *Johannes und die Synoptiker*; Weidemann, *Der Tod Jesu im Johannesevangelium*; Zumstein, "L'interprétation de la mort de Jésus dans les discours d'adieu," 95–119.

will briefly discuss these works and point out this investigation's uniqueness compared to them.

In an analysis of the cosmic battle motif in three passages (John 12:20–36; 14:30–31; 16:8–11), Judith Kovacs endeavors to demonstrate that "the Fourth Evangelist sees the death, resurrection and ascent of Jesus as the turning point between God and the forces of evil."[50] Kovacs notes that the themes of "casting out," "judgment," and "the ruler of the world" in these passages create resonances with the eschatological visions in a number of apocalyptic texts, which envisage Satan's defeat by God at the end of time (e.g., *1 En.* 10:9; *4 Ezra* 13:2–11; *T. Mos.* 10:1, 7; 1QM 1:15–19).[51] She argues that John's portrait of Jesus as the Son of Man draws directly on the cosmic-combat myths in the apocalyptic tradition. In particular, an important source of the idea of "the crucifixion as a victorious enthronement" is the apocalyptic portrayal of the Son of Man as a royal, glorified, and messianic figure on a "throne of glory" in the *Similitudes* (e.g., *1 En.* 45:3; 51:3; 55:4; 62:2–7; 69:29).[52]

Building on the results of Kovacs's work, John Dennis examines the Johannine articulation of Jesus' death as bringing about the defeat of the devil in John 12:31–32.[53] His examination in particular deals with (1) the association between Satan and sin in the Fourth Gospel and Second Temple Judaism, as well as (2) the role of Isaiah's Servant in the "lifting up" of the Son of Man (John 12:23–32). An earlier publication of Dennis also deserves mention. Dennis finds three motifs in the pericope John 11:47–52—the gathering of the dispersed, the unification of God's people, and the restoration of the "place"—that he believes take root in and reflect Jewish hopes for the eschatological restoration.[54] In Dennis's judgment, this pericope "functions as a crucial peak in the story of Jesus' restoration ministry to Israel."[55] Starting with these motifs, he explores the Johannine appropriation of Jewish restoration theology with particu-

---

50. Kovacs, "'Now Shall the Ruler of This World Be Driven Out,'" 231.

51. Kovacs examines four thematic parallels between the Gospel of John and the Jewish apocalyptic texts: cosmic combat, victory and judgment, the Son of Man and glorification.

52. Ibid., 244–45.

53. Dennis, "The 'Lifting Up of the Son of Man' and the Dethroning of the 'Ruler of This World,'" 677–91.

54. Idem, *Jesus' Death and the Gathering of True Israel.*

55. Ibid., 3.

lar attention to God's end-time installation of his people. According to Dennis, restoration motifs in the Gospel of John (e.g., John 1:14; 2:14–22; 4:4–26; 6:1–71; 7:37–38; 8:31–47; 10:1–42; 12:23–24, 31–32; 9:1—11:57) serve to invoke Israel's historic plight of foreign domination and the nation's hopes for divine reinstatement. Dennis concludes his analysis by affirming that the Gospel's formulation of the "effects" of the cross has a social function, which seeks to legitimize the Johannine community's self-perceived identity as the true Israel.[56] One obvious weakness of Dennis's research on the significance of the cross is that it pays little attention to the portrayal of Jesus' death in the passion narrative, in which he is overtly proclaimed Messiah-King of Israel. Despite this, Dennis's observation concerning the apologetic function of the "effects" of Jesus' death is worth underlining and our analysis in subsequent chapters will glean insight from this observation. However, we will take an approach which diverges methodologically from Dennis's work. Instead of focusing on the cross's ecclesiological function within the broad restoration scheme, we will concentrate specifically on the christological matrix of the Messiah-King's death. As Lindars correctly emphasizes, John's "interest in the passion is primarily christological." [57]

Brant Pitre's research analyzes the significance of Jesus' death in the Gospels with special attention to the motifs of the tribulation and the end of the exile.[58] Gleaning insights from Albert Schweitzer's proposal that underlines the connection between atonement and messianic tribulation, Pitre attempts to demonstrate that "Jesus did in fact speak and act on the basis of the Jewish expectation of the eschatological tribulation."[59] According to Pitre, Jesus believed that his death as the Messiah was a part of this tribulation, and that it would atone for Israel's sins leading to the end of her exile, the gathering of the scattered tribes, and the coming of God's kingdom. Pitre's treatment of the materials in Jewish writings and Mark's narrative is in-depth and comprehensive, yet he pays very little attention to relevant Johannine texts in spite of his acknowledgment that the Fourth Gospel is a useful source for understanding how Jesus would

---

56. See the chapter "The Social Function of John 11.47–52" in Dennis's monograph (esp. ibid., 324–31).

57. Lindars, "The Passion in the Fourth Gospel," 74.

58. Pitre, *Jesus, the Tribulation, and the End of the Exile*.

59. Ibid., 4.

have perceived his death.[60] Nevertheless, Pitre's research regarding the link between Jesus' death and Jewish restoration hopes will be useful to our investigation, although his view that forgiveness of sins is tantamount to end of exile seems to be too narrow. Also, diverging from Pitre's unilateral emphasis on the continuity of Jesus' teaching with first-century CE Judaism,[61] we will give due notice to pertinent elements of discontinuity in the Gospel of John that would show the evangelist's reinterpretation and transformation of Jewish royal-messianic traditions.

In conclusion, while a few scholars have investigated the death of Jesus against the background of Jewish eschatology, none of them concentrate on the particular background of the eschatological hope for the royal Messiah. The present study is distinct from existing scholarly works in that it seeks to relate Jesus' death adequately and specifically to the Johannine assertion that the crucified Jesus is Israel's Messiah-King. Further, previous research that touches upon the kingship-cross link has interacted largely with the texts in the trial and crucifixion scenes. We will expand the scope of inquiry by examining selected passages that contain this link (explicit and implicit) prior to the passion narrative.

Method and Approach

We will attempt to accomplish our objective by using an eclectic method that integrates literary, intertextual, and socio-historical approaches. On the one hand, we will conduct an intensive analysis of the thematic dynamics and interplay between Jesus' messianic kingship and death within the narrative context of John's Gospel. On the other hand, we will undertake a detailed examination of how John's royal depiction of the crucified Jesus resonates with pertinent texts and motifs in the Jewish royal-messianic traditions. By combining these two approaches, we will seek to incorporate the explicit and implicit kingship-cross connections in the Gospel into a holistic portrait of the Messiah-King's death, as well as to explicate clearly the tradition-historical background of this portrait. Some specific aspects of this approach must now be clarified.

One of the assumptions of our study is that the Gospel of John in its present form is a unified piece of literature.[62] While form, source, and re-

---

60. Ibid., 23–24.

61. Cf. Dennis, review of *Jesus, the Tribulation, and the End of Exile*.

62. As the literary theorist Northrop Frye says, "The primary understanding of any work of literature has to be based on an assumption of its unity. However mistaken such

daction criticisms have offered valuable insights into the Gospel's formative period before it assumed its final literary shape, a downside of these critical methods is that they tend to fracture the document into separate and distinct pieces without analyzing the text in its own right.[63] Critical for our analysis is that whatever sources, traditions, and layers of redactions may be buried underneath this Gospel, the narrative as recounted in it must be read as a unified whole in order to attain a logical comprehension of the Johannine perspective on a crucified Messiah-King. Thus, discussions in the subsequent chapters will center on the Johannine narrative as it now stands, not on the sources or possible stages of composition that reside in the world behind the extant text.

Affirmation of the Fourth Gospel's holistic character has implications for how we will handle Synoptic parallels of some of the selected Johannine passages (e.g., the temple account in John 2 and the passion narrative in John 18–19). Scholars have debated for a long time whether the Johannine story of Jesus is influenced—directly or indirectly—by materials from one or more of the Synoptic Gospels, and the debate is far from resolved regarding the Johannine-Synoptics relation.[64] Without denying the possibility of John's knowledge of the other three canonical Gospels or their traditions, we will take as a working hypothesis that his presentation of Jesus neither depends literarily on the Synoptics nor requires the aid of another literature to render its message comprehensible.[65] Therefore, mention of Synoptic passages in subsequent chapters will serve only to highlight distinctive features of the Johannine accounts, with no intention to investigate into matters pertaining to the evangelist's possible use and modification of Synoptic materials.

---

an assumption may eventually prove be, nothing can be done unless we start with it as a heuristic principle." This citation is taken from Rabinowitz, *Before Reading*, 147. Some important studies on the literary character of John's Gospel are Wead, *The Literary Devices of John's Gospel*; Culpepper, *Anatomy of the Fourth Gospel*; Stibbe, *The Gospel of John as Literature*; Culpepper and Black, *Exploring the Gospel of John*, 193–254; Nissen and Pedersen, *New Readings in John*.

63. For instance, see the treatments of Johannine passages in Bultmann, *The Gospel of John*; Fortna, *The Gospel of Signs*; idem, *The Fourth Gospel and Its Predecessor*.

64. For the Johannine-Synoptics relation, see Kysar, *Voyages with John*, 53–75; Smith, *John Among the Gospels*; Denaux, *John and the Synoptics*.

65. See the chapter "John, an Independent Gospel" in Smith, *John Among the Gospels*, 195–241.

On the basis of the literary unity of John's Gospel, our investigation will proceed on the assumption that the presentation of Jesus' death within this Gospel is thematically and conceptually coherent. We will demonstrate that sundry notions and expressions of the cross in the Johannine story cohere integrally and function synergistically within the Gospel's theological framework in order to identify the crucified Jesus as the expected royal Messiah. As will be seen, a number of references to the cross outside the passion account are laden with royal overtones. This account's explicit depiction of Jesus' death as the Messiah-King will help bring to light implicit kingly connotations that are bound up with the cross in other parts of the Gospel. Seen through the lens of the passion account, these kingship-cross interactions that are subtly at work will come into sharper focus. In fact, each of these kingship-cross interactions that occur before the passion account can be shown to play a part in constructing the Johannine picture of a crucified Messiah-King.

Another important issue that requires comment is the genre of John's Gospel.[66] In a thorough comparison of its generic features with ancient biographies, Richard Burridge has shown that the genre of the Johannine story of Jesus can be classified under the broad category of ancient Greco-Roman *bios*. Reading this story as a biography has three bearings on the interpretive orientation of this study.[67] First, since the focal point of an ancient *bios* centers upon a figure, it is reasonable to assume that the christological thrust is central to John's presentation of Jesus' death.[68] Second, on account of a literary convention in antiquity that the scene of the protagonist's death often represents the climax of a biography,[69] and given the kingship theme's prominence in the passion account, it is justified to explore possible royal connotations present in the cross motif outside this account. Third, if "the purpose of the author is essential to any concept of genre as a set of expectations or contract

66. For the importance of genre for interpreting literature, see Osborne, *The Hermeneutical Spiral*, 26, 181; cf. Rabinowitz, "What Readers Do When They Read/What Authors Do When They Write," 48–72.

67. Burridge, *What Are the Gospels?*

68. As Burridge says, "biography is a genre written by a person about a person for other people. Therefore the hermeneutical key for understanding the gospel as biography is not to be found in presumed problems in hypothetical communities, settings or textual relationships, but rather in their Christology" (ibid., 289).

69. Ibid., 160–63, 174–75.

between the author and the reader or audience,"[70] it is legitimate to ask about the intention of the evangelist who "encoded" his perception of Jesus specifically in the genre of *bios*. This leads our discussion to the controversial subject of authorial intention.

The literary theorists, Tom Kindt and Hans-Harald Müller, announced in 2006 an "obvious renaissance that intentionalistic approach to interpretation has now been experiencing for ten years or so."[71] Despite this, "new currents" through the Gospel of John have not yet witnessed such a renaissance, with the hermeneutical spotlight still being cast primarily on "readers and readings."[72] Without denying the interpretive insights offered by the reader-oriented approach, we will attempt an intentionalistic reading of this Gospel by utilizing the concept of "implied author" that is understood in the following ways. (1) The implied author "stands for images that authors produce of themselves in their works"[73] or for a "conscious representation of the real author."[74] (2) Unlike a form of narrative criticism that holds that "the implied author's point of view can be determined without considering anything extrinsic to the narrative,"[75] we affirm that pertinent extratextual evidence (historical background, cultural milieu, and linguistic conventions) are vital and indispensable within the interpretive program. This affirmation requires that the historically contingent nature of the ancient work concerned be taken seriously, so that the work will not be domesticated through the imposition of an anachronistic reading on it.[76] (3) Our approach, however, will differ from conventionalism/contextualism which bases textual meaning solely on social practices and linguistic conventions of the time that surrounded the text's creation.[77] In this study, how the author intended his or her text to be read will serve as a critical "filter" to properly assess the bulk of

---

70. Ibid., 121, cf. 48–52, 247–48. Osborne rightly stresses that the meaning of a text is "genre-dependent." See Osborne, *The Hermeneutical Spiral*, 26.

71. Kindt and Müller, *The Implied Author*, 168.

72. Lozada and Thatcher, *New Currents Through John*. Part 2 of this book is entitled "The New Current of Readers and Readings."

73. Ibid., 180. See Kindt and Müller's comment on Wayne Booth's understanding of the implied author (p. 8) and on a reception approach to this concept (pp. 152–55).

74. Osborne, *The Hermeneutical Spiral*, 519.

75. Powell, *What Is Narrative Criticism?* 5.

76. See Levinson's comment in his *The Pleasures of Aesthetics*, 184.

77. Kindt and Müller, *The Implied Author*, 162–67.

circumstantial materials and keep the interpretive efforts relevant. The reconstructed meaning of the text, analyzed within the literary setting and against the historical backdrop, is then ascribed to the implied author, who stands for the real author's self-representation.[78] (4) At the theoretical level the implied author and the actual author must remain distinct. The reason is that the latter author may fail to achieve his/her composition purpose or may express, through the implied author, a view that violates his/her own conviction. For the biblical documents, however, "there is no reason to believe that the real authors did not fully accept the ideas expressed in their books"[79] or that they lacked the necessary capability to achieve the literary goals. Thus Francis Moloney's supposition that the implied and the real authors of the NT narratives—particularly the narrative of the Gospel of John—"speak with the same voice" is sound and reasonable, albeit unverifiable.[80] Even so, our arguments in subsequent chapters will not be undermined if one does not take the step to ascribe the "reconstructed" authorial intent (the implied author's intent), established by a proper interpretation of the text, to the evangelist who penned this Gospel or shaped its final form. To avoid terminological clumsiness, we will not insist on a differentiation between the implied and the real authors.

Turning to the concept of Jewish royal messianism, we have already noted our working definition of the "Messiah" at the beginning of this chapter: "A messiah is a figure who acts as the agent of the final divine deliverance, whether or not he is specifically designated as 'messiah' or 'anointed.'"[81] We shall use the term "royal messianism" when the Jewish expectation is for a future king. In the following chapters, our discussion will focus on the relevant motifs of royal messianism in the biblical and extra-biblical Jewish documents and in the Gospel of John. Some scholars object to connecting the OT with messianism, based on the absence of an unambiguously eschatological sense in which the term מָשִׁיחַ is used in the OT.[82] However, Chester rightly emphasizes that though the OT

---

78. Ibid., 167–81.

79. Powell, *What Is Narrative Criticism?* 5.

80. Moloney, *The Gospel of John*, 16. Even for non-canonical writings, Levinson believes that "in many cases . . . , artistic meaning and author's actual concrete intent happily coincide" (*The Pleasures of Aesthetics*, 212).

81. Chester, *Messiah and Exaltation*, 201.

82. E.g., Becker, *Messianic Expectation in the Old Testament*.

texts concerned (e.g., 2 Sam 7:1–17) often speak of a particular historical situation, "they transcend this situation completely, and look far beyond it."[83] In fact, these OT texts which are interpreted messianically in post-biblical Judaism and early Christianity are the foundation and the root of the Jewish royal-messianic traditions. Because the OT references in John's Gospel exhibit a general tendency of aligning with the textual form in the Septuagint, examination of the evangelist's use of scriptural materials will focus mainly on the Greek instead of the Hebrew Scripture.[84] Analysis of Jewish writings will deal with those that pertain to the expectation for the royal Messiah. While the kingship of Jesus in this Gospel entails divine and prophetic notions, we will not examine Jewish writings that address the kingship of Yahweh, Moses, or some other figures without linking them to royal messianism (e.g., *Pss. Sol.* 2:30; 8:8; 15:12; *1 En.* 90:28–29; 91:13; Philo's *Moses* 1).[85] The reason for laying aside these writings is that they do not directly pertain to the subject matter under our investigation, namely the royal messiahship of the crucified Jesus.

We will pay considerable attention to the Johannine intertextual references to, and resonances with, royal-messianic texts in the OT and post-biblical Jewish writings. Whereas there are various methods of discerning and analyzing "intertextuality" in a given text, intrinsic to "intertextuality" as a concept is the notion that every text in some way interrelates with another text, or host of texts, in the tradition. Intertextuality rightly calls attention to the important fact that a NT author does not employ only the form of a citation to evoke and dialogue with an earlier text. [86] Rather, textual linkages can be created by allusion and echo, invoked by the use of elusive signs, codes, symbols, and conventions shared by texts in the tradition. In this way, intertextuality in its broadest sense can encompass all possible intertextual connections and linkages—explicit and

83. Chester, *Messiah and Exaltation*, 229.

84. Köstenberger, "John," 417–18; Schuchard, *Scripture Within Scripture*, 151.

85. For the kingship of Moses, see Meeks, *The Prophet-King*, 107–11.

86. For discussions of intertextuality in the field of biblical studies, see Fishbane, "Inner Biblical Exegesis: Types and Strategies of Interpretation in Ancient Israel," 19–37; Hays, *Echoes of Scripture in the Letters of Paul*; Evans and Sanders, *Paul and the Scriptures of Israel*; Litwak, "Echoes of Scripture?" 260–88; Chae, *Jesus as the Eschatological Davidic Shepherd*, 6–17.

Some recent intertextual studies on the Gospel of John are McWhirter, *The Bridegroom Messiah and the People of God*; Winsor, *A King is Bound in the Tresses*; Brunson, *Psalm 118 in the Gospel of John*.

implicit, intentional and unintentional—that can be drawn among texts within the whole textual web.[87] While this broad intertextual approach (involving all possible textual ties) holds potential for shedding light on the dynamic interconnections between texts, it is nonetheless not fitting to our research. This is partly because we are concerned with the notion of authorial intentionality and will employ this notion as a methodological control to confine interpretive focus and to keep the volume of textual and extra-textual material manageable. In other words, we will be mainly interested in intentional intertextual connections or references.[88]

In this study, the term "citation" or "quotation" will be used to denote an explicit reference to another text—"explicit" in the sense that the reference is introduced by a quotation formula or comprises a reasonable amount of correspondent words with that text (with little or no variation in wording). The term "allusion" or "echo" will be used to denote an "implicit" or elusive reference to another text. An indication of authorial intent is obvious in the use of a citation/quotation, which has the clear indicator of a quotation formula or even some measure of verbal parallel with another text. Richard Hays remarks that "the concept of allusion depends both on the notion of authorial intention and on the assumption that the reader will . . . recognize the source of the allusion."[89] Based on this definition, authorial intention is involved in the use of allusion. While determining textual relevance, we will basically employ Hays's seven criteria for an intertextual connection as general guidelines for discerning Johannine references to, and thematic links with, other texts.[90]

---

87. Fewell says, "there is no end to the making of texts, or to the making of connections" (*Reading between Texts*, 17).

88. According to Porter, any research on a NT author's use of the OT presupposes an interest in the author's intended purpose regarding the textual interactions with the Scripture. See Porter, "The Use of the Old Testament in the New Testament," 79–96.

89. Hays, *Echoes of Scripture in the Letters of Paul*, 29.

90. These seven criteria are: (1) Availability: Is the proposed referent available to the author and the original readers? (2) Volume: How explicit is the alleged intertextual connection? (3) Recurrence: Does the author make reference to the same biblical passage elsewhere? (4) Thematic coherence: Does the proposed echo cohere with the composition's overall train of thought? (5) Historical plausibility: Could the author have alluded to the proposed referent and could the original readers have perceived it? (6) History of interpretation: Did other interpreters hear the same intertextual echo? (7) Satisfaction: Does the proposed echo make sense within the immediate context and help enhance the thoughts of the surrounding text? See Hays, *The Conversion of the Imagination*, 34–45; idem, *Echoes of Scripture in the Letters of Paul*, 29–32.

Finally, it is necessary to discuss the criteria for selecting Johannine passages. Broadly speaking, we will employ two basic criteria to determine pertinent passages prior to the passion narrative that contain a kingship-cross intersection. These passages will be our interpretive focus in the remainder of this study. The first criterion is that the passage must contain a motif that occurs in relation to royal messianism in Jewish texts. Presumably the greater the number of attestations in the biblical and the extra-biblical Jewish writings, the greater is the likelihood that a royal-messianic notion is present in John's use of the motif and that his original audience would have perceived this notion. The motif in question may appear through an overt reference to Jesus' kingship (e.g., a royal epithet) or an implicit reference to it by means of a citation/quotation/allusion/echo that invokes Jewish royal-messianic hopes. The second criterion is that the theme of Jesus' death, which carries strong overtones of royal messianism in the passion narrative, must appear in conjunction with the proposed royal-messianic motif within the passage's immediate context. Based on these two criteria, the principal passages that will receive attention in the subsequent chapters are John 1:43–51; 2:13–22; 3:1–21; 10:14–18; 12:12–19. There are three passages (John 6:1–15; 11:46–53; 12:30–36) that do not meet the criteria but can be related to the subject of Israel's unification under the crucified Jesus as the Messiah-King; this subject will be treated in chapter 6. The first passage refers to Jesus as "king" (John 6:15) but contains no readily noticeable reference to the cross. The second passage speaks of the death of Jesus, but there is no perceptible reference to his kingship. The third passage does not directly refer to the death or kingship of Jesus, but it contains sundry themes that can be linked to the subject mentioned above. We will look at these three passages in an excursus of chapter 6 and briefly discuss their implications for our research.

Plan of This Study

Chapter 2 will lay a foundation of this study by establishing the link between Jesus' kingship and messiahship within the conceptual framework of John's Gospel. We will show evidence from late Second Temple Judaism and this Gospel in order to justify a royal-messianic understanding of Johannine Christology. Chapter 3 will examine the text John 1:45–51, where the theme of Jesus' messianic kinship occurs in conjunction with the motif of his death for the first time in the Gospel narrative. Chapters 4 to 6 will deal with three episodes respectively (John 2:13–22; 3:1–21; 10:14–18), in which the cross motif is connected with certain notions concerning the arrival of the royal Messiah in Jewish thought. Chapter 7 will analyze the passage John 12:12–19. We will seek to elucidate the Johannine idea regarding the scriptural witness to the crucified Jesus' royal messiahship. In the course of our discussion in these chapters, considerable attention will be given to the Johannine intertextual resonances with the royal-messianic motifs in the OT and Second Temple Judaism. Finally, chapter 8 will present a concluding synthesis of our research and point out some important implications for Johannine studies.

2

Linking Jesus' Kingship
and Messiahship

O UR FIRST TASK IS to lay a foundation for the subsequent investigation by establishing the linkage between Jesus' kingship and messiahship in the Gospel of John. As we have already seen, several studies have propounded various interpretations of the Johannine kingship theme that tend to divorce the notion of Jesus' kingship from that of his messiahship. This tendency would relegate any remaining notion of Jesus' royal-messianic status to an inconsequential position in John's Christological scheme. In response to these challenges, we will set forth contextual evidence from late Second Temple Judaism and internal evidence from the Gospel of John in order to demonstrate the Johannine interest in Jesus' royal-messianic legitimacy.

Contextual Evidence: Jewish Royal Messianism (ca. 200 BCE–100 CE)

This section will present a summary overview of the phenomena of Jewish royal messianism during the period ca. 200 BCE—100 CE,[1] and in particular it will highlight the widespread influence of royal-messianic

---

1. The reason for setting the *terminus a quo* as 200 BCE is that there is meager evidence of Jewish messianism during the period 500–200 BCE. The *terminus ad quem* (100 CE) is based on the majority of scholarly opinions (e.g., Köstenberger, Keener, Moloney, and Carson) that the Gospel of John was written sometime during the last two decades of the first century CE. See Köstenberger, *John*, 6; Keener, *The Gospel of John*, 1:140–42; Moloney, *The Gospel of John*, 5; Carson, *The Gospel according to John*, 82–87.

expectations and the major themes associated with them. The contention for a prominence of Jewish royal messianism does not mean that this kind of messianism was a single form of messianic manifestation or that messianism was central to the thought-worlds of all Second Temple Jewish groups. Recent studies on Second Temple Judaism have called attention to the diversity of messianic expectations, which took sundry forms of expression including royal, priestly, and prophetic.[2] However, as multifaceted as the character of the messianic hopes was, the plurality of these hopes should not be overstated. As a number of scholars correctly remark, there is evidence that the royal- or Davidic-messianic hope was gaining currency within the Jewish world, at least from the middle of the first century BCE onwards.[3] In charting the milieu of Judaism that surrounded the Fourth Gospel's creation, we will attempt to situate the Johannine portrayals of Jesus as king and as Messiah within their first-century context and thereby to buttress the claim that John conceives of Jesus as the Messiah-King. Two aspects of this background material will be examined. First, we will look for possible Davidic connotations that are expressed within the framework of typological correspondences between the Messiah and David.[4] The presence of such Davidic connotations in Jewish royal messianism opens up the possibility that the Johannine Jesus may be correlated typologically with David.[5] This possibility will then be explored further in the subsequent discussion. Second, since the Johannine profile of Jesus does not emphasize his Davidic pedigree, it will

---

2. Horsley, "Palestinian Jewish Groups and Their Messiahs in Late Second Temple Times," 14–29; Charlesworth, "From Messianology to Christology," 3–35; Neusner et al., *Judaisms and Their Messiahs at the Turn of the Christian Era*.

3. Chester, *Messiah and Exaltation*, 276–97, 329–63; Dunn, *Jesus Remembered*, 619–22; Horbury, *Messianism Among Jews and Christians*, 35–64; idem, *Jewish Messianism and the Cult of Christ*; Collins, *The Scepter and the Star*, 1–19.

4. In this study, "typology" refers in a broad sense to an intertextual approach to establish a relationship between two texts. This approach discerns the relationship in terms of an analogical correspondence between the "type" in a text and the "antitype" in a later text. The two texts may be (1) two OT texts, (2) an OT text and a post-biblical Jewish text, or (3) an OT text and a Johannine text. For the concept of typology, see Hoskins, *Jesus as the Fulfillment of the Temple in the Gospel of John*, 18–36; Hasel, *New Testament Theology*, 190–203 (esp. 190–95); Goppelt, *Typos*. Goppelt's work includes a section about the use of typology in Judaism.

5. Miura stresses the typological character of Davidic messianism in the OT and Second Temple Judaism. See Miura, *David in Luke-Acts*.

be worthwhile considering in our analysis whether this feature is likewise missing from some of the royal-messianic presentations in Judaism.

The Psalms of Solomon

The *Psalms of Solomon* were probably written during the Pompeian period in the latter half of the first century BCE, on account of a number of perceptible allusions in psalms 2, 8, and 17 to Pompey's conquest of Jerusalem (63 BCE) and his death in Egypt (48 BCE).[6] In designating the expected king "son of David" (υἰὸν Δαυίδ, *Pss. Sol.* 17:21) and "Lord Messiah" (χριστὸς κύριος, *Pss. Sol.* 17:32),[7] the seventeenth psalm bears an important witness to the Jewish hopes for a Davidic Messiah in the pre-Christian era.[8] The author(s) of the *Psalms of Solomon* leveled criticisms

---

6. Wright, *The Psalms of Solomon*; idem, "Psalms of Solomon," in *OTP* 2:639–70; Nickelsburg, *Jewish Literature Between the Bible and the Mishnah*, 238–47; Atkinson, *I Cried to the Lord*; Schreiber, *Gesalbter und König*, 161–90; Collins, *The Apocalyptic Imagination*, 143–44; idem, *The Scepter and the Star*, 49–56; Trafton, "The *Psalms of Solomon* in Recent Research," 3–19; Winninge, *Sinners and the Righteous*; Jonge, *Jewish Eschatology, Early Christian Christology and the Testaments of the Twelve Patriarchs*, 3–27; Davenport, "The 'Anointed of the Lord' in Psalms of Solomon 17," 67–92; Ryle and James, *ΨΑΛΜΟΙ ΣΟΛΟΜΩΝΤΟΣ. Psalms of the Pharisees, Commonly Called the Psalms of Solomon*.

Most scholars date the *Psalms of Solomon* to the Pompeian period. Atkinson argued for a Herodian date for the seventeenth psalm, but he seems to have changed his view recently to support a Pompeian date (cf. *I Cried to the Lord*, 129–79). In his earlier article, Atkinson says that "*Ps. Sol.* 17 actually describes the siege of Jerusalem by Herod the Great and the Roman general Sosius in 37 B.C.E." See Atkinson, "Herod the Great, Sosius, and the Siege of Jerusalem (37 B.C.E.) in *Psalm of Solomon* 17," 313–22 (314). According to Hengel, Adolf Schlatter dated *Psalms of Solomon* 17 to the early Herodian era. See Hengel, *The Zealots*, 321 n.53.

7. The Greek text and the English translation of the *Psalms of Solomon* are from Wright, *The Psalms of Solomon*. Scholars debate the authenticity of the phrase χριστὸς κύριος in *Pss. Sol.* 17:32. On the affirmative side, see Wright, *The Psalms of Solomon*, 48–49; Evans, "Messianic Hopes and Messianic Figures in Late Antiquity," 21–22; Hann, "Christos Kyrios in PsSOL 17.32," 620–27. If the nominative form is original, the title "Lord" (κύριος) expresses the Messiah's royalty rather than divinity. Some scholars believe that the original word is in the genitive case (i.e., κυρίου). On this view, see Schreiber, *Gesalbter und König*, 176–77; Atkinson, "On the Herodian Origin of Militant Davidic Messiah at Qumran," 435–60 (440 n. 15); Jonge, *Jewish Eschatology, Early Christian Christology and the Testaments of the Twelve Patriarchs*, 14–15, 21 n. 25; Davenport, "The Anointed of the Lord," 77–79.

8. Messianic references are also found in *Pss. Sol.* 18:5 and 18:7 and in the superscription of this eighteenth psalm, but these references do not receive any further elaboration there.

against the Hasmonean priest-kings, the Romans, and the impious Jews who accommodated their lifestyle to pagan cultures. The priests and the inhabitants of Jerusalem have profaned the temple (*Pss. Sol.* 1:7–8; 2:3–5; 8:11–13, 22) and the city (*Pss. Sol.* 8:22). In adopting the Gentiles' wicked practices (*Pss. Sol.* 17:15), the unrighteous Jews committed "every kind of sin" (*Pss. Sol.* 17:20, cf. 17:14–15, 19), specifically sexual immorality (e.g., prostitution [*Pss. Sol.* 2:11], adultery [*Pss. Sol.* 2:13; 4:4–5; 8:10], and incest [*Pss. Sol.* 8:9]).[9] In keeping with the Deuteronomistic concept of a causal relation between sin and punishment,[10] the *Psalms of Solomon* give explanation of the Roman conquest of Jerusalem and the Jewish exile as God's chastisement of his unfaithful people (*Pss. Sol.* 2:6–14; 4:21–25; 8:14–15; 9:1–2; 17:5, 19).

The main features of royal messianism in *Psalms of Solomon* 17 are as follows. (1) The Messiah is the "king of Israel" (v. 42, cf. vv. 4, 21, 32), but his royal authority is subordinate to God's sovereign kingship (vv. 1–3, 34, 46; cf. *Pss. Sol.* 2:30, 32; 5:19). (2) The Messiah is a descendant of David (vv. 4, 21). Emphasis on the Messiah's Davidic descent serves not only to denounce the illegitimate Hasmonean regimes (v. 6), which lacked Davidic status, but also to affirm God's commitment to the promises he made to David.[11] (3) The messianic profile exhibits certain characteristics that suggest a typological relationship between the Messiah and David. Yuzuru Miura discerns four such messianic characteristics that correspond to the portrayal of David in 1 Sam 2:1–10; 2 Sam 22:1–51; 23:1–7— the Messiah as a "chosen" (*Pss. Sol.* 17:32), "pious" (*Pss. Sol.* 17:34, 39–40), "righteous" (*Pss. Sol.* 17:22–25) and "warrior (triumphant)" king (*Pss. Sol.* 17:23, 26–29, 32–43).[12] Sundry thematic similarities between *Psalms of Solomon* 17 and several texts in the Prophets (Isaiah 11, Jeremiah 23, and Ezekiel 34 and 37) and the canonical Psalm 72 also advocate the view that

9. Winninge says that the two chief iniquities condemned in the *Psalms of Solomon* are cultic and sexual sins (*Sinners and the Righteous*, 126).

10. For this Deuteronomistic concept, see Dennis, *Jesus' Death and the Gathering of True Israel*, 89–93.

11. Davenport, "The 'Anointed of the Lord' in Psalms of Solomon 17," 72. Several terms or phrases (e.g., ὤμοσας, σπέρματος, and τοῦ μὴ ἐκλείπειν) in *Pss. Sol.* 17:4 (cf. v. 21) evoke the Davidic dynasty traditions (e.g., ὤμοσα in Ps 88:4 LXX [89:4 MT and Eng.] and σπέρμα in Ps 88:5 LXX [89:5 MT and Eng.; cf. 2 Sam 7:12]). See the examples in Pomykala, *The Davidic Dynasty Tradition in Early Judaism*, 160–61, esp. n. 157; also Miura, *David in Luke-Acts*, 57–58; Burger, *Jesus als Davidssohn*, 18.

12. Miura, *David in Luke-Acts*, 14–21, 55–58.

Davidic typology is probably at work in the royal-messianic formulation of this pseudepigraphic psalm.[13] These biblical texts, which look forward to the coming of a perfect Davidic monarch, are laden with inspirational ideas for the Jewish development of Davidic messianism. (4) The messianic hope is this-worldly and centers on the reinstatement of Jerusalem on earth.[14] While the Messiah is a political figure, he will not fight against his enemies with military weapons but his "word" (v. 24, cf. vv. 35, 43).[15] (5) The Messiah will purge Jerusalem from the Gentiles and all unrighteousness (vv. 22, 26, 29, 30, 32, 43; cf. *Pss. Sol.* 18:5, 7) and thereby restore to the land "a holy people" (v. 26; cf. v. 43). In light of this, the Messiah's task comprises a priestly component in that it aims to cleanse Israel of sin, which has defiled the people, the temple, and the land of Israel.[16] (6) The Messiah will assemble the scattered people of God (vv. 18, 26, 31) and "distribute them upon the land according to the tribes" (v. 28, cf. v. 43). This gathering not only includes the Jews but also the Gentiles (vv. 31–32).[17] As the eschatological shepherd appointed by God, the Messiah will lead the restored Israel ἐν πίστει καὶ δικαιοσύνῃ (v. 40; cf. Ezek 34:23; 37:24; Mic 5:4). (7) Lastly, the Messiah will enjoy universal dominion (vv. 31–34).

13. Ibid., 58. For the thematic correspondences between the *Psalms of Solomon* and Psalm 72, see Wright, *The Psalms of Solomon*, 7; Ryle and James, *The Psalms of Solomon*, lv.

14. Chester, *Messiah and Exaltation*, 342; Tan, *Zion Traditions and the Aims of Jesus*, 34.

15. Cf. Isa 11:4 LXX and the allusions to Ps 2:9 in *Pss. Sol.* 17:23b. See Chae, *Jesus as the Eschatological Davidic Shepherd*, 121; Jonge, *Jewish Eschatology, Early Christian Christology and the Testaments of the Twelve Patriarchs*, 12. By contrast, Atkinson emphasizes the Messiah's militant role. See Atkinson, "On the Use of Scripture in the Development of Militant Davidic Messianism at Qumran," 106–23.

16. In the *Psalms of Solomon*, the royal and priestly offices are not neatly separated (cf. the Hasmoneans' combination of these two offices). See Stuckenbruck, "Messianic Ideas in the Apocalyptic and Related Literature of Early Judaism," 95; Davenport, "The 'Anointed of the Lord' in Psalms of Solomon 17," 75.

17. Cf. Isa 2:2–4; 66:18–23; Jer 3:17; Zech 2:11; 8:20–23. See Pitre, *Jesus, the Tribulation, and the End of the Exile*, 83; Tan, *Zion Traditions and the Aims of Jesus*, 28.

The Dead Sea Scrolls

Like the *Psalms of Solomon*, a number of Qumran documents anticipate the advent of a royal Messiah from the Davidic line.[18] Three main
epithets in these documents refer to this figure: (1) "Messiah of Israel"
(משיח ישראל), (2) "Branch of David" (צמח דויד), and (3) "Prince of the
Congregation" (נשיא העדה).[19] The first epithet occurs a total of six times in
the Dead Sea Scrolls (1QS IX, 11; 1QSa II, 11-20; CD-A XII, 23—XIII, 1;
XIV, 18–19; CD-B XIX, 10–11; XIX, 33—XX, 1).[20] In each case, the Messiah
of Israel (presumably the royal Messiah) appears in an eschatological scene
and is accompanied by a priestly figure, often the "Messiah of Aaron"
(אהרן משיח).[21] The appearance of the Messiah of Israel will mark the end
of "the time of wickedness" and the dawn of the latter-day (CD-A XII,
23—XIII, 1). In the *Damascus Document*, his arrival is associated with
the expiation of sin (CD-A XIV, 18–19) and the divine judgment (CD-B
XIX, 10–11). Aside from its occurrences in 1QS, 1QSa and CD, the term
משיח (without ישראל or אהרן) denotes the Davidic Messiah in 4Q252 V, 3
(משיח הצדק) and perhaps an eschatological royal figure in 4Q458 frg.
2 II, 6.[22]

Four Qumran texts (4Q252, 4Q174, 4Q161, and 4Q285), all of which
can be dated to the first century BCE, mention the "Branch of David." In
4Q252 V, 1–7, he is identified with "the Messiah of righteousness" (cf. Jer

---

18. Davies and Strawn, *Qumran Studies*; Wolters, "The Messiah in the Qumran
Documents," 75–89; Chester, *Messiah and Exaltation*, 230–97, 525–29; Xeravits, *King,
Priest, Prophet*; Schreiber, *Gesalbter und König*, 99–121, 199–245; Evans, *Jesus and His
Contemporaries*, 83–154; Zimmermann, *Messianische Texte aus Qumran*; Charlesworth
et al., *Qumran-Messianism*; Oegema, *The Anointed and His People*, 86–97, 108–27;
Collins, *The Scepter and the Star*, 56–83.

The Qumran text and the English translation are from Martínez and Tigchelaar, *The
Dead Sea Scrolls*. Our terminology diverges from *The Dead Sea Scrolls* in that we translate
the Hebrew word צמח as "branch" instead of "bud."

19. The equivalences of these three epithets in some writings of the DSS indicate
that the epithets refer to the same figure. See VanderKam, "Messianism in the Scrolls,"
212; Collins, *The Scepter and the Star*, 60–63. Contra Pomykala, *The Davidic Dynasty
Tradition in Early Judaism*, 232–46.

20. Xeravits, *King, Priest, Prophet*, 130; Evans, "Qumran's Messiah."

21. For diarchic (royal and priestly) messianism at Qumran, see Xeravits, *King,
Priest, Prophet*; Evans, "Qumran's Messiah," 146–49; Zimmermann, *Messianische Texte
aus Qumran*.

22. Xeravits, *King, Priest, Prophet*, 130–32; Evans, *Jesus and His Contemporaries*, 102–
103, 137–38; Zimmermann, *Messianische Texte aus Qumran*, 113–27, 205–10.

23:5; 33:15) and Jacob's blessing to Judah in Gen 49:10 is interpreted as a prophecy speaking of the perpetuity of the Davidic line and kingdom. In depicting the scenarios of "the last days" (I, 2, 12, 15, 19), 4Q174 strings together various scriptural passages from 2 Samuel (e.g., 7:10, 11, 12, 13, 14), the Pentateuch (e.g., Exod 15:17–18), the Psalter (e.g., Pss 1:1; 2:1), and the Prophets (e.g., Amos 9:11; Isa 8:11). This Qumran document envisions the eschatological appearance in Jerusalem of the Branch of David and the Interpreter of the Law, who is probably the priestly Messiah (I, 11–13).[23] Chae suggests that the messianic expressions in 4Q174 summon the Davidic shepherd tradition in Ezekiel 34 and 37, despite a lack of explicit shepherd terminology in this scroll.[24] As indicated in 4Q174 I, 13, the mission of the Branch is "to save" Israel; this mission probably refers to the messianic deliverance of God's people from both their enemies and sin, which is the cause of the temple's impure state (cf. I, 6).[25] In light of the identification of Israel's enemies as "the sons of Belial" (I, 7–9), the redemption brought by the Branch entails not only an earthly but also a cosmic aspect, namely the eschatological defeat of Satan. The remaining two texts—4Q161 frgs. 8–10, III, 10–25 and 4Q285 frg. 5, 1–6—draw on the motifs of Isa 10:34—11:5 and present the Branch as a mighty warrior slaying his foes in the final battle.[26] To some degree, then, the idealized Davidic king as a victorious warrior in Isaiah 11 serves as a prototypal counterpart for the "Branch of David" at Qumran.[27]

The titular formulation "Prince of the Congregation" or simply "Prince" occurs in several Qumran scrolls. In 4Q285 (frg. 4, lines 2 5, 10 and frg. 5, line 4), the "Prince" is a military figure who will fight for Israel

---

23. That is, the Messiah of Aaron. See Fitzmyer, *The One Who Is to Come*, 99.

24. Chae, *Jesus as the Eschatological Davidic Shepherd*, 134–37. By contrast, Willitts finds the Davidic shepherd-king motif in only 11Q5 and 4Q504 in the DSS. See Willitts, *Matthew's Messianic Shepherd-King*, 72–79.

25. Atkinson stresses the Branch's militaristic function in 4Q174. Against Atkinson, Chae underlines that this document describes the Branch as "saving" God's people from their sins. See Atkinson, "On the Use of Scripture"; Chae, *Jesus as the Eschatological Davidic Shepherd*, 136–37. It is probable that the Branch executes *both* militaristic (externally to Israel's foes) and redemptive (internally to Israel) functions.

26. As for the matter of whether 4Q285 frg. 5 portrays a "slaying" or a "slain" Messiah, see Zimmermann, *Messianische Texte aus Qumran*, 83–88; Bockmuehl, "A 'Slain Messiah' in 4Q Serekh Mil'amah (4Q285)?" 155–69; Vermes, "The Oxford Forum for Qumran Research Seminar on the Rule of War from Cave 4 (4Q285)," 85–90.

27. Miura, *David in Luke-Acts*, 84–88, 134–36.

in the final war and annihilate all the adversaries. Whereas1QM (late first-century BCE or early first-century CE) accentuates the role played by the priests in the eschatological battle, the Prince (V, 1) is probably messianic on account of the allusions to David's defeats of Goliath and the Philistines in XI, 1–3 and the quotation of Num 24:17–19 in XI, 4–7. If this understanding is correct, David's victories in the past foreshadow the messianic Prince's triumph at the end of times.[28]

In summary, the royal Messiah in Qumran thought is a Davidic figure whose principal functions are militaristic and judicial. The Davidic royal Messiah will be the chief leader of God's people in the latter-day battle and will destroy all their pagan enemies, who represent the forces of evil. His arrival is further associated with the inauguration of the eschaton and probably with the reparation of Israel's sin (CD-A XIV, 18–19; 4Q174).[29]

The Similitudes of Enoch

The *Similitudes of Enoch* (1 *Enoch* 37—71) unfold a series of Enoch's visions and heavenly journeys.[30] To Enoch is disclosed the divine plan about the final judgment and resurrection, the punishment of the evil angels, and the coming of a royal-messianic figure. The term "Messiah" occurs only twice in the *Similitudes* (1 *En.* 48:10; 52:4);[31] but three other designations are used to describe this messianic figure: the "Son of Man" (1 *En.* 46:2, 3, 4; 48:2; 62:5, 7, 9, 14; 63:11; 69:26, 27, 29 [2x]; 70:1; 71:14, 17),[32]

28. Chester, *Messiah and Exaltation*, 337; Evans, "Qumran's Messiah," 144.

29. Other Qumran writings that may be pertinent to royal or Davidic messianism include 1QM, 4Q175, 4Q246, 4Q287 (?), 4Q369, 4Q458, 4Q491c (?) and 4Q504. Thus potential royal-messianic documents in the DSS are 1QS, 1QSa, 1QSb, 1QM, CD, 4Q161, 4Q174, 4Q175, 4Q246, 4Q252, 4Q285, 4Q369, 4Q458, 4Q491c (?) and 4Q504. These documents will receive attention in the subsequent chapters as necessary.

30. Boccaccini, *Enoch and the Messiah Son of Man*; Chester, *Messiah and Exaltation*, 344–45; Elliot, *The Survivors of Israel*, 491–502; Schreiber, *Gesalbter und König*, 324–43; Collins, *The Apocalyptic Imagination*, 177; Oegema, *The Anointed and His People*, 140–47; Nickelsburg, "Salvation without and with a Messiah," 49–68; VanderKam, "Righteous One, Messiah, Chosen One, and Son of Man in 1 Enoch 37—71," 169–91. There is a lack of scholarly consensus on the date of the *Similitudes*; however, it is likely that the book was composed before 70 CE. See the relevant discussions in the studies above.

31. The English translation of the *Similitudes* is from Nickelsburg and VanderKam, *1 Enoch*.

32. Most scholars believe that Enoch is the Son of Man in 71:14, but Collins finds traits of redactional work in this verse. See his recent comment on the identity of this

the "Chosen One" (*1 En.* 39:6; 40:5; 45:3, 4; 48:6 [an adjectival form]; 49:2, 4; 51:3, 5; 52:6, 9; 53:6; 55:4; 61:5, 8, 10; 62:1), and the "Righteous One" (*1 En.* 38:2; 53:6).[33] The last two designations underscore the Messiah's special relationship to God and his righteous character (cf. *1 En.* 39:6–7; 46:3; 62:2), which is a characteristic of the awaited Davidic ruler in Jewish conceptualization.[34] There is no reference to the Messiah's Davidic ancestry in the *Similitudes*, within which he appears as the preexistent, transcendent Son of Man (*1 En.* 48:2–3, 6; 62:7).[35] Yet the Messiah of the *Similitudes* apparently enjoys royal status, in view of the recurrent theme of his enthronement in the heavenly court (*1 En.* 45:3; 51:3; 55:4; 61:8; 62:1–3, 5; 69:27–29;[36] cf. the notion of the Messiah's universal jurisdiction [e.g., *1 En.* 46:4; 48:5; 55:4; 62:6, 9]).

On the whole, the messianic portrait in the *Similitudes* integrates the motifs drawn from various scriptural traditions surrounding the Davidic king (e.g., Ps 2:2 [*1 En.* 48:8–10]; Isa 11:2–3 [*1 En.* 49:2–4]), the Danielic Son of Man (Dan 7:13), and the Isaianic Servant (Isa 42:6; 49:6; 53:11 [*1 En.* 48:4, 8–10]).[37] In this portrait, the exalted Son of Man acts as the divinely appointed agent to reward the "holy" and "righteous" and "chosen" ones and to mete out judgment on the kings and the nations, who oppress God's people (e.g., *1 En.* 45:3–6; 46:4–6; 47:1–2; 48:8–10; 50:1–3). He also receives judicial authority from God to exercise judgment on the evil angels—even their head, Satan (*1 En.* 54:1–6; 55:4; 64:2; 67:4; cf. 53:3; 69:2–12). These angelic beings rebelled against God and are held responsible for seducing the humans to commit sin (*1 En.* 64:2; 65:6; 69:6).

"Son of Man" in "Enoch and the Son of Man," 216–27; cf. idem, *The Scepter and the Star*, 178–81.

33. It is generally held that these titles refer to the same figure. The designation "Judge" appears once in 41:9. See VanderKam, "Righteous One, Messiah, Chosen One, and Son of Man in 1 Enoch 37—71," 185–86; Oegema, *The Anointed and His People*, 142.

34. Cf. Isa 9:6–11; 11:33–34; Jer 23:5; Zech 9:9; *Pss. Sol.* 17:29, 32, 37, 40; *2 Bar.* 40:2. See Schreiber, *Gesalbter und König*, 334–35; Oegema, *The Anointed and His People*, 144.

35. Horbury believes that the expectation of a heavenly Messiah is rooted in the Jewish concept that the Davidic Messiah will be "the manifestation and embodiment of a spirit sent by God." Horbury, *Jewish Messianism and the Cult of Christ*, 90.

36. Most of these passages employ the messianic title "the Chosen One." Two texts, namely *1 En.* 62:5 and 69:27–29, speak of the enthronement of "the Son of Man."

37. Fitzymer, *The One Who Is to Come*, 86–87; Schreiber, *Gesalbter und König*, 330 n. 27, 331–32; VanderKam, "Righteous One, Messiah, Chosen One, and Son of Man in 1 Enoch 37—71," 187–90. According to Fitzmyer, the idea of the "hidden" Son of Man (*1 En.* 62:7) may draw on the depiction of the Servant in Isa 49:2.

In brief, the royal-messianic hopes of the *Similitudes* concentrate on the heavenly Son of Man, who is associated with the ideas of the dawn of the eschatological age, the annihilation of the hostile Gentiles, the judgment of Satan, and the vindication of God's righteous people.

Fourth Ezra

In the wake of the national catastrophe in 70 CE, the apocalypse *Fourth Ezra* bears witness to the persistence of Jewish messianic hopes.[38] In unfolding a fictional story against the background of the fall of Jerusalem in 587/586 BCE, this apocalypse (similarly, *Second Baruch*; see the next section) raises questions regarding theodicy and God's justice in allowing the Romans to devastate Jerusalem and his people.[39] Although the Messiah appears in only a few passages in *Fourth Ezra* (7:28–29; 11:37—12:1; 12:31–34; 13:3–13; 13:25–52 and 14:9), he plays a significant role in the book's eschatology.[40] Michael Stone asserts that the Messiah's portrayal in this book lacks royal characteristics, notwithstanding his identity as David's offspring (*4 Ezra* 12:32a).[41] Against Stone's assertion, Steven Bryan claims that the description of the Messiah as a "conqueror (*4 Ezra* 13:8–12) and gatherer of the Gentiles and exiles (*4 Ezra* 13:12–13) suggests his possession of royal dominion."[42] Jonathan Moo argues that the mysteriously royal figure of *4 Ezra* 5:6–7, who will reign over all earthly inhabitants, is the Messiah. Moo further underlines that "the Messiah's role in the book must be seen to encompass both judgment and rule."[43] In Stefan Schreiber's view, the depiction of the Davidic Messiah in *Fourth*

---

38. Chester, *Messiah and Exaltation*, 345–47; Schreiber, *Gesalbter und König*, 346–74; Elliot, *The Survivors of Israel*, 502–14; Oegema, *The Anointed and His People*, 216–20; Collins, *The Apocalyptic Imagination*, 195–212; Hayman, "The Man from the Sea," 1–16; Pomykala, *The Davidic Dynasty Tradition in Early Judaism*, 216–21; Stone, *Fourth Ezra*; idem, "The Question of the Messiah in 4 Ezra," 209–24; Zimmermann, "The Language, the Date, and the Portrayal of the Messiah in IV Ezra," 203–18; Metzger, "The Fourth Book of Ezra," in *OTP* 1:517–59.

39. For the literary relationship between *Fourth Ezra* and *Second Baruch*, see Sayler, *Have the Promises Failed?* 123–34; Collins, *The Apocalyptic Imagination*, 222–23.

40. Stone, *Fourth Ezra*, 41, 207–13. It is a scholarly agreement that the first two and the last two chapters of *Fourth Ezra* (i.e., chapters 1, 2, 15, and 16) are not original but Christian products.

41. Ibid., 41; also Stone, "The Question of the Messiah in 4 Ezra," 215.

42. Bryan, *Jesus and Israel's Traditions of Judgment and Restoration*, 195 n. 26.

43. Moo, "A Messiah 'Whom the Many Do Not Know'? Reading 4 Ezra 5:6–7," 525.

Ezra has an implicit ruling function.[44] If these observations of Bryan, Moo and Schreiber are accurate, the royal features of the Davidic Messiah in *Fourth Ezra* are more prominent than have been alleged by Stone.

In *4 Ezra* 7:28–29 the Messiah is called God's "Son"[45] (cf. *4 Ezra* 13:32, 37, 52; 14:9).[46] After a period of worldwide tribulations, he will come and make the people who have survived "rejoice" for 400 years; then, he and all human beings will die. The subsequent eagle vision and the interpretation of this vision depict the Messiah as a lion (*4 Ezra* 11:37; 12:32a; cf. Daniel 2), a symbol that hints at his Judahite ancestry (cf. Gen 49:9–10; 1QSb V, 29 [lion = Prince]). In spite of his human nature, the Messiah existed prior to the creation of the world (*4 Ezra* 12:32; cf. 13:25).[47] The explication of this eagle vision stresses the lion-Messiah's functions as the judge of the Romans and the liberator of the remnant of Israel (*4 Ezra* 12:32b–34).[48] In the sixth vision, "something like the figure of a man" arises from the sea and flies with the clouds (*4 Ezra* 13:3; cf. 13:26, 32; Dan 7:2–3, 13). These images probably serve to portray this man, identified as the "Son" of God in *4 Ezra* 13:32 (cf. vv. 37, 52), as a triumphant figure overthrowing the evil forces.[49] In a similar fashion, the

44. Schreiber, *Gesalbter und König*, 350.

45. The Israelite king is referred to as God's "son" in Ps 2:7; 89:26-7 and the Messiah is referred to as God's "son" in 1QSa II, 11-12. The use of "son" terminology with respect to the Messiah is attested in the Latin and Syriac versions of *Fourth Ezra*. The Latin word *filius* (son) may reflect the Greek word παῖς ("son" or "servant"). For "son" as the preferable meaning, see the excursus "The Messiah: Son or Servant of the Most High?" in Hogan, *Theologies in Conflict in 4 Ezra*, 195–98; Collins, *The Scepter and the Star*, 165–67; cf. Stuckenbruck, "Messianic Ideas," 90–113 (106); Hayman, "The 'Man from the Sea' in 4 Ezra 13," 8. However, Stone prefers the reading "servant" instead of "son" (*Fourth Ezra*, 207–208); similarly, Elliot, *The Survivors of Israel*, 504.

46. The English translation of *Fourth Ezra* is from Metzger, "The Fourth Book of Ezra," in *OTP* 1:517–59.

47. The idea of the Messiah's preexistence does not contradict his Davidic lineage. See Stone, "The Question of the Messiah in 4 Ezra," 211.

48. Elliot, *The Survivors of Israel*, 502–14.

49. Beale, "The Problem of the Man from the Sea in IV Ezra 13 and Its Relation to the Messianic Concept in John's Apocalypse," 182–88 (185). In the OT, "sea" is often associated with the notions of chaos and evils (e.g., Hab 3:15; Isa 7:12–14). The idea that the sea will be destroyed at the eschaton is present in *Sib. Or.* 5:155 and Rev 21:1. Contra Zimmermann's view that from the "sea" is a mistranslation of from the "west," i.e., the Messiah will come from Palestine ("The Language, the Date, and the Portrayal of the Messiah in IV Ezra," 212); also contra Hayman's view that the "man" refers to Yahweh as the Divine Warrior ("The 'Man from the Sea in 4 Ezra 13," 9–16). Hogan offers a brief

messianic Son (or Servant) appears as a warrior annihilating the foes of God's people with the "fiery breath" (i.e., the law [*4 Ezra* 13:38]) from his mouth (*4 Ezra* 13:26–27; cf. Isa 11:4). Faced with the assault of the nations (cf. Ps 2:2), the Messiah takes his victorious stand "on the top of Mount Zion" (*4 Ezra* 13:35–36; cf. Isa 11:4; 66:15) and assembles the dispersed ten (or nine and one half) tribes of Israel (*4 Ezra* 13:40). They will be reunited with the remnant of Israel who survives within the borders of the holy land (*4 Ezra* 13:46–50).[50] Simply put, the Davidic (royal) Messiah in *Fourth Ezra* performs primarily these dual tasks: destruction (of the nations) and restoration (of Jerusalem and the righteous of Israel).

Second Baruch

In Syriac *Second Baruch*, messianic references are found in 29:3; 30:1; 39:7; 40:1; 70:9; 72:2.[51] Unlike *Fourth Ezra*, *Second Baruch* does not link the Messiah genealogically to David. While the Messiah's Davidic lineage is unclear, his royalty is implied in the references to his "dominion" (*2 Bar.* 39:7) and enthronement in the kingdom (*2 Bar.* 73:1–7).[52] As portrayed in *Second Baruch* 29—30, the Messiah will be manifested after an era of worldwide chaos and disasters. Further, his advent will usher in a glorious age characterized by prosperity and material abundance (*2 Bar.* 29:3–7). When this messianic era is completed, the Messiah will return with glory and thereafter "the end of times" will begin (*2 Bar.* 30:1–5; cf. *4 Ezra* 7:28–29).[53] Chapters 39 and 40 provide an interpretation of the seer's earlier vision, in which he sees a powerful fountain uprooting "the great forest except one cedar" (*2 Bar.* 36:5–6); this represents "the last ruler" in the world (*2 Bar.* 40:1). The fountain and the vine in the vision are symbolic descriptions of the Messiah (*2 Bar.* 39:7), who will exercise his juridical

---

critique of Hayman's divine identification of the "man" in *Theologies in Conflict in 4 Ezra*, 186 n. 67.

50. Fuller, *The Restoration of Israel*, 80; Elliot, *The Survivors of Israel*, 509.

51. See Chester, *Messiah and Exaltation*, 347–48; Nickelsburg, *Jewish Literature Between the Bible and the Mishnah*, 277–85; Schreiber, *Gesalbter und König*, 363–74; Collins, *The Apocalyptic Imagination*, 212–25; Oegema, *The Anointed and His People*, 220-6; Murphy, "The Temple in the Syriac Apocalypse of Baruch," 671–83; idem, *The Structure and Meaning of Second Baruch*; Sayler, *Have the Promises Failed?*

52. The English translation of *Second Baruch* is from Klijn, "2 Baruch." in *OTP* 1:615–52.

53. Sayler, *Have the Promises Failed?* 60 n.41.

authority to reprove this ruler for his "wicked deeds" and then kill him (*2 Bar.* 40:1–2). Messianic emphasis in chapters 68—70 lies on the "Servant" (*2 Bar.* 70:9–10) as a warrior-judge, who will punish the nations—especially the Romans—and deliver Israel from their foreign oppression.[54] Not all the Gentiles will be destroyed, however. The nations who did not attack Israel will be spared by the Messiah (*2 Bar.* 72:2–3). The author of *Second Baruch* anticipates the eschatological restoration of Jerusalem and the temple, to which all the nations will come to pay their homage (*2 Bar.* 68:5). As with several writings addressed above (e.g., *Sibylline Oracles* 3 and *Psalms of Solomon* 17), the messianic age is described in terms of the glorious fulfillment of the scriptural prophecies with respect to the Davidic dynasty (*2 Bar.* 73:1–7; cf. Isa 11:6–9).[55]

Third Sibylline Oracles

The first example of royal messianism is from the third book of the *Sibylline Oracles*,[56] a book containing a collection of oracles written by Jews in Egypt in the middle of the second century BCE.[57] According to John Collins, a major theme of this book is "royal eschatology."[58] The importance of this theme is evident in the recurrent pattern "sin–tribulation–king/kingdom" (i.e., sin results in tribulation which ends with the coming of a king/kingdom) that forms the structures of four main oracles of the book: (1) vv. 162–95, (2) vv. 196–294, (3) vv. 545–656, and (4) vv. 657–808.[59] The fourth oracle in particular presages the advent of a royal-messianic liberator, who will come "from the sun" (ἀπ' ἠελίοιο, v. 652).[60]

---

54. Oegema, *The Anointed and His People*, 220–24.

55. Chester, *Messiah and Exaltation*, 348; Stuckenbruck, "Messianic Ideas," 112.

56. Chester, *Messiah and Exaltation*, 348–50; Collins, "The Third Sibyl Revisited," 3–19; idem, *The Sibylline Oracles of Egyptian Judaism*; Buitenwerf, *Book III of the Sibylline Oracles and Its Social Setting*; Schreiber, *Gesalbter und König*, 260–64; Oegema, *The Anointed and His People*, 81–85; Pomykala, *The Davidic Dynasty Tradition in Early Judaism*, 256–58; Nolland, "Sib. Or. III. 265–94," 158–67; Klausner, *The Messianic Idea in Israel*, 370–81.

57. Contra Buitenwerf's contention for an Asia provenance and a first-century BCE date (*Book III of the Sibylline Oracles*). See Collins's criticism of Buitenwerf's proposal in "The Third Sibyl Revisited."

58. Collins, *The Sibylline Oracles of Egyptian Judaism*, 35.

59. Ibid., 37.

60. The Greek text of the *Sibylline Oracles* is from Geffcken, *Die Oracula Sibyllina*. The English translation is from Collins, "Sibylline Oracles," *OTP* 1:317–472.

It has been suggested that the phrase ἀπ’ ἠελίοιο hints at the Ptolemaic identity of this liberator.[61] This view, which considers the messianic king of third *Sibylline Oracles* as a Gentile, finds support in the identification of "the seventh king" of Egypt (= the royal liberator in v. 652) as a Greek in vv. 193, 318, 608.[62] Some scholars, however, argue that ἀπ’ ἠελίοιο is an abbreviated expression for ἀφ’ ἡλίου ἀνατολῶν and so the former phrase actually refers to a ruler "from the sunrise/east" (cf. Isa 41:2, 25 LXX).[63] Furthermore, the royal Messiah is not Gentile but Jewish.[64] Either way, in this case, it is important for our purpose to observe that the sibyl makes no mention of the Messiah's Davidic ancestry.

As envisaged in *Sib. Or.* 3:652–56, the messianic king will bring all wars to an end and consequently make peace in the world. Aside from his political role, this passage stresses the king's piety with a reference to his trust in God (v. 656). Several scholars note that the earlier references to Cyrus (cf. Isa 45:1) and his release of the Jewish deportees in *Sib. Or.* 3:286–94 may serve to "provide a typology for the eschatological time."[65] If this typological conception is correct, the royal Messiah would likely enact Cyrus' role as the divine instrument to bring the exiles back and to re-establish Jerusalem and the temple. An oracle of the eschatological kingdom (vv. 767–95), near the end of the book, prophesies that all nations will bring tribute to the restored temple and worship the God of Israel.[66] This oracle does not speak of the Messiah but draws heavily on the motifs in the prophecy of Isa 11:1–12 (esp. 11:6–9).[67] This biblical prophecy envisions the transformation of the earth under the wise and righteous leadership of an ideal, Davidic king. While it remains unclear

---

61. Collins, "Sibylline Oracles," *OTP* 1:356.

62. Collins, *The Apocalyptic Imagination*, 121; Pomykala, *The Davidic Dynasty Tradition in Early Judaism*, 257.

63. E.g., Buitenwerf, *Book III of the Sibylline Oracles*, 272–74.

64. On this view, see Gruen, *Heritage and Hellenism*, 277–78; Nolland, "Sib. Or. III.265–94."

65. Collins, *The Apocalyptic Imagination*, 122. See also Chester, *Messiah and Exaltation*, 349–50; Pitre, *Jesus, the Tribulation, and the End of the Exile*, 77–78; Buitenwerf, *Book III of the Sibylline Oracles*, 275; Nolland, "Sib. Or. III. 265–94."

66. It is likely that *Sib. Or.* 3:776 ("for mortals will invoke the son of the great God") is a Christian interpolation. See Collins, "Sibylline Oracles," *OTP* 1:379; Buitenwerf, *Book III of the Sibylline Oracles*, 289–90; contra Pitre's view that this verse is original (*Jesus, the Tribulation, and the End of the Exile*, 77).

67. Oegema, *The Anointed and His People*, 83–85.

whether the expected king of the third *Sibylline Oracles* will be Gentile or Jewish/Davidic, it is notable that the royal eschatology of this document of the Diaspora conceives the kingdom of God in terms of an actualization of the traditional hope for an eternal Davidic dynasty.

Fifth Sibylline Oracles

The fifth book of the *Sibylline Oracles* represents a Jewish response in the Diaspora to the destruction of the temple in 70 CE.[68] Collins observes that four literary blocks (*Sib. Or.* 5:52–110, 111–78, 179–285, 286–434) dated to the period 70–120 CE display a common pattern: the oracles against the nations—the appearance of a Nero-like tyrant—the advent of a liberator—the annihilation of the wicked.[69] It is uncertain whether the expected messianic king will be David's descendant. Throughout the book, the sibyl denounces the sins of the Gentiles and declares imminent doom against the nations, particularly Rome.[70] Two oracles, *Sib. Or.* 5:155–61 and 5:247–85, are relevant to royal messianism.[71] In an allusion to the "star from Jacob" in Num 24:17, the "great star" from the sky in the first oracle (v. 155) symbolizes the heavenly Messiah who will destroy the wicked forces ("sea") and Rome ("Babylon").[72] Anti-Roman polemics reflect the Jewish exasperation against the Romans, who subjugated the Jews and desolated Jerusalem and the temple in 70 CE. In the second oracle, the coming of "one exceptional man" (*Sib. Or.* 5:256) will set in motion the eschatological renewal of Jerusalem, which will stand "in the middle of the earth" (*Sib. Or.* 5:250).[73]

In *Sib. Or.* 5:414–27, the "blessed man" ($\dot{\alpha}\nu\dot{\eta}\rho$ $\mu\alpha\kappa\alpha\rho\dot{\iota}\tau\eta\varsigma$) from heaven is probably messianic. The "scepter" in his hands (v. 415) signifies his

---

68. Chester, *Messiah and Exaltation*, 398–405; Felder, "What Is the Fifth Sibylline Oracle?" 363–85; Collins, *The Apocalyptic Imagination*, 233–38; Oegema, *The Anointed and His People*, 226–69; cf. the earlier bibliographical references of third *Sibylline Oracles*.

69. Collins, *The Apocalyptic Imagination*, 234.

70. The sins of the Gentiles are mainly idolatry (*Sib. Or.* 5:75–85, 278–80, 353–56, 403–5, 495–96) and sexual immorality (*Sib. Or.* 5:386–93, 496–96).

71. It is uncertain whether the king sent by God in *Sib. Or.* 5:108–9 is messianic.

72. For the symbolic connotation of "star" in the Hellenistic and the Jewish traditions, see Collins, *The Apocalyptic Imagination*, 236; idem, *The Sibylline Oracles of Egyptian Judaism*, 90–91.

73. The Greek text of fifth *Sibylline Oracles* is from Geffcken, *Die Oracula Sibyllina*. The English translation is from Collins, "The Sibylline Oracles" in volume 1 of *OTP*. Line 257 is probably a Christian emendation ("The Sibylline Oracles," *OTP* 1:390).

royalty and legal authority granted by God to mete out punishment on nations and evildoers (vv. 418–19). The eschatological hopes of fifth *Sibylline Oracles* concentrate on the final destiny of the Jewish people and their city and temple. At the eschaton immoral deeds (adultery, homosexuality, bloodshed, and injustice) will be completely banished from Jerusalem, where the "holy temple" (*Sib. Or.* 5:420) will stand and the "holy people of God" will dwell (*Sib. Or.* 5:432). Whereas God is the "founder" of the temple (*Sib. Or.* 5:433; cf. vv. 420–22), it is likely that the Messiah will be the divine agent to accomplish its building project.[74]

Political Movements

So far our overview has examined late Second Temple Jewish writings that explicitly mention the expectation that a kingly Messiah will come. In addition to these writings, prominence of royal messianism during the late Second Temple era is supported indirectly in Josephus's reports of certain political movements in Palestine.[75] These movements were led by various individuals, who hankered for royal status and pejoratives. While it is unclear whether any of these individuals ever made messianic claims, the movements instigated by them may be relevant to our investigation on account of the fact that the religious and the political domains in antiquity overlapped.[76] Furthermore, Josephus on one occasion speaks of an "ambiguous oracle" in Scripture that foretells the coming of a worldwide ruler. This oracle was misinterpreted by the insurgents, who believed that it predicted the Jewish victory over the Romans and so rebelled against them in 66 CE (*J. W.* 6.312–13). If this "ambiguous oracle" refers to Balaam's royal prophecy in Num 24:17 (cf. the omen of a "star" in *J. W.* 6.289), there is good reason to believe that royal-messianic ambitions partly provoked the first Jewish revolt and probably other uprisings.[77] As

74. See chapter 4.

75. Chester, *Messiah and Exaltation*, 418–23; Evans, *Jesus and His Contemporaries*, 53–81; Pomykala, *The Davidic Dynasty Tradition in Early Judaism*, 258–64; Horsley and Hanson, *Bandits, Prophets, and Messiahs*, 110–34; Hengel, *The Zealots*, 237–40.

76. Evans, *Jesus and His Contemporaries*, 53–58; Tan, *Zion Traditions and the Aims of Jesus*, 43; Hengel, *The Zealots*, xv. As Evans says, "any Jewish claim to Israel's throne is in all probability a messianic claimant in some sense" (55). However, Brown objects to a "messianic" description of these non-Davidic, royal aspirants (*The Death of the Messiah*, 1:681–82).

77. For a messianic interpretation of this "ambiguous oracle" (though Josephus considers it a prophecy about Vespasian), see relevant discussions in the studies mentioned in n. 75.

far as our investigation is concerned, the scale of these revolutionary movements and the popularity of their leaders provide evidence of the far-reaching influences of royal messianism in the first century CE, which extended outside literate circles to the masses.

Five revolutionaries who are mentioned in Josephus's writings merit attention. Three of them rose in armed rebellion against the government after the death of Herod the Great in 4 BCE: (1) Judas the son of Hezekiah (*Ant.* 17.271–72; *J.W.* 2.56), (2) Simon, a slave of King Herod (*Ant.* 17.273–76; *J.W.* 2.57–59), and (3) Athronges the shepherd (*Ant.* 17.278–84; *J.W.* 2.60–65). According to Josephus, Simon and Athronges put the diadem on their heads and were proclaimed king by their followers. All three of these rebels came from the lower class in society and their supporters were primarily peasants.[78] The remaining two revolutionaries were commanders of the first Jewish revolt (66–70 CE): (4) Menahem was the son of Judas the Galilean (*J.W.* 2.433–48). After raiding the royal armory at Masada, he returned like a king to Jerusalem and became the leader of the political revolution. (5) Simon bar Giora (i.e., Simon, son of a proselyte), from Gerasa, earned wide support by "proclaiming liberty for the slaves and rewards for the free" in the hill areas (*J.W.* 4.508). After the failure of the revolt, Simon, dressed in white and a purple mantle, appeared unexpectedly before the Romans at the location of the desolate temple.[79] Simon was captured and then executed as part of the Romans' ceremonial celebration at the temple of Jupiter Capitolinus during their triumphant procession in the capital (*J.W.* 7.153–55).

No evidence indicates that any of the five insurrectionists claimed Davidic pedigree.[80] Yet, as Richard Horsley and John Hanson emphasize, the way in which Simon surrendered himself to the Romans "reveal[s] both that Simon understood himself as the messiah and the conquering Romans recognized him as the leader of the nation."[81] It is notable that Josephus's description of Simon bar Giora is reminiscent of the bibli-

---

78. Horsley and Hanson, *Bandits, Prophets, and Messiahs*, 114–17.

79. Tan stresses the importance of Jerusalem (and, by extension, the temple) for these "royal-messianic" pretenders, who held fast to the conviction that "the redemption of Israel *depended* on the redemption of Jerusalem" (*Zion Traditions and the Aims of Jesus*, 47 [emphasis his]). See also Hengel, *The Zealots*, 117–18, 297.

80. But see Hengel, *The Zealots*, 298–300; Bauckham, "Messianism according to the Gospel of John," 48 n. 51.

81. Horsley and Hanson, *Bandits, Prophets, and Messiahs*, 126–27.

cal picture of David, though Simon had a pagan lineage as the son of a proselyte.[82] The Simon-David similarities include: (1) both launched their military careers as the chiefs of desperate villains; (2) both had great physical strength; and (3) Simon captured the city Hebron, where David was anointed as king of Judah (2 Sam 2:4; 5:7).[83] It is possible that Simon's self-perception as the royal liberator, and his reception as such by the Jews, were reinforced by his embodiment of certain Davidic features.

The New Testament

Despite their Christian character, the New Testament documents are an important source for Jewish royal-messianic phenomena in the first century CE.[84] Especially significant are the Gospel narratives, according to which both the religious elites and the ordinary people look forward to the arrival of the Davidic Messiah (Matt 22:42; Mark 12:35, 37; Luke 1:69; John 7:42). A number of Jewish people in the Gospels designate Jesus as the "Son of David," a title which carries strong royal-messianic overtones. These people include two blind men (Matt 9:27), a crowd (Matt 12:23), two other blind men (one is Bartimaeus; Matt 20:30–31; Mark 10:46–48; Luke 18:38–39), and a group of exulted Jews in Jerusalem (Matt 21:9; cf. Mark 11:10). Some Jews associate the "Son of David" with the blessings of physical healing (Matt 9:27; 15:22; 20:30–31);[85] whereas others expect him to play a militant role to annihilate Israel's enemies (Luke 1:71, 74) and reinstate the Davidic monarchy (Mark 11:10; Acts 1:6; cf. Luke 1:31–32). It is likely that political ambitions lie behind the Jewish attempt to make Jesus king, after he miraculously feeds more than five thousand people (John 6:15). Broadly speaking, Jewish royal messianism as seen in the Gospels revolves around the hopes for a Davidic king who will carry out political, and to a lesser degree, healing tasks.

82. Hengel notes that Athronges and the young David had the same occupation, i.e., shepherd (*The Zealots*, 292).

83. Horsley and Hanson, *Bandits, Prophets, and Messiahs*, 121–22.

84. Chester, *Messiah and Exaltation*, 310–24; Bauckham, "Messianism according to the Gospel of John," 35; Strauss, *The Davidic Messiah in Luke-Acts*, 48–49; Jonge, *Jesus*, 77–116.

85. Chae discusses the healing function of the eschatological Davidic shepherd in Judaism and Matthew's Gospel. See *Jesus as the Eschatological Davidic Shepherd*.

The Septuagint, the Testaments of the Twelve Patriarchs, the Targumim, and the Shemoneh Esreh

Finally, we will briefly comment on royal messianism in the Septuagint, the *Testaments of the Twelve Patriarchs*, the *Targumim*, and the *Shemoneh Esreh*. For the Septuagint, scholars generally agree that there is no homogenous tendency in the (royal) messianic treatment among the Greek biblical books.[86] A study of Jewish royal-messianic ideas in the LXX is also hampered by the fact that all its extant copies were preserved and copied by Christian scribes, who might have "messianized" certain passages that they understood as prophecies of Jesus the Messiah.[87] Nonetheless, royal-messianic elements are probably present in some LXX passages including Num 24:7, 17 and Amos 4:13. The former two Greek verses construe Balaam's third and fourth oracles as foretelling the advent of a "man" (ἄνθρωπος). As envisaged in Num 24:7 LXX, this person will possess dominion and "rule over many nations." The future drift in the Greek text can be seen in the interpretation of the Amalekite king Agag in the MT as Gog, who is an eschatological figure according to Ezekiel 38—39. In Num 24:17 LXX, the royal emblem שבט ("scepter") in the MT is construed as symbolizing a "man" who will arise out of Israel.[88] In Amos 4:13 LXX, the Greek reading, ἀπαγγέλλων εἰς ἀνθρώπους τὸν χριστὸν αὐτοῦ, is overtly messianic.[89]

Various passages in the *Testaments of the Twelve Patriarchs* mention the future coming of a royal figure from the tribe of Judah (e.g., *T. Sim.* 7:1–2; *T. Jud.* 24:1–6; *T. Dan.* 5:10; *T. Naph.* 8:2–3; *T. Gad* 8:1).[90] While the

86. For messianism in the Septuagint, see Fitzmyer, *The One Who Is to Come*, 65–81; Fabry, "Messianism in the Septuagint," 193–205; Lust, *Messianism and the Septuagint*; Jobes and Silva, *Invitation to the Septuagint*, 96–97, 297–300; Horbury, *Jewish Messianism and the Cult of Christ*, 46–59. Among these scholars, Horbury places great emphasis on the royal-messianic elements in the LXX.

87. Lust gives two examples: Lam 4:20 and Ezek 17:23. See *Messianism and the Septuagint*, 9, 14.

88. Fabry, "Messianism in the Septuagint," 202; Jobes and Silva, *Invitation to the Septuagint*, 298–99; contra Lust, "Messianism and Septuagint," in *Messianism and the Septuagint*, 13–14. The passage Num 24:17 is interpreted messianically in various late Second Temple Jewish writings including CD-A VII, 20; 1QM 11:4–9; *T. Jud.* 24:1–6.

89. Jobes and Silva, *Invitation to the Septuagint*, 297.

90. The *Testaments* mention not only a future ruler from the tribe of Judah but also the arrival of an ideal priest from the tribe of Levi (e.g., *T. Sim.* 7:1–2). This latter figure may be the priestly Messiah. For messianism in the *Testaments of the Twelve Patriarchs*,

Vorlage of the *Testaments* was probably composed before the Common Era, its extant form display obvious traits of Christian redaction (e.g., *T. Jos.* 19:11; *T. Ben.* 3:8) that make the task of discerning authentic Jewish royal-messianic notions from later Christian interpolations very difficult. For this reason, we will not give primary weight to royal-messianic texts in the *Testaments*, but rather will consider them as secondary evidence of Jewish royal-messianic phenomena during the late Second Temple period. Subsequent chapters will only briefly touch on the relevant texts as necessary.

For the *Targumim*, the hope for the messianic king is obviously present in a number of Aramaic biblical texts.[91] Some of them will receive attention in the following chapters. Although the targumic writings are dated to the post-NT age, some of their traditions might have been in circulation within the circles of first-century CE Judaism. Of special importance is *Isaiah Targum*, which bears witness to a Jewish royal-messianic identification of the Servant in Isaiah 53 during the period 70–135 CE.[92] At any rate, it is sufficient for the present purpose to note that royal messianism in the *Targumim* at the very least points to the existence of Jewish royal-messianic hopes among first-century CE synagogues.

For the *Shemoneh Esreh*, the fourteenth and fifteenth benedictions contain petitions to God that ask him to raise up an offspring of David. This offspring will be the agent through whom the fortunes of Jerusalem will be restituted:

> And to Jerusalem Thy city return with compassion, and dwell therein as Thou hast promised; and rebuild her speedily in our days, a structure everlasting; and the throne of David speedily establish therein. Blessed art Thou, O Lord, the builder of Jerusalem. (The fourteenth benediction)

---

see Oegema, *The Anointed and His People*, 73–81, 208–12; Jonge, *Jewish Eschatology, Early Christian Christology and the Testaments of the Twelve Patriarchs*, 147–79; Hultgård, "The Ideal 'Levite,' the Davidic Messiah and the Savior Figure in the Testaments of the Twelve Patriarchs," 93–110.

91. For messianism in the *Targumium*, see Shepherd, "Targums, the New Testament, and Biblical Theology of the Messiah," 45–58; Fitzmyer, *The One Who Is to Come*, 146–81; Evans, *Jesus and His Contemporaries*, 155–81; Levey, *The Messiah: An Aramaic Interpretation*.

92. Chilton, *The Glory of Israel*, 94–96; contra the view of Levey and Churgin that *Isaiah Targum* 53 implicitly points to the revolution of Bar Kokhba. See Levey, *The Messiah*, 67; Churgin, *Targum Jonathan to the Prophets*, 26, 83–84.

The offspring of David Thy servant speedily cause to flourish, and let his horn be exalted in Thy exaltation; for Thy salvation do we hope daily. Blessed art Thou, O Lord, who causest the horn of salvation to flourish. (The fifteenth benediction) [93]

Most likely the *Shemoneh Esreh* took shape during the last few decades of the first century CE. This is supported by the fact that the destruction of Jerusalem is alluded to and the fact that this collection of Jewish prayers was known by the rabbi of the early second century CE (cf. *m. Ber.* 4:3; *m. Ta'an.* 2:2).[94] If the references to a future Davidic king in the fourteenth and fifteenth benedictions are taken as messianic, the *Shemoneh Esreh* provides evidence of Jewish royal messianism during 70–100 CE and particularly the royal Messiah's connection with the restoration of the Davidic monarchy and Jerusalem.

Summary

The prominence of Jewish royal messianism (albeit with diverse manifestations) is supported directly or indirectly in a number of late Second Temple writings, whose dates of composition span from the middle of the second century BCE to the turn of the first century CE. The presence of royal messianism in the writings addressed above, which vary considerably in genre (poems, apocalypses, and narratives) and provenance (inside and outside Palestine), indicates the prevalence of the royal-messianic hopes in first-century CE Judaism—among both educated and uneducated people.[95] What is the importance of royal messianism in Judaism for our study? Of foremost importance is that it significantly increases the probability that the Gospel of John, in its twin assertions of Jesus as king and as Messiah, intends to portray him as the Messiah-King of Israel. This understanding of Johannine Christology as royal-messianic will be confirmed in the next section, which probes relevant Gospel ma-

---

93. The texts are from Schürer, division 2 of *A History of the Jewish People in the Age of Jesus Christ*, 2:87.

94. Ibid., 2:87–88.

95. This is not to say that royal messianism occupies the central position in the thought-world of Second Temple Judaism. The writings discussed above constitute only a portion of Jewish literature of the Second Temple period, apart from the NT. Moreover, it is widely observed that the figure of a messianic king does not appear in some literary works of this period (e.g., Sirach and 1 and 2 Maccabees).

terials in light of the circumstantial Jewish royal-messianic phenomena as delineated in the preceding analysis.

Internal Evidence: Jesus as the Messiah-King in the Gospel of John

We will first refute the scholarly arguments that undermine the conceptual tie between Jesus' kingship and messiahship in Johannine thought. Next we will put forward further evidence from the Gospel of John in order to strengthen such a tie in the Johannine conception of Jesus' identity.

Johannine Christology as Non-Davidic?

In chapter 1, we mentioned several Johannine studies that tend to downplay Davidic-messianic or messianic entailments in the royal Christology of John's Gospel. To grasp the thrust of this tendency, it is adequate to recapitulate the principal arguments propounded in Lierman's recent essay, which may be taken as representative. Underlying Lierman's contention is the argument that there is a "dearth of Davidic claims in the Fourth Gospel."[96] Throughout this Gospel "John makes nothing of Jesus' Davidic ancestry, and never refers to Jesus as the Son or descendant of David."[97] Lierman emphasizes that even at the single place in the Gospel story where David's name surfaces (John 7:42), no indication hints at the Johannine intention of associating Jesus with David.[98] In Lierman's judgment, the various proposals for Davidic messianism in Johannine Christology lack convincing power because they build upon a shaky foundation: "John makes Jesus the messiah; to be the messiah was to be a Davidic figure; therefore, John makes Jesus a Davidic messiah."[99] Instead of David, Lierman contends that Moses is the best precedent for the Johannine portrayal of Jesus.

In response to Lierman's challenges and similar ones posited by other scholars, it is crucial to note that the idea of Davidic lineage is not ubiquitous in all royal-messianic profiles in the late Second Temple age. Among the writings addressed in the preceding section, only the *Psalms of Solomon*, the DSS, *Fourth Ezra*, and the New Testament (and

96. Lierman, "The Mosaic Pattern of John's Christology," 217.
97. Ibid.
98. Ibid.
99. Ibid., 233.

the *Targumim* and the *Shemoneh Esreh*) contain *explicit* references to the Messiah's Davidic descent. Such references are missing from third and fifth *Sibylline Oracles*, the *Similitudes of Enoch, Second Baruch,* and Josephus's reports of the political rebels who sought kingship.[100] Whether or not the royal-messianic figures in these documents are in fact genealogically non-Davidic, it is apparent that a Davidic-genealogical notion is not necessary for the expression of Jewish royal messianism. Thus, the absence of such a notion in the Johannine portrait of Jesus does not in itself imply that this portrait does not conceive of Jesus as the royal Messiah.

The allegation of Lierman and other scholars that the Gospel of John lacks Davidic materials is also questionable. It is correct to say that overt Davidic references are scant in this Gospel, which mentions David by name only twice (John 7:42). However, a careful examination of John's narrative presentation of Jesus reveals that it draws much of its substance from the rich Davidic traditions in the Jewish Scriptures. For instance, most scholars agree that Ezekiel 34 is one of the inspirations of the Johannine depiction of Jesus as the good shepherd (John 10:1–18, 22–30).[101] In the context of Ezekiel 34, God rebukes the unfaithful shepherds of Israel (i.e., the Jewish leaders) and promises that he as the divine Shepherd will tend his own sheep and place them under the care of one Davidic shepherd (Ezek 34:23–24; cf. 37:22–25; Jer 3:15; 23:4–6; Zech 13:7–9). Several Jewish texts in the late Second Temple age (e.g., *Pss. Sol.* 17:24, 40; Ps 2:9 LXX) take up and develop the Davidic shepherd motif in the OT to construct a Davidic-messianic shepherd, through whom the biblical promises of Israel's restoration will be realized. In this respect, the Johannine description of Jesus as "one shepherd" gathering his own flock (John 10:16; cf. 11:47–51; *Pss. Sol.* 17:18, 26–28, 31–32) stands in line with the OT and post-biblical Jewish messianic traditions. Nevertheless, John transforms the traditional materials by combining the roles of God and the Davidic shepherd into one divine-messianic individual. It is probable that the Johannine shepherd discourse employs a Davidic-typological

100. In the *Testaments of the Twelve Patriarchs*, the future ruler from the tribe of Judah is not explicitly referred to as David's descendant, although the ruler's Davidic status can be inferred from his Judahite ancestry.

101. E.g., Laniak, *Shepherds After My Own Heart*, 210–11; Beutler, "Der alttestamentlich-jüdische Hintergrund der Hirtenrede in Johannes 10," 18–32. Contra Bultmann's claim: "[T]he shepherd is not thought of as the Messianic ruler; there are no traces whatsoever of the kingly figure" (*The Gospel of John*, 367).

scheme to implicitly present Jesus as fulfilling the scriptural prophecies regarding the eschatological Davidic shepherd.[102]

In her study on the Johannine appropriation of the Psalms, Margaret Daly-Denton detects sundry subtle Davidic motifs present in the Christology of John's Gospel, which cites frequently from this biblical book.[103] Daly-Denton argues that Davidic connotations are powerfully expressed in the Gospel narrative through direct and indirect references to the Psalms, whose Davidic authorship was taken for granted in first-century CE Judaism and early Christianity.[104] Thus the quotation of Ps 68:10 LXX (Ps 69:10 MT; 69:9 Eng.) in John 2:17 in the temple pericope would naturally conjure up the idea of the psalmist's (David's) zeal for God's temple (cf. 2 Sam 7:5, 11b–16). The Johannine citations from Psalms 21 LXX (22 MT/Eng.), 68 LXX (69 MT/Eng.), and 33 LXX (34 MT/Eng.) in the passion narrative would have the effect of likening Jesus' death to David's righteous suffering and thereby strengthening the claim that crucified Jesus is the rightful king of Israel. In fact, Daly-Denton notes that these analogical patterns are suggestive of a typological relationship between Jesus and David.[105] The correctness of some of these proposed Jesus-David ties will be scrutinized more closely in the remainder of our study, which will expand the scope of investigation in order to address royal messianism in general. Even at this preliminary stage, it is evident—to say the least—that the Davidic presence in the Gospel of John is not confined to a single verse, i.e., John 7:42.

Several other motifs in this Gospel are highly evocative of the Jewish expectations for a royal, but not necessarily Davidic, Messiah. For the present purpose two examples of such motif are sufficient. The first motif relates to the future hope concerning the eschatological temple. There is evidence that some Jews in the late Second Temple era expected the royal/Davidic Messiah to perform the task of restoring/cleansing/rebuilding the temple (cf. *Sib. Or.* 5:414–433; *Tg.* Isa. 53:5; *Tg.* Zech 6:12). Seen in this light, it is possible that a purpose of the Johannine accounts, which unfold Jesus' ardent actions in the temple (John 2:13–17) and his announcement

102. Köstenberger, "Jesus the Good Shepherd Who Will Also Bring Other Sheep (John 10:16)," 67–96.

103. Daly-Denton, *David in the Fourth Gospel*, 38–46. See also Köstenberger, "John," 415–512.

104. Daly-Denton, *David in the Fourth Gospel*, 59–113.

105. Ibid., 208–42.

of its imminent destruction and reconstruction (John 2:18–22), is demonstration of Jesus' royal-messianic validity. The second Johannine motif that is potentially pertinent to royal messianism is the inauguration of the kingdom of God (John 3:1–14; cf. 18:36). In the thoughts of the OT and some Jewish circles, the appearance of the royal or Davidic Messiah will set in motion the actualization of the longed-for kingdom of God (e.g., Isa 9:1–7; 11:1–11; Ezek 34:23–24; Zech 9:9–10; *Pss. Sol.* 17:21; 4Q252; 4Q174; 4Q285). In the context of John's realized eschatology, this kingdom anticipation may be echoed when Jesus avers that his "lifting up" on the cross will effect the bestowal of the life of God's eternal kingdom (John 3:1–15).

Still unanswered is the puzzling question of why John never makes a reference to Jesus' Davidic pedigree, if he really wants to present Jesus as the Messiah-King of Israel. In response to this question it is noteworthy that Jesus' heavenly origin (cf. John 3:8; 8:14, 23), which itself qualifies him to disclose the divine revelation, is one of the key themes of the Gospel of John.[106] In order to shine the spotlight on Jesus' heavenly provenance, it is unsurprising that the evangelist remains silent on Jesus' earthly lineage as David's son.[107] In fact, an irony may be subtly at work in the pericope John 7:40–44, which narrates the Jewish schism over Jesus' identity and the Messiah's birthplace. In other words, the evangelist deliberately brings up Jesus' Galilean background so as to highlight the Jewish ignorance of Jesus' true origin.[108] Another viable explanation is that John attempts to distance Jesus from the nationalistic expectation—Israel's political freedom from the Roman rule—that was intrinsically bound up with Davidic messianism during the late Second Temple era (cf. *Psalms of Solomon* 17; 4Q174; 4Q285; *4 Ezra* 13:26–27; Luke 1:71, 74; Acts 1:6).[109] In his investigation of the motif of "Jesus' Davidic Suffering" in Mark's passion narrative, Stephen Ahearne-Kroll claims that the passage Mark 12:35–37 tones down the prominence of the Messiah's Davidic ancestry in order to dissociate "Jesus from the earthly, militaristic aspects of a Davidic messiah."[110]

---

106. Smith, *The Theology of the Gospel of John*, 91–93.

107. Schnackenburg, *The Gospel according to St. John*, 2:158–59.

108. Beasley-Murray, *John*, 118; Carson, *The Gospel according to John*, 330; Duke, *Irony in the Fourth Gospel*, 66–67.

109. Cf. Schreiber, *Gesalbter und König*, 472–73; Smith, *The Theology of the Gospel of John*, 86–87; Hay, *Glory at the Right Hand*, 110–15.

110. Ahearne-Kroll, *The Psalms of Lament in Mark's Passion*, 168; cf. Daly-Denton, *David in the Fourth Gospel*, 104–5.

If Ahearne-Kroll's judgment is accurate, the Johannine effort to downplay the Davidic lineage of Jesus as the Messiah is not without Christian precedent. It is probable that John, like Mark, wants to distance Jesus from the national-militant connotations of contemporary Davidic messianism, rather than distance David from being a messianic type for Jesus.

Johannine Christology as Royal-Messianic

Underlying the Johannine portrayal of Jesus is the idea that he is the promised Messiah-King of Israel. The centrality of Jesus' messiahship in the structure of Johannine Christology is evident in the Gospel's purpose statement (John 20:31), which Jean Zimmermann underscores as one of Johannine "paratexts."[111] This purpose statement indicates clearly that John's narrative presentation of Jesus aims to elicit belief in him as "Messiah" and "Son of God." The word χριστός ("Christ") occurs 19 times in the Gospel of John,[112] compared to only 16 times in Matthew, 7 times in Mark, and 12 times in Luke. Two of these 19 occurrences are in the compound phrase Ἰησοῦς χριστός ("Jesus Christ"; John 1:17; 17:3). In this Gospel, the transliterated Aramaic term Μεσσίας ("Messiah") appears twice in John 1:41 and 4:25, but nowhere in the narratives of the other three canonical Gospels. Throughout the Johannine story, the subject of whether Jesus is the expected Messiah surfaces repeatedly in various settings in the main plotline (e.g., John 1:42; 4:29; 7:26, 27; 9:22; 12:34). Schreiber is right when he notes that the Jewish search for the Messiah at the outset of the Gospel story (John 1:20) and the Johannine conclusion of Jesus as the Messiah (John 20:31) together form an *inclusio*, within which Jesus' messianic identity and mission gradually unfold.[113] In fact, one can give a *précis* of the Johannine story as "the quest for the Messiah."[114]

Turning to the kingship motif, it is evident that this motif occupies a vital position within the framework of John's messianic Christology. Nineteen of the 21 instances of the terms βασιλεύς ("king") and βασιλεία ("kingdom") in the Fourth Gospel occur with respect to Jesus' kingship.

111. Zimmermann, "Intratextuality and Intertextuality in the Gospel of John," 121–35 (123). Zimmermann discerns three "paratexts" in the Gospel of John, namely the prologue (1:1–18), the conclusion (20:30–31), and the epilogue (21:1–25).

112. John 1:17, 20, 25, 41; 3:28; 4:25, 29; 7:26, 27, 31, 41 (2x), 42; 9:22; 10:24; 11:27; 12:34; 17:3; 20:21.

113. Schreiber, *Gesalbter und König*, 483.

114. Painter, *The Quest for the Messiah*.

Further, John adeptly places the Christological title "king of Israel/the Jews" at critical junctures of the Gospel plot so as to bring Jesus' royal status to prominence. As Frey comments, "[d]as vierte Evangelium stellt die Königstitulatur für Jesu mit besonderem Nachdruck heraus."[115] The first occurrence of "king of Israel" is in Nathanael's acclamation of Jesus (John 1:49), at the narrative point after Jesus has just launched his public ministry. The next "king of Israel" title (John 12:13) is strategically located in the transition from the book of signs (John 1:19—12:50) to the book of glory (John 13:1—20:31), at the critical juncture where Jesus' public career is coming to an end.[116] The majority (15 occurrences) of kingship terminology, including the remaining four instances of the epithet "king of the Jews" (John 18:33, 39; 19:19, 21), are lodged within the trial and crucifixion scenes.[117] Here the Johannine plot rises toward its summit. Aside from these titular references, the kingship theme appears in John 6:15 and finds expression in sundry Davidic or royal-messianic motifs. Royal overtones are also probably implied in certain Christological formulations such as ὁ σωτὴρ τοῦ κόσμου ("the Savior of the world"; John 4:42) and the Jesus-Caesar comparison in the passion account.[118] In support of the evangelist's interest in royal messianism, it may be significant that the Johannine story of Jesus unfolds primarily in the geographical setting of Jerusalem.[119] In the Jewish belief the eschatological stage of the royal Messiah will be in Zion, the chosen city of God.

In view of the strategic placement of the royal appellation "king of Israel/the Jews" in John's narrative portrayal of Jesus, and granted the internal coherence of this portrayal, there is little doubt that the royal-messianic status of Jesus is a central theme of the Fourth Gospel. We do not deny that the kingship of Jesus in Johannine thought entails divine and prophetic nuances. It is unlikely, however, that a work whose composition

115. Frey, *Die eschatologische Verkündigung in den johanneischen Texten*, 272; cf. Brunson, *Psalm 118 in the Gospel of John*, 223–25.

116. The terms "the book of signs" and "the book of glory" are borrowed from Brown's *The Gospel according to John*.

117. These 15 kingship terms are in John 18:33, 36 (3x), 37 (2x), 39; 19:3, 12, 14, 15 (2x), 19, 21 (2x).

118. Sailer, "Jesus, the Emperor, and the Gospel according to John," 284–301; Busse, "Metaphorik und Rhetorik im Johannesevangelium," 304–5; Koester, "The Savior of the World (John 4.42)," 665–80.

119. In this respect, the observation of Fee and Stuart is correct (*How to Read the Bible for All Its Worth*, 141).

purpose centers on Jesus' messiahship (John 20:31) would have perceived and articulated his kingship as lacking strong messianic overtones. It merits notice that the first occurrence of the title "king of Israel" in the Fourth Gospel is juxtaposed with another title "Son of God" (John 1:49; cf. the connection between "Son of God" and "king" in John 19:7, 12), which links with "Christ" elsewhere in Martha's confession (John 11:27) and in the summary conclusion of the entire Gospel (John 20:31). These titular associations within the Gospel narrative support the view that the designations "Son of God" and "king of Israel" in John's usage are of messianic importance. Brunson alleges that the messianic significance is peripheral in the second "king of Israel" epithet that occurs in the quotation of Ps 118:25 in John 12:13. In his view, John deliberately tempers the messianic connotation in this epithet in order to depict Jesus' entrance in Jerusalem as Yahweh's new exodus theophany. Without rejecting the idea of Jesus' divine kingship, it is noteworthy that the royal designation in that context accompanies the participial phrase ὁ ἐρχόμενος ("the coming one"). In Johannine treatment, when this phrase (with variations of form) is used for christological purpose, it often appears in close proximity to the epithet "Christ/Messiah" (John 4:25; 7:27, 31, 41, 42; 11:27; cf. 1:15, 27, 30).[120] On account of this general usage, the occurrence of ὁ ἐρχόμενος in connection with "king of Israel" in John 12:13 would hardly constitute an exception. Most likely, John portrays the Jewish crowd as welcoming Jesus' arrival as the messianic king, while at the same time insinuating his divine royalty.

Conclusion

The aim of this chapter was to lay the foundation of our research by demonstrating the conceptual linkage between Jesus' kingship and messiahship in Johannine Christology. In order to achieve this aim, we first put forward royal-messianic evidence from late Second Temple Judaism. To different degrees of importance, the advent of the messianic king holds a place in the eschatological frameworks of the *Psalms of Solomon*, certain Qumran scrolls, third and fifth *Sibylline Oracles*, *Fourth Ezra*, and *Second Baruch*. Aside from these Jewish writings, we noted possible royal-messi-

---

120. Köstenberger, *The Missions of Jesus and the Disciples according to the Fourth Gospel*, 94. The phrase ὁ ἐρχόμενος also refers to Jesus as the "light" (John 1:9), as one from heaven (John 3:31 [2x]), and as the eschatological prophet (John 6:14).

anic implications of five insurrectionists who are mentioned in the works of Josephus. Analysis of relevant Gospel materials in the New Testament also yielded insights in understanding the Jewish expectation for the royal Messiah (more specifically, the Davidic Messiah) in Palestine during the first century CE. In addition to the writings above, we briefly looked at the relevant materials (though their relevance is debatable) from the LXX, the *Testament of the Twelve Patriarchs*, the Targumim, and the *Shemoneh Esreh*, and pointed out some possible corollaries for our investigation. In short, the result of our survey broadly affirmed the growing influences of royal messianism during the late Second Temple era and its prevalence in the times of Jesus and John.

In addition to external evidence from late Second Temple Judaism, we underlined that the kingship-messiahship connection in Johannine Christology is supported by internal evidence from the Gospel itself. Aside from noting that the notion of Davidic ancestry is not essential to a Jewish royal-messianic portrait, we called attention to sundry Johannine motifs that may resonate with the rich Davidic traditions in the OT; these intertextual resonances may hint at the outworking of a Davidic typology in Johannine thought. Furthermore, it is very probable that several Christological themes (e.g., Jesus' resurrected body as the eschatological temple) create strong resonances with the Jewish hope for the royal Messiah. Given the Gospel's overriding messianic focus (John 20:31) and the consistent associations of certain royal and messianic epithets, all these Davidic- and royal-messianic elements point to an interconnection between Jesus' kingship and messiahship in the Gospel of John.

In view of the external and internal evidence, we conclude that the twin notions of Jesus' kingship and messiahship are intimately woven together within the scheme of Johannine Christology. In the following chapters, we will proceed carefully to examine the kingship-cross interplays in a number of pericopae prior to the passion narrative.

3

The Anticipation of the Death
of the Messiah-King (John 1:43–51)

IN JOHN'S GOSPEL, THE royal epithet "king of Israel" makes its first appearance in the pericope John 1:43–51, where Nathanael acknowledges the royal dignity of Jesus. In the ensuing analysis, we will first observe the royal-messianic notions that emerge in the narrative before Nathanael comes on the scene. Next, we will examine relevant motifs in this pericope in order to demonstrate that it exemplifies the Johannine undertaking to redefine royal messianism in relation to the cross.

Textual Setting: Royal-Messianic Notions (John 1:19–42)

The passage John 1:43–51 is part of the literary unit John 1:19–51, which narrates the events that happen at the beginning of Jesus' public career. The scene commences with the Jewish embassy's exchanges with John the Baptist (John 1:19–28), who refuses to seize a messianic homage that is not rightfully his (v. 21). This scene sets a clear messianic tone for the following episodes and prepares for the appearance of Jesus the Messiah. In John 1:29–34 and 1:35–36, the Baptist gives his witness to Jesus as (1) the lamb of God (vv. 29, 36), (2) the one who will baptize with the Spirit (vv. 30, 32–33; cf. 1:27; Isa 11:2; 42:1), and (3) the Son or chosen one of God (v. 34). For the present purpose the first and the third epithets require comment.

Titular usage of the expression ὁ ἀμνὸς τοῦ θεοῦ ("the lamb of God") occurs only twice in the NT and exclusively in the Gospel of John (1:29,

36).[1] Various backgrounds have been proposed to account for the evangelist's peculiar employment of this expression. Two plausible backgrounds are the Passover lamb in Exodus 12 and the Isaianic Servant as the obedient lamb in Isa 53:7.[2] In addition, the apocalyptic proposal of C. H. Dodd merits attention. Dodd argues that the "lamb of God" designation, which concerns one function of Jesus taking away the sin of the world (John 1:29; cf. 1 John 3:5), is deeply rooted in the Jewish messianic traditions.[3] Dodd finds support from the "horned lambs" symbol in *1 Enoch* 90 and the messianic portraits of *T. Jos.* 19:8; *T. Lev.*18:9; *Pss. Sol.* 17:29; *2 Bar.* 73:1–4. The last two writings in particular envisage the royal or Davidic Messiah eradicating wickedness and delivering God's righteous people.[4]

Scholars' reactions to an apocalyptic approach to the "lamb of God" epithet vary.[5] For the present aim an appraisal of these reactions is unnecessary. It is sufficient to note that despite the limited pre-Christian evidence of the use of "lamb" as a messianic title, the strong messianic tenor surrounding the Baptist's testimonies in John 1:29 and 1:36 suggest that these testimonies most likely pertain to Jewish messianic hopes. This messianic consideration of "lamb of God" is espoused by the scholarly consensus that emerged from the 2005 Colloquium in Leuven, namely

1. The term ἀμνός ("lamb") refers to Jesus in an OT citation in Acts 8:32 (Isa 53:7) and in a simile in 1 Pet 1:19, but these two references do not connote a titular sense. This term also appears in the *Testaments of the Twelve Patriarchs* (*T. Jos.* 19:8; *T. Ben.* 3:8) and two early Christian texts (*1 Clem.* 16:7; *Barn.* 5:2). See BDAG 54; TDNT 1:338–40.

2. Other suggested backgrounds include the "lamb" in Gen 22:8, the gentle "lamb" in Jer 11:19, the scapegoat in Leviticus 16, and the guilt offering in Lev 14:10–31 and Num 6:9–21. See Keener, *The Gospel of John*, 1:452–54; Knöppler, *Sühne im Neuen Testament*, 239–44; Morris, *The Gospel according to John*, 144–47.

3. Dodd, *The Interpretation of the Fourth Gospel*, 230–32, 236–38. Beasley-Murray proposes a similar apocalyptic view of the Johannine title "lamb of God." See Beasley-Murray, *John*, 24–25.

4. Dodd calls attention to the image of Jesus as the slain but mighty warrior-lamb in the book of Revelation, which is associated with the Gospel of John in early Christianity. The book of Revelation is also the only other NT writing that uses the "lamb" symbol as a title for Jesus, albeit with the different term ἀρνίον. In Revelation, Jesus is denoted as "lamb" a total of 28 times (Rev 5:6, 8, 12, 13; 6:1, 16; 7:9, 10, 14, 17; 12:11; 13:8; 14:1, 4 [2x], 10; 15:3; 17:14 [2x]; 19:7, 9; 21:9, 14, 22, 23, 27; 22:1, 3). In Rev 13:11, the beast has two horns like a "lamb." See Dodd, *The Interpretation of the Fourth Gospel*, 236; cf. Bruce, *The Gospel of John*, 52.

5. Scholars who show support for Dodd's proposal (at least part of it) include Carson (*The Gospel according to John*, 150) and Brown (*The Gospel according to John*, 1:58–59).

that this title on the Baptist's lips in all probability carries messianic connotations.[6]

In keeping with the "lamb of God" designation, the other epithet "Son/chosen one of God" (v. 34) in the Baptist's speech is also of messianic importance. The original reading of this epithet is debatable. The Nestle-Aland 27th edition advocates the variant ὁ ἀμνὸς τοῦ θεοῦ as authentic.[7] Against this textual choice, a number of scholars contend that the variant ὁ ἐκλεκτὸς τοῦ θεοῦ ("the chosen one of God") is the *lectio difficilior* and so this variant should be original.[8] In this view, the expression ὁ ἐκλεκτὸς τοῦ θεοῦ draws on the Isaianic description of the Servant as God's elect who receives the Spirit's anointing (Isa 42:1).[9] Proponents of this view argue that ancient scribes would more likely have altered the word ἐκλεκτός ("chosen"), which never occurs elsewhere in the Fourth Gospel, to the usual Johannine term υἱός ("son"; 54x in this Gospel; excluding John 1:34) than vice versa. If the Baptist really utters "the chosen one of God," Nathanael's declaration in John 1:49 attests the first instance of the "Son of God" title in the Johannine story. Moreover, the fact that this title's first and last occurrences in this Gospel overtly link with Jesus' kingship (John 1:49) and his messiahship (John 20:31) respectively reinforces an underpinning of our research, namely that Johannine Christology is royal-messianic (see chapter 2).

Andrew's announcement to Peter that he has found the "Messiah" (v. 41) recalls and contrasts with the Jewish deputation's earlier unsuccessful quest for the "Christ" (Χριστός in v. 20; cf. John 1:25). The term Μεσσίας, which occurs in the NT only in John 1:41 and 4:25, is the Greek translit-eration of the Aramaic term משיחא. In both verses the Greek equivalent

---

6. Coloe, *Dwelling in the Household of God*, 24 n. 22. The papers presented in the 2005 Colloquium in Leuven are collected in Belle, *The Death of Jesus in the Fourth Gospel*.

7. Metzger says that this variant coheres with the Johannine language and is supported by the majority of manuscript witnesses including 𝔓⁶⁶ and 𝔓⁷⁵. See Metzger, *A Textual Commentary on the Greek New Testament*, 172; cf. Moloney, *The Gospel of John*, 59; Bultmann, *The Gospel of John*, 92–93.

8. Scholars who endorse the authenticity of this reading include Burge (*John*, 74–75), Schreiber (*Gesalbter und König*, 457–58), Carson (*The Gospel according to John*, 152), Barrett (*The Gospel according to St. John*, 178), and Schnackenburg (*The Gospel according to St. John*, 1:305–306).

9. Note that the Messiah is designated the "Chosen One" in the *Similitudes of Enoch* (e.g., *1 En.* 39:6; 40:5; 45:3–4; 49:2–4) and there are allusions in the Synoptic Gospels to Isa 42:1 (Matt 3:17; Mark 1:11; Luke 3:22).

of this term, χριστός, is provided. The need for translation reveals that the original audience of John's Gospel was probably incompetent in the Semitic dialect (cf. John 1:38, 42; 9:7; 20:16). In light of this audience background, John's deliberate inclusion of the epithet Μεσσίας, instead of using χριστός alone, hints at his intention to retain and heighten the traditional overtones that are bound up with Jewish messianic hopes. If this judgment is correct, it lends support to a (royal) messianic interpretation of the Baptist's testimonies in John 1:29 and 1:36 and of Philip's and Nathanael's declarations in John 1:45 and 1:49 respectively.

The Prelude to Nathanael's Confession (John 1:43–48)

The temporal phrase τῇ ἐπαύριον at the outset of John 1:43 (cf. 1:29, 35) signals the commencement of a new scene, in which Jesus gains two of his earliest disciples, Philip and Nathanael. In John 1:45, Nathanael responds with skepticism to Philip's witness, which identifies Jesus of Nazareth with the one whom Moses and the prophets have foretold. In Philip's speech, M.-É. Boismard divorces the testimony of Moses from that of the prophets and claims that the former testimony refers specifically to the prophet like Moses (Deut 18:18), whom Boismard correlates with the "king of Israel" in John 1:49.[10] The implication is that this royal title serves to identify Jesus as the Mosaic prophet-king rather than as the royal Messiah.[11]

Several observations, however, temper the view that sees little royal-messianic import in Philip's speech to Nathanael. First, Johannes Beutler comments that the compound expression Μωϋσῆς ἐν τῷ νόμῳ καὶ οἱ προφῆται,[12] which follows the third-person aorist indicative verb ἔγραψεν in John 1:45a, has the intimation of summing up "the whole of Scripture."[13] Given this intimation, it seems unwarranted to separate the witness of Moses from that of the prophets. Second, the perfect indicative verb εὑρήκαμεν in John 1:45 echoes the same verb in John 1:41, where Jesus

10. Boismard, *Moses or Jesus*, 25–30 (esp. 30).

11. Ibid., 30.

12. The two-fold division of the Scripture into the Torah and the Prophets is attested in both of the Jewish and the Christian traditions (e.g., 2 Macc. 15:9; 4 Macc. 18:10; Matt 5:17; 7:12; 11:13 [= Luke 16:16]; 22:40; Acts 13:15; 24:14; 28:23; Rom 3:21). Luke 24:44 mentions a three-fold division—the Law, the Prophets, and the Psalms. See Keener, *The Gospel of John*, 1:482 n. 496; Bultmann, *The Gospel of John*, 103.

13. Beutler, "The Use of 'Scripture' in the Gospel of John," 152–53.

is referred to as the "Messiah."[14] This textual linkage between these two verses is also suggested in their shared use of a first-person plural verbal form, which in effect binds together Andrew's and Philip's declarations. More important, this linkage indicates that Philip's utterance most likely functions to enhance the "Messiah" theme that has been introduced in Andrew's announcement. One way Philip's utterance develops this theme is that it propounds the assertion that Jesus is the Messiah *promised in the Scripture*. Nonetheless, further revelation in the cross is necessary to unveil that the Scripture actually predicts a *crucified* Messiah (cf. John 2:22; 20:9). Third, there is evidence that certain passages in the Torah were considered as messianic prophecies during the Second Temple era. For example, the passage Gen 49:10–11 is interpreted messianically in 4Q252 V, 1–7; 1QSb V, 29 (the lion-Prince); *4 Ezra* 11:37 (the lion-Messiah); 12:32. Balaam's oracle in Num 24:17 is understood as presaging the Messiah's coming in 1QM XI, 4–7; 4Q175 9–13; *Sib. Or.* 5:155. These messianic examples suggest that the belief that Moses has spoken of the Messiah is not foreign to first-century CE Judaism, which surrounded the creation of John's Gospel.[15] Simply put, all that was said points to a messianic significance in the Nathanael-Philip conversation in John 1:44–46.

The description of Jesus as ἀπὸ Ναζαρέτ ("from Nazareth") in John 1:45 deserves notice. In the Johannine context, this description will be reiterated in the scornful question of Nathanael, who thinks it absurd that the Messiah would have originated from such an inconsequential region (John 1:46; cf. 7:41, 52). The Galilean village "Nazareth," which was located to the southeast of the city Sepphoris, is not mentioned in the OT, Second Temple Jewish literature, or rabbinic writings.[16] In the Gospel of John, the term Ναζαρέτ (2x) appears only in the Philip-Nathanael dialogue. It is possible that, in an ironic fashion typical of this Gospel's literary style,[17] this term's double occurrences in John 1:45–46 point forward

---

14. The same historical present εὑρίσκει also occurs in both of John 1:41 and 1:45. See the grammatical analysis in Urban, *Das Menschenbild nach dem Johannesevangelium*, 202–205, 223; cf. Bultmann, *The Gospel of John*, 103.

15. In the NT, the passages of Gen 49:10–11 (cf. Rev 5:5) and Num 24:17 (cf. Matt 2:2; Rev 22:16) are interpreted as prophecies concerning Jesus the Messiah.

16. Riesner, "Archaeology and Geography," in *DJG* 33–46 (36); cf. Wise, "Nazarene," in *DJG* 571–74.

17. For Johannine irony, see Duke, *Irony in the Fourth Gospel*; Culpepper, *Anatomy of the Fourth Gospel*, 165-80.

to the designation of the crucified Jesus as ὁ Ναζωραῖος in the passion narrative (John 19:9; cf. 18:5, 7). Mary Coloe proposes that this designation in the cross-inscription is a royal-messianic title.[18] According to Coloe, this expression accentuates the identity of the crucified Jesus as the messianic builder of the eschatological temple. This being the case, a Johannine irony is plausibly in play in the Johannine description of Nathanael's derisive comment. While Nathanael disdains Jesus' Nazarene origin as subverting his messianic credentials, the crucifixion narrative will unfold that Jesus' Nazarene identity turns out as a verification of his royal messiahship.[19]

Nathanael's misgiving changes to amazement and admiration upon his encounter with Jesus. In John 1:47b, the evangelist contrasts the "guileless" Nathanael with the "deceitful" Jacob, who shrewdly expropriates the birthright of his older brother Esau (Gen 27:35–36). This Jacob later receives from God the new name "Israel" and eventually becomes the ancestor of the Israelites (Gen 32:28–30). It is noteworthy that the description of Nathanael as "under the fig tree" (John 1:48, 50) may bear a messianic overtone.[20] Gleaning insight from the metaphorical depiction of Israel as the fruits on a fig tree in Hos 9:10, J. Ramsey Michaels claims that this Johannine "fig tree" reference underlines Nathanael's symbolic role as the "new Israel."[21] Undermining Michaels' contention, similar references (i.e., Israel as a fig tree or the figs) in the biblical traditions often surface in a judgment context regarding Israel's unfaithfulness to God (e.g., Hos 9:10; Jer 8:13; 24:1–8; 29:17; cf. Matt 21:18–20; Mark 11:12–14, 20–21; Luke 13:6–9).[22] By contrast, Jesus is not reprimanding Nathanael or pronouncing judgment on him as Israel's representative. Delbert Burkett (followed by Alan Kerr) modifies Michaels' view and suggests that the "fig tree" reference symbolically denotes Nathanael as "an Israelite by natural descent."[23] However, in the Johannine setting Nathanael is not

---

18. Coloe, "The Nazarene King: Pilate's Title as the Key to John's Crucifixion," 839–48; idem, *God Dwells with Us*, 171–74.

19. Boismard says that "son of Joseph" (John 1:45) is a royal title (*Moses or Jesus*, 32–38).

20. For various interpretations of the Johannine reference to "the fig tree," see Barrett, *The Gospel according to John*, 185; Brown, *The Gospel according to John*, 1:83.

21. Michaels, "Nathanael under the Fig Tree," 182–83.

22. Burkett, *The Son of the Man in the Gospel of John*, 113–14.

23. Ibid., 114; Kerr, *The Temple of Jesus' Body*, 142.

compared to the fig tree. Some scholars think that the "fig tree" in John 1:48 signifies prosperity or tranquility (cf. 1 Kgs 4:25; 5:5; Mic 4:4; 1 Macc 14:12), whereas other interpreters, in light of certain rabbinic texts about the scribes studying the Torah under fig trees (e.g., Rabbi Hiyya, Aqiba, and Hoshaia in *Gen. Rab.* 62:2), propose that Nathanael is mediating on the Scripture.[24] Yet the relatively late date of the rabbinic sources subverts the attractiveness of this proposal.

More promising is Craig Koester's messianic approach to the Johannine "fig tree" references.[25] Koester argues that the fig tree in John 1:48 (and 1:50) alludes to the eschatological vision of Zech 3:10 (cf. 1 Kgs 4:25; Mic 4:4; 1 Macc 14:12), which envisages every man "calling" his neighbor to sit under his vine and fig tree (cf. Philip's "calling" Nathanael). In the context of Zech 3:8–10, this vision will be actualized on the last days when the Branch of David arrives (cf. Zech 6:12; Jer 23:5; 33:15 [MT]). As Koester observes, the evangelist quotes the book of Zechariah twice—Zech 9:9 in John 12:15 and Zech 12:10 in John 19:37—and plausibly alludes to Zech 14:21 in John 2:16 and Zech 14:8 in John 7:38 (cf. John 19:34).[26] Given the evangelist's acquaintance with this biblical book, it is very probable that he draws on its messianic motifs in the early part of his story in order to identify Jesus as the messianic king predicted in Zechariah. This is probable especially because John has just affirmed the OT prophets' messianic witness to Jesus (John 1:45). The summoning of the messianic prophecy of Zech 3:8–10 near the closing of John 1 paves the way for the subsequent temple account, in which Jesus is portrayed as the builder of God's eschatological temple (John 2:19–21; see chapter 4). It is notable that the other oracle about the "Branch" in Zech 6:12, aside from the passage Zech 3:8–10 which mentions a fig tree, speaks of this figure as God's agent who will rebuild the temple. With Koester, it seems likely that the Johannine "fig tree" locale in the Nathanael-Jesus conversation is to some extent inspired by the messianic prophecy of Zechariah. While at this narrative point before Easter Nathanael has not yet fully grasped the essence of Jesus' royal messiahship which entails crucifix-

24. For the rabbinic references, see Keener, *The Gospel of John*, 1:486 n. 528; cf. Neusner, vol. 3 of *Genesis Rabbah*.

25. Koester, "Messianic Exegesis and the Call of Nathanael (John 1:45–51)," 23–34; cf. idem, "Jesus' Resurrection, the Signs, and the Dynamics of Faith in the Gospel of John," 47–74 (56).

26. Idem, "Messianic Exegesis and the Call of Nathanael," 25–26.

ion, he will soon recognize that Jesus is the one of whom Moses and the prophets have testified.

Nathanael's Acclamation of Jesus (John 1:49)

In John 1:49, Nathanael, apparently impressed by Jesus' supernatural knowledge and messianic revelation, professes his faith in Jesus as the "Son of God" and the "king of Israel." Given that the Messiah's identity is a recurrent motif that runs throughout the entire literary section John 1:19–51 (vv. 20, 25, 41, 45, 49),[27] this declaration of Nathanael most likely bears a messianic connotation and represents his *royal-messianic* confession of Jesus' identity. This reading of Nathanael's titular acclamation of Jesus is supported by the biblical basis of the Messiah-King's divine sonship and the contextual evidence of this concept and of the use of "king" as a messianic title in late Second Temple Judaism. Without denying John's divine Christology, the following paragraphs will elaborate on these arguments.

"Son of God" as a Messianic Title

The concept that the messianic king is God's "son" is rooted in the Davidic dynasty promise as delineated in the Nathan oracle in 2 Sam 7:4–16 (cf. 1 Chr 17:1–15; Pss 2:7; 89:26–27; 132:1–18).[28] As indicated in 2 Sam 7:14, God declares through Nathan that Solomon, David's successor, will enjoy the privileged status as the deity's "son" (בֵן). Similar ideas with regard to the king's filial relationship to God are present in Ps 2:7 and Ps 89:27–28 (89:26–27 Eng.). In Psalm 2, God speaks to the king as "my [his] son" (בְּנִי) and one "begotten" (יָלַד) by God (Ps 2:7). In Psalm 89, the king summons help from God "my [his] father" (אָבִי; Ps 89:27 MT [89:26 Eng.]) and consequently receives the divine consolation that he will be exalted as God's "firstborn" (בְּכוֹר; Ps 89:28 MT [89:27 Eng.]). Significantly, Psalms 2 and 89 not only affirm the Davidic king's divine sonship but also refer to him as the Lord's "anointed" (מָשִׁיחַ in Pss 2:2; 89:39, 52 MT [89:38, 51 Eng.]).[29] These OT passages, which speak of the king's special relationship

---

27. Painter, *The Quest for the Messiah*, 177–88; Wright, *The Resurrection of the Son of God*, 672.

28. Collins and Collins, *King and Messiah as Son of God*, 25–33; Strauss, *The Davidic Messiah in Luke-Acts*, 35–37.

29. See Wilson, "King, Messiah, and the Reign of God," 391–406; Tournay, *Seeing and*

to God as his father, provide the theological foundation of the affirmation of the Messiah-King's divine sonship in post-biblical Judaism and early Christianity.

Joseph Fitzmyer alleges that there is no extant evidence of a pre-Christian messianic use of the designation "Son of God."[30] If this allegation is accurate, it would significantly undermine a (royal) messianic understanding of the Johannine "Son of God" title. Yet, aside from the above-mentioned scriptural texts, the late first-century BCE Aramaic document 4Q246 bears witness to this title's messianic usage.[31] In 4Q246, the opening lines of column I unfold a seer falling before an enthroned king, who is greatly terrified of the disastrous events that he has seen in a vision. The remaining lines offer the exposition of this vision, which announces the rise of this king's heir. As envisaged in line 1 of column II, all the earthly inhabitants will hail this royal heir as the "Son of God" (ברה דר אל) and the "Son of the Most High" (בר עליון).[32] He will destroy the wicked rulers, who are represented by the kings of Assyria and Egypt (I, 6; cf. 1QM I, 2, 4). Further, this "Son of God" will reign on the whole earth (I, 7–8; II, 7–9) and his kingdom will perpetuate eternally (II, 5, 9).[33]

Fitzmyer and Schreiber object to a messianic identification of the Son of God in 4Q246, on account of its lack of the Aramaic word משיחא.[34] This objection is worth considering, but it is not decisive unless one

---

Hearing God with the Psalms, 199–229; Durham, "The King as 'Messiah' in the Psalms," 425–35.

30. Fitzmyer, The Dead Sea Scrolls and Christian Origins, 74. For Schreiber, "[e]in Nachweis der Bezeichnung des Gesalbten als Sohn Gottes im frühen Judentum gestaltet sich aufgrund des Quellenbefundes schwierig" (Gesalbter und König, 504). In Schreiber's view, only 4Q174 plausibly attests the idea of the Messiah as God's Son in pre-Christian times.

31. Xeravits, King, Priest, Prophet, 82–89; Zimmermann, Messianische Texte aus Qumran, 129; Collins, "The Son of God Text from Qumran," 65–82.

32. It is feasible that the lacuna at the beginning of I, 9 originally speaks of the royal successor's divine sonship, on the basis of the parallel structures within 4Q246 I, 9–II, 1. See the discussions in Zimmermann, Messianische Texte aus Qumran, 135 (his proposed restoration of the lacuna is בר מלכא רבא); Xeravits, King, Priest, Prophet, 85–86 (his proposed restoration of the lacuna is בר רבא).

33. If the third-person masculine suffixes and verbs in 4Q246 II, 4–9 refer to the people of God instead of the "Son of God," he will probably rule on behalf of God's people. See Zimmermann, "Observations on 4Q246—The 'Son of God,'" 184–85; Fitzmyer, "4Q246," 153–74 (164).

34. Fitzmyer, The One Who Is to Come, 105; Schreiber, Gesalbter und König, 506. For various proposals of the identity of the Son of God in 4Q246, see Fitzmyer, The One

adopts the view that equates a term with a concept. Some scholars think that this Son of God is an evil ruler (either human or angelic).[35] The "negative" identification of the Son of God builds upon the assumption that 4Q246 unfolds its incidents according to a linear, historical sequence. Yet the weakness of this assumption has been exposed by Zimmermann. He observed that the internal development of 4Q246 displays a concentric structure, within which negative (I, 4–6 and II, 1–3) and positive events (I, 7–II, 1 and II, 4–9) unfold alternatively.[36] Since the Son of God (I, 9–II, 1) takes the center stage of a "positive" scene (I, 7–II, 1), it is unlikely that he is a wicked ruler. Fitzmyer rightly recognizes the positive character of the Son of God, but his insistence that this figure is merely a future Jewish king is at variance with 4Q246's heavily apocalyptic tenor, which Fitzmyer acknowledges.[37] Although Florentino García Martínez considers the Son of God as an angelic or heavenly being (cf. 11QMelch; 1QM XIII, 10), he nonetheless attributes a messianic character to this figure.[38] In fact, the editor of 4Q246, Emile Puèch, has finally expressed his approval of a messianic identification of the Son of God in this document.[39]

The "Son of God" of 4Q246 should be identified as the royal Messiah for three reasons. First, his profile exhibits certain central elements in the Davidic traditions, specifically 2 Sam 7:5–14 and Isa 10:20—11:16.[40] Pertinent motifs include the regal successor's divine sonship, his everlasting kingdom, worldwide authority, and subjugation of foreign enemies. The fact that these two biblical passages are interpreted messianically in several writings at Qumran (e.g., 1QSb; 4Q174; 4Q285; 4Q161) reinforces

---

Who Is to Come, 104–7; Zimmermann, *Messianische Texte aus Qumran*, 160; Collins, *The Scepter and the Star*, 155–57.

35. E.g., Horbury thinks that the Son of God is an evil ruler. For Vermes, the Son of God is "the last historico-apocalyptic sovereign of the ultimate world empire." Flusser proposes that this figure is the Anti-Christ. See Horbury, *Messianism among Jews and Christians*, 134; Vermes, *The Complete Dead Sea Scrolls in English*, 617; Flusser, *Judaism and the Origins of Christianity*, 207–17.

36. Zimmermann, *Messianische Texte aus Qumran*, 136, 161–62; idem, "Observations on 4Q246," 184; cf. Xeravits, *King, Priest, Prophet*, 87.

37. Fitzymer, *The One Who Is to Come*, 105; idem, "4Q246," 173–74.

38. Martínez, "Divine Sonship at Qumran," 127–29; idem, *Qumran and Apocalyptic*, 172–79.

39. Puèch, "Le 'Fils de Dieu' en 4Q246," 143–52 (cited from Martínez, "Divine Sonship at Qumran," 130 n. 88; Fitzmyer, *The One Who Is to Come*, 106).

40. Chester, *Messiah and Exaltation*, 232; Evans, *Jesus and His Contemporaries*, 108–9.

the likelihood that the author of 4Q246 seeks to depict the Son of God as a messianic conqueror. Second, a messianic construal of the Son of God accords with Qumran's expectation that the Davidic Messiah will fight for God's people in the final war and annihilate all their foes (cf. 4Q174; 4Q285). Third, Luke 1:32–35 attest the utilization of "Son of God" and "Son of the Most High" as messianic titles in the first century CE. This infancy account displays several textual parallels with 4Q246, including the use of passive verbal forms.[41] The Lukan employment of these twin epithets suggests that they probably carry messianic connotations in first-century CE Judaism. Otherwise, the third evangelist would not have applied them to accentuate the messianic importance of the birth of Jesus.

Two other Qumran scrolls (4Q174 and 1Q28a) may be relevant to our investigation. In expounding the Nathan oracle of 2 Sam 7:11–14, the author of 4Q174 frg.1 correlates David's son, whom God adopts to be his son, with the messianic "Branch of David" (I, 11; cf. 4Q252, 4Q161, 4Q285). Although 4Q174 does not employ the epithet "Son of God," the identification of the "Branch" with the "son" of 2 Samuel 7 supports the assertion that this epithet carries a royal-messianic connotation.[42] The fragmentary text 1Q28a (1QSa) depicts the eschatological banquet, where the Messiah of Israel (משיח ישראל in II, 14, 20; משיח in II, 12 [without ישראל]) will participate with the community at Qumran (I, 1). On the basis of a textual restoration, the lacuna at the end of II, 11 may originally read יוליד (cf. the link in Psalm 2 between the verb ילד [v. 7] and the Lord's "anointed" [משיח in v. 2]).[43] This reading plausibly gives the impression that God "begets" the Messiah.[44]

Aside from the DSS, *Fourth Ezra* 13 may bear witness to the Jewish conception of the (royal) Messiah as God's son at the end of the first century CE.[45] This apocalypse's Latin and Syriac versions denote the Messiah as the "Son" of God (4 Ezra 13:32, 37, 52; cf. 7:28–29; 14:9). Michael Stone

41. For the parallels between Luke 1:32–35 and 4Q246, see Zimmermann, *Messianische Texte aus Qumran*, 159; Evans, *Jesus and His Contemporaries*, 109.

42. Collins, *The Scepter and the Star*, 164.

43. Evans, *Jesus and His Contemporaries*, 94–98; Collins, *The Scepter and the Star*, 164–65.

44. Since there are other feasible ways to reconstruct the missing text (e.g., יוליד), the authenticity of the reading יוליד remains uncertain. See Fitzmyer, *The One Who Is to Come*, 92.

45. See chapter 2 for the debate regarding the Messiah's royal status in *Fourth Ezra*.

claims that the reading "son" results from Christian interpolation and the original texts actually speak of the Messiah as God's "servant" (i.e., παῖς/ עֶבֶד in Greek/Hebrew).[46] However, many scholars think that the variant "son" in these versions adequately renders the original denotation of the Greek or Hebrew *Vorlage*, i.e., υἱός or בֵּן.[47] It is crucial that the messianic portrayal of 4 *Ezra* 13:35–38 has sundry points of contact with Psalm 2, such as the foreign assault of the Davidic king or Messiah, his rebuke of the nations, and his triumphant stand on mount Zion. Since Psalm 2 is a key biblical inspiration for the idea of the Messiah's divine sonship, the textual resemblance with this psalm espouses the interpretation that the Davidic Messiah of *Fourth Ezra* 13 is designated God's "son".[48]

Lastly, the narrative of Mark 14:61 provides evidence of the Jewish belief concerning the Messiah's filial relationship to God. If the historicity of this narrative is assumed, it indicates that the high priest in Jesus' times most probably considered ὁ υἱὸς τοῦ εὐλογητοῦ and χριστός as interchangeable designations (cf. ὁ υἱὸς τοῦ θεοῦ and χριστός in Matt 26:63).[49]

"King of Israel" as a Messianic Title[50]

A messianic interpretation of the epithet "king of Israel" is based on the biblical traditions in which the title "king" is applied to the eschatological

---

46. Stone, *Fourth Ezra*, 207–8; similarly, Schreiber, *Gesalbter und König*, 508–9.

47. Collins and Collins, *King and Messiah as Son of God*, 96; Chester, *Messiah and Exaltation*, 346; Metzger, "The Fourth Book of Ezra," *OTP* 1:551–53. See the excursus "The Messiah: Son or Servant of the Most High?" in Hogan, *Theologies in Conflict in 4 Ezra*, 195–98.

48. Hogan, *Theologies in Conflict in 4 Ezra*, 196; Collins, "The Son of God Text," 76–77.

49. For the historicity of this Markan account, see Bock, "Blasphemy and the Jewish Examination of Jesus," 626–38.

50. In several Second Temple Jewish writings, the Messiah is not explicitly designated "king" but his profiles display sundry features that point to a royal status. These features may be the Messiah's heavenly enthronement (*1 En.* 45:3; 51:3–5; 55:4; *2 Bar.* 73:1–7), his universal dominion (e.g., *4 Ezra* 5:6 [if the royal figure there is messianic; see chapter 2]; *2 Bar.* 39:7), and the symbols "scepter" and "star" (e.g., *Sib. Or.* 5:155, 415). At Qumran, the messianic title "Prince" connotes a regal, albeit not overtly royal, sense (e.g., 1QSb V, 20; 1QM V, 1; 4Q285 frgs. 4, 5). It must be remarked that the lack of the title "king" in these Jewish royal-messianic texts is unsurprising. In fact, even in the LXX there is a translation tendency that favors the diminutive term ἄρχων (or its cognate words) rather than the royal title βασιλεύς, when translating the Hebrew word מֶלֶךְ (e.g., Num 24:7; Ezek 37:22–24; Mic 5:3). Political sensitivity might have played a role in the Jewish re-

David (e.g., Jer 30:9; Ezek 37:22, 24). In Mic 5:1, the regal description of the new David as מוֹשֵׁל בְּיִשְׂרָאֵל ("ruler in Israel") is not far from the conspicuously royal title "king of Israel." In chapter 2, we called attention to the growing prevalence of Jewish royal messianism during the late Second Temple era. Of special importance for the present discussion, the first-century BCE writing *Psalms of Solomon* 17 contains a clear reference to the Messiah as "the king of Israel" (τοῦ βασιλέως Ἰσραήλ; v. 42). This writing further designates him as "son of David" (υἱὸν Δαυίδ; v. 21) and "Lord Christ" (χριστὸς κύριος; 17:32; cf. the title χριστός in the superscription of *Psalms of Solomon* 18 and *Pss. Sol.* 18:5, 7). Associations of these messianic titles within *Psalms of Solomon* 17 and 18 suggest that "king of Israel" was a current appellation for the royal Messiah at the turn of the Common Era, at least in the Palestinian region. The royal title "king" (βασιλεύς) also occurs with reference to a messianic savior in the pre-Christian Diaspora document third *Sibylline Oracles* (e.g., *Sib. Or.* 3:193, 608, 652 [βασιλῆα]).[51]

Summary

There is solid biblical basis and adequate circumstantial evidence to bolster our interpretation that the designations "Son of God" and "king of Israel" in John 1:49 are meant to be royal-messianic. In line with the messianic focus of the surrounding episodes, these designations represent Nathanael's salutation to Jesus as the Messiah-King of Israel.

Jesus' Response to Nathanael's Acclamation (John 1:50–51)

In John 1:50–51, Jesus utters his summative response to Nathanael's messianic acclamation and, by extension, to other characters in the earlier narrative. The response of Jesus begins with a rhetorical question being tantamount to a positive assertion. In his following speech, Jesus promises Nathanael that he will see "greater things" (μείζω τούτων; John 1:50b). The exact referent of these "greater things" is partly dependent on the textual relationship between John 1:50 and 1:51. Some commentators reject the authenticity of John 1:51 and slacken this verse's textual connection with

---

straint of explicitly designating the royal Messiah as "king." For the LXX, see Freund, "From Kings to Archons," 58–72.

51. The Greek text is from Geffcken, *Die Oracula Sibyllina*.

John 1:50 accordingly.[52] By contrast, a number of other scholars assert that John 1:51 aptly serves as the climatic ending of John 1.[53] From our perspective, whether or not 1:51 is a redactional product, this verse must be analyzed as an integral part of the Johannine narrative if the literary coherence of this narrative's extant form is affirmed. On this basis, the "greater things" in John 1:50 and the "Son of Man" vision in John 1:51 will be treated as interrelated promises of Jesus.

The "Son of Man" vision commences with the image of a heaven opened. In the canonical and extra-canonical Jewish writings, the image of an open heaven often heralds God's revelation or announcement (e.g., Gen 28:12; Ezek 1:1; *2 Bar.* 22:1; *T. Lev.* 2:8).[54] Such usage of this image is also found in several NT writings (e.g., Matt 3:16 pars.; 26:64 pars.; Acts 7:56; 10:11; Rev 4:1; 19:11).[55] In the Johannine context, an open heaven likewise signals the disclosure of a divine revelation. This revelation, which links with the "greater things" in John 1:50, unveils the role and function of the Son of Man. Brown says that Jesus' promise of a greater revelation will be fulfilled in the Cana "sign," in which the disciples will glimpse the glory of Jesus (John 2:11).[56] Yet it is more likely that this "sign" represents only the initial realization of this promise. The reason this interpretation is more likely is that although the "signs" in John's Gospel have a revelatory function of displaying Jesus' glory, the supreme manifestation of divine revelation must take place in the cross. As several scholars rightly underline, Jesus' utterance in John 1:50–51 serves as an internal prolepsis in anticipating his death that will be unfolded in the subsequent narrative.[57] Therefore this utterance of Jesus in John 1 adroitly brings the cross motif into play.

The cross motif's subtle presence in John 1:50–51 is more perceptible when seen in light of this passage's preparatory function for the temple theme in John 2, where the temple is redefined as Jesus' crucified and

52. E.g., O'Neill, "Son of Man, Stone of Blood (John 1:51)," 374; Brown, *The Gospel according to John,* 1:88–89.

53. Keener, *The Gospel of John,* 1:489; Moloney, "The Johannine Son of Man Revisited," 188–89; idem, *The Johannine Son of Man,* 36–41; Carson, *The Gospel according to John,* 165–66.

54. Rowland, *The Open Heaven,* 53, 359.

55. See ibid. The "Son of Man" is mentioned in Matt 3:16 and 26:64.

56. Brown, *The Gospel according to John,* 1:89–91.

57. Coloe, *Dwelling in the Household of God,* 49; Hoskins, *Jesus as the Fulfillment of the Temple in the Gospel of John,* 134–35; Moloney, *The Johannine Son of Man,* 37–40.

risen body (vv. 19–22). Most scholars agree that the "Son of Man" saying of John 1:51 alludes to Jacob's dream at Bethel (Gen 28:12). In the setting of Gen 28:12, Jacob beholds a ladder that reaches the sky, and the angels of God ascending and descending בו. According to Gen 28:17–19, Jacob perceives his dream as a vision from God and names the place where he stands "Bethel" and the "gate of heaven." The prepositional term בו in Gen 28:12 can be translated as either "on him [i.e., on Jacob]" or "on it [i.e., on the ladder]," because both of the Hebrew nouns יעקב and סלם are masculine.[58] The former reading gives the impression that the traffic of the angels is between heaven and Jacob (cf. *Gen. Rab.* 68:12; 69:7).[59] This being the case, John probably wants to stress that Jesus as the Son of Man takes the place of Jacob and represents the new Israel.[60] This view is attractive, but its plausibility is subverted by the relatively late date of the only textual evidence from the targumic writings, which are dated no earlier than the third century CE. While these writings may preserve an earlier tradition of the first century CE, there is no extant evidence to confirm such preservation. The evangelist will bring the Jesus-Jacob comparison to the fore in John 4:12. Yet it is unclear that this comparison is at work early in the allusions to Genesis 28 in John 1:51, particularly because John introduced the Nathanael-Jacob contrast shortly before in John 1:47.

The Hebrew term בו in Gen 28:12 probably means "on it." That is to say, in his dream Jacob sees the angels ascending and descending "on the ladder."[61] A strong evidence of this reading is in Gen 28:12 LXX, where the feminine pronoun in the phrase ἐπ' αὐτῆς refers to κλῖμαξ. This LXX evidence is crucial for the exegesis of John 1:51, not only because the LXX is pre-Christian, but also because this Johannine verse exhibits a substantial lexical resemblance with Gen 28:12 LXX. Also important, most of the scriptural quotations in the Gospel of John come closer to the textual

58. For other proposed interpretations, see Brown, *The Gospel according to John*, 1:89–91.

59. For Jacob's dream in the targumic or rabbinic traditions, see Clarke, "Jacob's Dream at Bethel as Interpreted in the Targums and the New Testament," 367–77; Dodd, *The Interpretation of the Fourth Gospel*, 245–46; Kim, *The Son of Man as the Son of God*, 82–83.

60. On this view, see Carson, *The Gospel according to John*, 163–64; Clarke, "Jacob's Dream at Bethel," 374–75; Dodd, *The Interpretation of the Fourth Gospel*, 245–46.

61. On this view, see Hoskins, *Jesus as the Fulfillment of the Temple*, 132–33; Keener, *The Gospel of John*, 1:490; Burkett, *The Son of the Man in the Gospel of John*, 118.

form of the LXX than that of the MT.[62] This tendency within the Gospel gives credence to the interpretation that the Son of Man corresponds to the ladder, which is the earthly destination of the angels' transit according to Gen 28:12 LXX. Thus the Son of Man, akin to the ladder at Bethel that bridges heaven and earth, is the intermediary that connects God and human. In other words, analogous to Jacob's reception of the divine revelation at Bethel, Nathanael and the disciples will behold a revelation of greater things concerning the Son of Man. While the temple theme *per se* does not surface in John 1:50–51,[63] the notion of Jesus as the locus of God's presence and revelation apparently anticipates the ensuing redefinition in John 2:19–22 of the temple as Jesus' resurrected body. In the latter text, the death of Jesus is unequivocally mentioned for the first time in the Johannine story. So the cross motif in John 1:50–51, which is subtly evoked by this passage's revelation theme, gains strength through this connection with the temple theme in John 2. In response to Nathanael's royal-messianic acclamation, Jesus' rejoinder in terms of the "Son of Man" vision anticipates the revelation of his true identity that will take place in the cross.

"Son of Man" and Royal Messianism

So far we have brought to light the Johannine attempt as early as in John 1:50–51 that seeks to reinterpret royal messianism in relation to the death of Jesus. But, why is the expression "Son of Man" (v. 51) employed in this attempt? Given that most of the thirteen "Son of Man" instances in the Gospel of John appear in association with the cross motif (John 1:51; 3:13, 14; 5:27; 6:27, 53, 62; 8:28; 9:35; 12:23, 34 [2x]; 13:31),[64] this expression's royal-messianic overtone (if there is any) bears on this study in that it impinges on the conceptual coherence of the Johannine presentation of the Messiah-King's death. To complicate the issue, a number of scholars claim that there is no such thing as a "Son of Man" title or a stock "Son

---

62. Köstenberger, "John," 417–18; Schuchard, *Scripture Within Scripture*, 151.

63. Kerr, *The Temple of Jesus' Body*, 166; Morgan, "La Promesse de Jésus à Nathanaël (Jn 1, 51)," 3–21 (esp. 21).

64. John usually uses the expression ὁ υἱὸς τοῦ ἀνθρώπου (with the definite articles). The only exception is in John 5:27, where the anarthrous form υἱὸς ἀνθρώπου is employed. For the Johannine understanding of the "Son of Man," see Moloney, *The Johannine Son of Man*; Lindars, "The Son of Man in the Johannine Christology," 43–60.

of Man" concept in first-century CE Judaism.[65] If this claim is valid, it would diminish the possibility that the Johannine "Son of Man" statement in John 1:51 carries a royal-messianic overtone. Yet, undermining this scholarly claim, John Collins and Yabro Collins note that the case for an absence of "Son of Man" title or common "Son of Man" concept in first-century CE Judaism should not be overstated.[66] They emphasize that although the Aramaic phrase בר (א)נש or ברנ(א) נשא in conventional vernacular denotes a human being or humanity in general, the "Son of Man" vision of Daniel 7 was increasingly associated with Jewish royal-messianic hopes during the first century CE. For the purpose of our study, demonstration of this association in late Second Temple Judaism will lend credence to the construal that John's christological use of "Son of Man" is of royal-messianic significance. Consequently, the thematic-conceptual tie between the "Son of Man" statement in John 1:51, which alludes to Jesus' death, and Nathanael's royal-messianic laudation of Jesus in John 1:49 will gain strength.

The late first-century BCE writing 4Q246, which received attention earlier, probably attests an emerging royal-messianic connection of a "Son of God" figure with the "Son of Man" vision of Daniel 7. Several features of this writing are redolent of this Danielic vision. In addition to the same language of composition (i.e., Aramaic), the shared features include (1) the literary setting of a prophet interpreting the dream of a king, (2) the prophecy of global warfare (4Q246 I, 4–6; Dan 7:17–27), (3) the prophecy of worldwide subordination to the Son of God/Man (II, 7; Dan 7:14, 27), (4) the use of the verb דוש (II, 3; Dan 7:23), and (5) the thematic resemblance of מלכותה מלכות עלם(II, 5) and שלטנה שלטן עלם(II, 9) in 4Q246 with Dan 3:33 and 7:27 (cf. Dan 2:34; 7:14).[67] There are also considerable similarities between 4Q246 and 1QM, which draws much of its substance from the book of Daniel. Two such similarities are (1) the reference to Assyria and Egypt as the oppressors of God's people (4Q246 I, 6; 1QM 1, 2, 4) and (2) the use of an uncommon Persian loanword (i.e.נחשירון

---

65. E.g., Kazen, "Son of Man as Kingdom Imagery," 87–108 (esp. 90–91); Vermes, *Jesus in His Jewish Context*, 81–90; Burkett, *The Son of the Man in the Gospel of John*, 38–45; Casey, *Son of Man*, esp. 197–98 (regarding John 1:51).

66. Collins and Collins, *King and Messiah as Son of God*, 75–100.

67. Zimmermann, "Observations on 4Q246," 185–87; Collins, *The Scepter and the Star*, 157–60.

4]Q246 I, 5]; 1] נחשיר‎QM 1:9–10]).[68] While the available evidence does not indicate a complete identification of the "Son of God" in 4Q246 with the "Son of Man" in Daniel 7,[69] the view that discerns a certain degree of Danielic influences on the portrayal of the "Son of God" in 4Q246 seems logical.[70]

The Son of Man is a prominent figure in the *Similitudes of Enoch* (*1 Enoch* 37—71), in which he appears a total of 16 times (*1 En.* 46:2, 3, 4; 48:2; 62:5, 7, 9, 14; 63:11; 69:26, 27, 29 [2x]; 70:1; 71:14, 17). Twice he is explicitly denoted as the Messiah (*1 En.* 48:10; 52:4). Notably, the early description in *1 En.* 40:1 of a large multitude of angels standing before God evokes the "Son of Man" vision of Dan 7:10.[71] In addition, Danielic allusions are perceptible in *1 En.* 46:1 and 47:3; both of these instances refer to God as the "Head of Days" (cf. Dan 7:9, 13, 22).[72] Despite the absence of the notion of Davidic lineage in the royal-messianic profile of the *Similitudes*, echoes of certain central texts of Davidic messianism ring in *1 En.* 48:10; 49:1–4; 62:2 (cf. the use of Isaiah 11 and Psalm 2).[73] In *Fourth Ezra* 13, the material of Daniel 7 coalesces with that of Isaiah 11 in giving a royal-messianic portrayal.[74] The integration of the constituents from Daniel 7 and Davidic-messianic texts suggests that the former passage was gradually connected with the Davidic- or royal-messianic hopes during the first century CE. In fifth *Sibylline Oracles*, the messianic king is referred to as a "blessed man" from heaven (*Sib. Or.* 5:414; cf. 5:246). William Horbury and George Beasley-Murray believe that the sibyl's depiction of this figure probably witnesses to a *messianic* understanding of

---

68. Collins, *The Scepter and the Star*, 159.

69. Collins and Collins remark that 4Q246 lacks certain basic elements of Daniel 7 (e.g., the beasts and one "coming with clouds"). See *King and Messiah as Son of God*, 72–73. By contrast, both Kuhn and Kim assert that the Son of God in 4Q246 is identified with the Son of Man in Daniel 7. See Kuhn, "The 'One Like a Son of Man' Becomes the 'Son of God,'" 22–42; Kim, *The Son of Man as the Son of God*, 20–22.

70. See esp. Zimmermann, "Observations on 4Q246," 188; *pace* Dunn, "'Son of God' as 'Son of Man' in the Dead Sea Scrolls?" 198–210.

71. VanderKam, "Daniel 7 in the Similitudes of Enoch (1 Enoch 37—71)," 293.

72. Ibid., 294–99. For the change of "Ancient of Days" to "Head of Days," see pp. 294–96.

73. Collins and Collins, *King and Messiah as Son of God*, 90.

74. Hogan, *Theologies in Conflict in 4 Ezra*, 188–89; Collins, "The Apocalyptic Son of Man Sayings," 224.

the Danielic Son of Man.[75] Lastly, the "Son of Man" references in the *Tg. Pss* 8:3; 80:18 (80:17 Eng.); 144:3 are evidently messianic, although these texts are dated to the post-NT age.[76]

On account of the Jewish linkage of Daniel 7 and its "Son of Man" with royal messianism during the late Second Temple period (at least since 100 BCE onwards), it can be reasonably concluded that some Jews in the first century CE referred to the coming royal Messiah as the "Son of Man." In view of this contextual factor, the Johannine juxtaposition in John 1:49–51 of "Son of Man" with the messianic epithets "Son of God" and "king of Israel" carries on the "Messiah" theme that has persisted in the narrative since verse 19. Assuming that Nathanael's confession in John 1:49 is royal-messianic in the traditional sense, it is probable that Jesus' self-reference as the Son of Man instead of either of these two epithets is partly due to the "Son of Man" expression's slighter degree of political connotations.[77] We proposed in chapter 2 that one reason for the Johannine lack in mentioning Jesus' Davidic sonship is that the evangelist wants to distance Jesus from popular nationalistic hopes, which were bound up with Davidic messianism during the late Second Temple era. A similar reasoning plausibly lies behind the Johannine designation of Jesus as the Son of Man in John 1:51, for his kingship is not of this world (John 18:36; cf. 6:15). Thus at both of the thematic and the conceptual levels, the "Son of Man" saying in John 1:51 intrinsically relates to Nathanael's acclamation of Jesus as the "Son of God" and the "king of Israel" (John 1:49)—despite the fact that these three christological designations gradually take on varied nuances as the Gospel story unfolds. In his reply to Nathanael, Jesus intimates through a saying about the Son of Man that the true substance of his royal messiahship will be revealed in the critical moment when he as the Messiah-King goes to the cross. Within the theological fabric of John's Gospel, this initial kingship-cross interplay in John 1:49–51—albeit implicit—hints at the cross's determinative role in the Johannine construction of royal messianism.

75. Horbury, *Messianism Among Jews and Christians*, 150; Beasley-Murray, *Jesus and the Kingdom of God*, 60–61.

76. Collins, "The Apocalyptic Son of Man Sayings," 223.

77. Köstenberger, *John*, 87; Burge, *John*, 79–80; Evans, "David in the Dead Sea Scrolls," 183–97 (esp. 195); Carson, *The Gospel according to John*, 164.

Conclusion

We have closely analyzed the initial occurrence of the kingship-cross link in the Nathanael pericope in John 1:43–51, where the royal epithet "king of Israel" makes its first appearance in the Gospel of John (v. 49). Nathanael's titular acclamation of Jesus is basically royal-messianic and it carries on the "Messiah" theme that predominates in the prior episodes. In support of our reading of this acclamation, we set forth the royal-messianic evidence concerning the twin epithets "Son of God" and "king of Israel" from the OT and late Second Temple Judaism. Further, we strengthened this royal-messianic tie between John 1:49 and 1:51 by providing circumstantial evidence from a number of post-biblical Jewish royal-messianic texts that make use of the constituents of Daniel 7 or explicitly designate the Messiah "Son of Man." As was underlined, Jesus' reply to Nathanael in terms of a "Son of Man" vision in John 1:51 hints at the forthcoming disclosure of the true essence of his royal messiahship, a disclosure which will take place in Jesus' crucifixion. Alertness to this royal-messianic tinge in John 1:51, which points to the christological revelation concerning the Son of Man in the cross, brought to light an implicit kingship-cross interaction in the passage John 1:43–51. In a nutshell, the kingship-cross link in the early part of the Gospel story exemplifies the Johannine undertaking to reinterpret royal messianism in relation to Jesus' death.

4

Temple Restoration and the Royal Messiahship of Jesus (John 2:13–22)

THE AIM OF THIS chapter is to demonstrate that the motif of Jesus' death as expressed in John 2:13–22 serves to corroborate his royal-messianic legitimacy. Whereas in Jewish thought the establishment of the eschatological temple does not necessarily hang on a royal-messianic figure,[1] it is very likely that the Johannine articulation of Jesus' death and resurrection as the temple's destruction and restoration carries royal-messianic overtones. We will first examine relevant scriptural texts so as to lay the biblical basis for the Messiah-King's connection with temple renewal. Next we will seek to show that this royal-messianic connection is present in the thought-world of late Second Temple Judaism. Finally, we will investigate the significance of Jesus' death in John 2 in light of the OT and Second Temple Jewish traditions regarding the Messiah-King and the eschatological temple.

Temple Restoration and the Messiah-King in the OT

The Nathan oracle of 2 Sam 7:4–16 (cf. 1 Chr 17:1–15) is foundational to the Jewish royal-messianic expectation for an ideal temple,[2] where

---

1. Some Jewish texts envision that God will rebuild the temple or Zion; e.g., *Tob.* 13:10, 15–18 (Zion); 14:5–6 (both temple and Zion); *Jub.* 1:17, 27, 29; *1 En.* 90:28–29; 91:13; *2 Bar.* 32:4 (Zion; cf. *2 Bar.* 68:5); 11QT XXIX, 8–10. See McKelvey, *The New Temple*, 15–20, 28–34.

2. A messianic understanding of the Nathan oracle is attested in 4Q174 and several NT passages (e.g., Luke 1:32–33; John 7:42; Acts 2:30; Heb 1:5).

God's presence and glory will reside perpetually in the midst of his people.[3] The twin motifs of temple and kingship are integrally connected in this oracle, which Niek Poulssen refers to as "die magna charta des Jerusalemer Königtums."[4] As 2 Sam 7:5 reveals (cf. v. 2), David desires to construct a בית ("house") as the deity's dwelling place but God rebuffs his proposal. Instead of David erecting a בית (i.e., temple), God declares through Nathan that he will establish a בית (i.e., dynasty) for the king (2 Sam 7:11). The LXX of 2 Sam 7:11 diverges from the MT in that it has subject and object altered and thus conveys the idea that David (presumably via Solomon) will build a "house" (οἶκος) for God. In both of the MT and the LXX, the Nathan oracle announces that David's "seed" will sit on the throne and build a "house" (בית/οἶκος) for the name of God (2 Sam 7:12–13; cf. 1 Kgs 5:17–19 MT [1 Kgs 5:3–5 Eng.]; 6:1). This descendant of David, moreover, will enjoy a filial relationship to God as his "son" (2 Sam 7:14). As God's sacred abode, the temple (and Zion)[5] will always be enfolded and safeguarded by the divine presence on the stipulation that the king and his people are loyal to God (1 Kgs 9:3–9; 2 Chr 7:16–22; cf. 2 Sam 7:15). Nonetheless, the history of ancient Israel witnesses to the nation's apostasy, the resulting departure of God's presence and glory from the temple (Jer 7:14–15; Ezekiel 8—11 [esp. Ezek 8:6; 10:18]), and its tragic demolition by the Babylonians in 587/586 BCE (2 Kgs 25:1–17; Jer 39:1–8; 52:12–23).

The return of the divine glory and presence to Zion, where a splendid temple will stand again, holds a consequential place in the OT prophetic hopes (e.g., Isa 44:28; 49:14; Ezek 43:4–7; Zech 1:16; 2:14–15 MT and LXX [2:10–11 Eng.]; Hag 2:9). Several prophetic texts are relevant to our investigation. In Ezekiel's vision of the new Jerusalem (Ezekiel 40—48), the temple appears as already erected and the glory of God returns to take lodging in it (Ezek 43:4–7; cf. Ezek 10:18).[6] Thomas Renz is probably correct that Ezekiel's accentuation of Yahweh's sovereignty

---

3. The biblical root of the eschatological temple can be traced back to the Mosaic institution of the tabernacle as God's lodging place among his people. For the tabernacle-temple connection, see Hoskins, *Jesus as the Fulfillment of the Temple*, 38–51; Koester, *The Dwelling of God*, 6–22.

4. Poulssen, *König und Tempel im Glaubenszeugnis des Alten Testamentes*, 55.

5. Ps 132:13–14.

6. Hoskins, *Jesus as the Fulfillment of the Temple*, 69–83; Coloe, *God Dwells with Us*, 47–48.

in reinstating the temple, without the involvement of any human mediator, seeks to underscore that Yahweh alone is king.[7] As the prophet envisages, the new sanctuary will be "holy" (Ezek 43:12) and "purified" (Ezek 43:26) and its sin will be "atoned for" (Ezek 43:20, 26; cf. the divine cleansing of Israel in Ezek 36:25–28). In this eschatological temple, the Davidic "Prince" will serve alongside the priests in reinstituting the proper worship of God (Ezek 45:17, 22–25; 46:1–12; cf. 34:24; 37:25). Although the role of the "Prince" is somewhat overshadowed by Ezekiel's emphasis on the priestly contribution, the Prince apparently plays a part in restoring the temple cult.[8]

In the prophecy of Zech 6:12–13, the "Branch" (cf. Zech 3:8) is designated twice as the builder of God's temple (vv. 12b, 13a).[9] This prophecy does not denote the Branch as king but implies his royal status in the enthronement motif of Zech 6:13. Sigmund Mowinckel alleges that the Branch does not prefigure a future king but rather refers only to Zerubbabel, who was the governor of Judea at the time of Zechariah and Haggai (cf. Hag 2:23). In confining the referent of Branch to Zerubbabel alone, Mowinckel interprets the prophetic hope of a new temple as being fulfilled in the building project under the leadership of Zerubbabel, who has laid the temple's foundation and will finish its construction (Zech 4:9; cf. Zech 1:16).[10] Building on Mowinckel's study, Lloyd Gaston claims that the prophecy of Zech 6:12–13 is totally irrelevant to the idea that the messianic king will build the eschatological temple.[11] Yet Mowinckel and Gaston's simplistic identification of the "Branch" with Zerubbabel faces a number of exegetical difficulties. As Wolter Rose notes, the Branch-Zerubbabel identification fails to offer a satisfactory explanation for the crowning of the high priest Joshua instead of Zerubbabel (Zech 6:11), as well as for the sense of discontinuity with the current situation that

---

7. Renz, *The Rhetorical Function of the Book of Ezekiel*, 128.

8. Block, "Bring Back David," 183–88.

9. Jeremiah also prophesizes the sprouting of a righteous "Branch" from David's line (Jer 23:5; 33:14–16 [the latter passage is absent from the LXX]), but the prophet does not ascribe the assignment of temple restoration to the "Branch." Nonetheless, Dennis supposes that the future reconstitution of Jerusalem will naturally include the temple (Jer 30:18). See Dennis, *Jesus' Death and the Gathering of True Israel*, 146.

10. Mowinckel, *He That Cometh*, 119–22. For Mowinckel, both Zechariah and Haggai believed that "the ideal king of the ancient line is already present" (120).

11. Gaston, *No Stone on Another*, 149 (esp. n. 2).

is intimated in the use of the name צֶמַח.[12] Also problematic is that this one-dimensional identification does not comport well with the consistently future orientation of the pertinent passages in Zechariah 3 and 6.[13] In view of the preceding considerations, the better construal is that the appearance of the "Branch" and the related temple expectation, from Zechariah's viewpoint, are forthcoming events that are yet to be realized.

The oracle of Isa 44:24–28 declares that the Persian ruler, Cyrus, will issue a regal decree and commission imperial endowment to aid in the reconstruction of Jerusalem and its temple (cf. Isa 45:13; Ezra 1:1–4; 6:4–5; 2 Chr 36:22–23). John Goldingay and David Payne comment that "[t]he first explicit reference to Cyrus is closely followed by the first explicit reference to the rebuilding of Jerusalem and of the temple." [14] Cyrus is referred to as "his [God's] anointed" (מְשִׁיחוֹ) in Isa 45:1 and "his [God's] servant" (עַבְדּוֹ) in Isa 44:26 (cf. Cyrus as "shepherd" [the Qal participle רֹעִי] in Isa 44:28a).[15] The anointing of Cyrus signifies that he is God's chosen instrument and is endowed with the Spirit's power, which enables him to execute the divine assignment of restoring the Jewish city and temple (Isa 44:28b). According to Horbury, it is possible that the Isaianic vision of a new temple rebuilt by Cyrus has furnished scriptural inspirations for later Judaism to formulate the concept of a messianic temple, notwithstanding the pagan identity of this מָשִׁיח.[16]

Temple Restoration and the Messiah-King in Late Second Temple Judaism

With varied degrees of certainty, a number of post-biblical Jewish writings attest the belief that the royal Messiah will take part in instigating or even building the eschatological temple.[17]

The first text to consider is *Psalms of Solomon* 17. As underlined in this text, the Davidic Messiah will carry out the mission of purging Jerusalem from the Gentiles and from all unrighteousness (vv. 22, 26, 30,

---

12. Rose, *Zemah and Zerubbabel*, esp. 248–49; cf. Chester, *Messiah and Exaltation*, 226–27.

13. Rose, *Zemah and Zerubbabel*, 248.

14. Goldingay and Payne, *Isaiah 40—55*, 2:16.

15. Ibid., 2:14–22.

16. Horbury, *Messianism among Jews and Christians*, 83–122 (92).

17. For the dating of the Jewish writings, see chapter 2.

32, 43). It is perplexing that this psalm makes no mention of the temple, given that the destiny of Jerusalem occupies a central position in the psalm's messianic vision. McKelvey asserts that the allusions in *Psalms of Solomon* 17 to Nathan's prophecy, as well as the whole document's strong cultic interest, indicate that the messianic consecration of Jerusalem as anticipated in *Pss. Sol.* 17:32 "must refer to the temple."[18] Jostein Ådna goes a step further and argues that the Messiah as depicted in *Pss. Sol.* 17:30c (καὶ καθαριεῖ Ἰερουσαλὴμ ἐν ἁγιασμῷ ὡς καὶ τὸ ἀπ᾽ ἀρχῆς) will not only purify but also rebuild the temple. Ådna finds support from the motif in the following verse 31 regarding the nations streaming to Zion to behold the glory of God, a motif which he believes draws heavily on the eschatological visions of Isa 2:2–4; 49:22f.; 60:1–14.[19] For Ådna, the parallel idea of the Gentile pilgrimage to the temple/Zion in Isa 2:2/*Pss. Sol.* 17:31 indicates that the Davidic Messiah of *Psalms of Solomon* 17 will erect a new temple.[20] Andrew Chester says that the notion of purging Jerusalem from sin may imply the purification of the defiled temple, but he disagrees with Ådna that the portrayal of the Messiah in *Pss. Sol.* 17:30 implies that he will be a temple founder.[21] I broadly agree with Chester's position. That is to say, there is no sufficient evidence from *Psalms of Solomon* 17 that confirms the statement that this psalm expects the Messiah to rebuild the temple. Yet we can be more affirmative than Chester in including temple consecration as part of the messianic mission in *Psalms of Solomon* 17. This affirmation primarily stems from an interpretative approach that seeks to read the seventeenth psalm intratextually with other poems that are conjoined together within the *Psalms*' extant literary form. Reading the *Psalms of Solomon* as a unified piece of literature, notwithstanding this writing's composite and redactional character, leads to the reasonable conclusion that the final editor would have likely considered the Messiah's advent as the theological solution to the profaned temple (cf. *Pss. Sol.* 1:7–8; 2:3–5; 8:11–13, 22).[22] To put the point succinctly, it is very likely

18. McKelvey, *The New Temple*, 17–18, esp. n. 3. McKelvey says that the purification of Jerusalem in *Pss. Sol.* 17:32f. is distinct from that in *Pss. Sol.* 17:14.

19. Ådna, *Jesu Stellung zum Tempel*, 69.

20. Ibid., 69–70.

21. Chester, *Messiah and Exaltation*, 298–99, 485.

22. For the *Psalms*' cultic concern, see Atkinson, *I Cried to the Lord*, 219; Embry, "The *Psalms of Solomon* and the New Testament," 109. Embry puts emphasis on analyzing the *Psalms of Solomon* as a unified piece of literature.

that the Messiah of *Psalms of Solomon* 17 will cleanse Jerusalem *and* its temple.

The text of 4Q174 (frg. 1 I, 2, 7–11) attests a pre-Christian Jewish messianic exegesis of 2 Sam 7:10–14, in which David proposes to build a temple for God. It is important that this text links the Nathan oracle with the promise of Exod 15:17–18, which is cited in lines 3 and 5 of the first column.[23] The textual linkage is established through the shared motif of the sanctuary that appears in these two biblical passages. In the context of 4Q174, the בית ("house") in 2 Sam 7:12 is identified with the מקדש ("sanctuary") in Exod 15:17. In so doing, 4Q174 enhances the idea that the fulfillment of this Exodus promise is indiscrete from the Davidic hope.[24] Yet the citation of Nathan's oracle lacks the prophetic words of 2 Sam 7.13a, which declare that David's son will establish a בית ("house") as God's residence. Donald Juel believes that the author of 4Q174 deliberately omitted 2 Sam 7:13a in order to "avoid the potential contradiction within the [Nathan] oracle," which envisions both of a "house" built by God (2 Sam 7:10) and a "house" built by David's offspring (2 Sam 7:13a).[25] Further, 4Q174 "perhaps even reflects a conscious correction of a traditional view according to which the Messiah was expected to build the temple."[26] For George Brooke, the quotation of Exod 15:17–18 in 4Q174 underscores the notion of divine sovereignty in restituting Israel, while shrinking the Messiah's role in the program of this restoration.[27] By contrast, N. T. Wright asserts that this quotation "confirms, rather than undermines, the fact that the text envisages the Davidic Messiah as the builder of the eschatological temple."[28]

In response, it is noteworthy that the citation of 2 Sam 7:10–14a in 4Q174 retains only certain constituents of the Nathan oracle: (1) David will experience rest from his foes (2 Sam 7:11b); (2) God will build up

23. There is no scholarly consensus on the meaning of the phrase מקדש אדם in 4Q174 I, 6. For various proposals, see Zimmermann, *Messianische Texte aus Qumran*, 107–8.

24. Watts, "The Lord's House and David's Lord," 310.

25. Juel, *Messiah and Temple*, 178–79. In Juel's understanding, 4Q174 reckons the two occurrences of בית in 2 Sam 7:10 and 7:13 as referring to the temple, although they originally render different meanings (p. 177).

26. Ibid., 179.

27. Brooke, "Kingship and Messianism in the Dead Sea Scrolls," 454. In his earlier work, Brooke says that 4Q174 seeks to convey the idea that "God has established both houses, the sanctuary and the shoot of David." See *Exegesis at Qumran*, 178.

28. Wright, *Jesus and the Victory of God*, 484.

David's "house" (2 Sam 7:11c); (3) God will raise up David's "seed" (2 Sam 7:12b); (4) God will establish David's kingdom forever (2 Sam 7:12c, 13b); and (5) David's "seed" will be God's son (2 Sam 7:14a).[29] Hence 4Q174 leaves outs three elements of 2 Sam 7:11–14a: (1) David's "seed" will rise after David's death; (2) this "seed" will come out of David's body; and (3) he will build a sanctuary for the divine name. Kenneth Pomykala observes that these three elements are of direct pertinence to Solomon, who succeeds David's throne and constructs the temple.[30] In view of these elements' "historical" implications, the author of 4Q174 probably omits them in order to better re-contextualize the Nathan prophecy within the scroll's eschatological setting (I, 11).[31] In fact, it is a false alternative that either God or the Messiah can be temple builder within a given writing, for in Jewish thinking the Messiah will act as God's intermediary (cf. both God and the Messiah are king in *Pss. Sol.* 17:1–3, 4, 21, 32, 34, 42, 46 and both of them are purifier of Jerusalem/Israel in *Pss. Sol.* 17:22, 30; 18:5). While 4Q174 does not assign the specific task of temple renewal to the Davidic Branch, his advent is evidently tied to the hope of the eschatological temple.

Steven Bryan proposes that a subtle connection between the Messiah and the temple is present in *1 En.* 53:6 and *Fourth Ezra* 13.[32] The first text declares that the Righteous and Chosen One will reveal the "house" of his congregation. Bryan claims that, at least from the perspective of the subsequent audience, this "house" in *1 En.* 53:6 relates to the heavenly temple that appears near the end of the *Similitudes* (*1 En.* 71:5–7).[33] Building on this thematic relation, Bryan further deduces that the royal Messiah of the *Similitudes* will build the eschatological temple. As for *Fourth Ezra* 13, Bryan contends that the description of *4 Ezra* 13:6 concerning the messianic "man" carving out a "great mountain," which symbolizes Zion (cf. Dan 2:34–35), implies the notion that the Davidic Messiah will partake in reinstituting the city and, by extension, its temple (cf. *4 Ezra* 10:56–57). These two proposals of Bryan are adopted as evidence of the messianic temple in Dennis's study of the Johannine treatment of Israel's restoration

---

29. Juel, *Messiah and Temple*, 177.

30. Pomykala, *The Davidic Dynasty Tradition in Early Judaism*, 194.

31. Ibid.

32. Bryan, *Jesus and Israel's Traditions of Judgment and Restoration*, 192–96; cf. Horbury, *Messianism Among Jews and Gentiles*, 92 n. 13.

33. Bryan, *Jesus and Israel's Traditions*, 192.

hopes.[34] Other scholars, however, show reservation in affirming the validity of such evidence.[35]

In chapter 2, we noted the possibility that within the conceptual fabric of *Sib. Or.* 3:286–94, the restoration of Israel after the Babylonian exile provides a typological pattern for the nation's eschatological redemption.[36] In line 285, the "king" who will be sent by God to reinstate the fortunes of Israel probably refers to Cyrus.[37] There are two references to the temple in *Sib. Or.* 3:286–94: (1) καινὸν σηκὸν θεοῦ (v. 290) and (2) ναός (v. 294). The first reference envisions the erection of a new shrine of God and the second one pertains to the restoration of the sanctuary as it was before. Thus both references look forward to the reversal of the temple's desolate state, which has just been mentioned in *Sib. Or.* 3:281. If the structure of *Sib. Or.* 3:286–94 really employs a Cyrus-typological scheme, this employment suggests that the messianic king will be God's instrument through whom a new temple will be established in Zion (see chapter 2; cf. Isa 44:28; 45:1).[38] Nevertheless, the evidence is admittedly indirect and deduced from an analogous structure.

The text of *Sib. Or.* 5:414–433 contains an important witness to the concept that the Messiah will rebuild the temple. This post-70 CE Diaspora text envisions the descent of a "blessed man" from heaven, with a "scepter" in his hands (vv. 414–415). In chapter 2, we noted that this "man" is most likely the royal Messiah, who appears as a "great star" (μέγας ἀστήρ; *Sib. Or.* 5:155) and an "exceptional man" (ἔξοχος ἀνήρ; *Sib. Or.* 5:256) elsewhere in the same document.[39] As indicated in *Sib. Or.* 5:422, the "blessed man" will reconstruct the sanctuary of God. Gaston discounts this messianic evidence and says that this figure is God rather than the Messiah, based on the description of God as κτίτης ναοῖο μεγίστου ("founder of the greatest temple") in the ensuing line 433.[40] Yet

---

34. Dennis, *Jesus' Death and the Gathering of True Israel*, 155–56.

35. E.g., Ådna, *Jesu Stellung zum Tempel*, 70–71.

36. Collins, *The Apocalyptic Imagination*, 122; Pitre, *Jesus, the Tribulation, and the End of the Exile*, 77–78; Buitenwerf, *Book III of the Sibylline Oracles and Its Social*, 275; Nolland, "Sib. Or. III. 265-94," 158–67.

37. Collins, "Sibylline Oracles," in *OTP* 1:368.

38. Horbury, *Messianism Among Jews and Christians*, 92.

39. It is uncertain whether the "king" sent by God in *Sib. Or.* 5:108 is the royal Messiah, but this royal figure is possibly associated with the messianic references in the remainder of the document.

40. Gaston, *No Stone on Another*, 148.

the twin assertions of God as temple founder and the Messiah as temple founder are not mutually exclusive, given that the Messiah undertakes the temple project on the divine behalf (cf. his "scepter" [i.e., royal authority] in v. 415 is from God).[41] Although it is possible that God is the subject of the three singular verbs in *Sib. Or.* 5:420–423 concerning temple building (ἐποίησεν [2x] and ἔπλασσεν), the more likely view is that the perpetrator of these verbal actions is the "blessed man" (ἀνὴρ μακαρίτης) in *Sib. Or.* 5:420. This view is preferred because this figure is consistently the subject of the verbs in the neighboring verses—ἐκράτησε (v. 416), εἷλεν (v. 418), and ἔφλεξε (v. 419).[42]

Given the relatively late date of the targumic and the rabbinic writings, pertinent materials from them will be addressed briefly. It is possible, however, that these materials might originate from older traditions of the first century CE. (1) In *Targum Jonathan* to Zech 6:12, the Hebrew term צמח is translated as the Aramaic term משיחא (cf. *Tg.* Zech 3:8; *Tg.* Jer 23:5; 33:15).[43] This targumic translation makes plain the future drift of the Hebrew text and announces that the Davidic Messiah will rebuild the temple in Zion.[44] (2) As indicated in *Tg.* Isa 53:5, the sanctuary was profaned by the sins of God's people and consequently it was relinquished to the pagans. The arrival of the Messiah will set into motion the ingathering of Israel's dispersed tribes, the forgiveness of sin, and the reinstatement of the temple (והוא יבני בית מקדשא).[45] The temple notion is not present

---

41. A number of scholars affirm that the Messiah in *Sib. Or.* 5:414–433 is portrayed as temple builder. These scholars include Chester (*Messiah and Exaltation*, 479–82), Hoskins (*Jesus as the Fulfillment of the Temple*, 99), Dennis (*Jesus' Death and the Gathering of True Israel*, 155–56), Ådna (*Jesu Stellung zum Tempel*, 71–76), Bryan (*Jesus and Israel's Traditions*, 194), and Horbury (*Messianism Among Jews and Gentiles*, 92 n. 13).

42. Ådna, *Jesu Stellung zum Tempel*, 75.

43. *Tg.* Zech 6:12 reads: "And you shall speak to him [Joshua], saying, 'Thus speaks the Lord of hosts, saying, Behold the man whose name is Anointed will be revealed, and he shall be raised up, and shall build the temple of the Lord." The English translation is from Cathcart and Gordon, *The Targum of the Minor Prophets*.

44. Gaston dismisses *Tg.* Zech 6:12 as evidence of the Messiah building the temple, on the grounds that this Aramaic verse exhibits minimal variation compared to its MT counterpart (*No Stone on Another*, 149). In contrary to Gaston's claim, the targumic text diverges from the MT in that it alters צמח to משיחא and construes the verb יצמח as יתגלי ("be revealed"; cf. *Tg.* Zech 3:8) and יתרבי ("be raised/exalted"). See Chester, *Messiah and Exaltation*, 483; Dennis, *Jesus' Death and the Gathering of True Israel*, 113–15.

45. Chilton, "The Temple in the Isaiah Targum," 251–62. In *The Isaiah Targum*, Chilton notes that "the focus of much of the Messiah's ministry is the Temple he is to restore." See Chilton, *The Isaiah Targum*, xvii.

in the Hebrew text but is added to this Isaianic passage, probably on the basis of a messianic exegesis of Zech 6:12–13 or a related tradition.[46] According to Bruce Chilton, "the focus of much of the Messiah's ministry [in *Isaiah Targum*] is the Temple he is to restore."[47] (3) In explicating the phrase "awake, O north" in Song 4:16, *Lev. Rab.* 9:6 (fifth-century CE) prophesies that the messianic king will erect the sanctuary of God (cf. *Num. Rab.* 18:21).[48] Similar to *Tg.* Isa 53:5, this messianic idea is probably derived from an established tradition which conceives of the Messiah as the builder of God's eschatological temple.[49]

Summary: The idea that the royal Messiah will rebuild the temple is perceptible in fifth *Sibylline Oracles* and some targumic and rabbinic writings. This idea is not readily observable in the *Psalms of Solomon*, the DSS, *Fourth Ezra*, the *Similitudes*, and third *Sibylline Oracles*. However, several scholars argue for a subtle presence of this idea in some of these documents. While few late Second Temple Jewish writings explicitly depict the Messiah-King as temple builder, it is notable that his advent is often associated with the eschatological restoration of the temple or Jerusalem.

Analysis of John 2:13–22

The pericope John 2:13–22 contains the first explicit reference to Jesus' death and resurrection in the Fourth Gospel (v. 22). The evangelist not only situates this reference in a temple setting, but also formulates it in terms of the temple's demolition and reconstruction. The dual "Passover" references in John 2:13 and 2:23 enclose the temple pericope and build to a crescendo in the passion narrative, where Jesus is crucified during the third and final Passover in this Gospel (John 11:55; 12:1; 13:1; 18:28, 39; 19:14; cf. 6:4 [the 2nd Passover]).[50] This "Passover" linkage not only ties together the temple pericope (John 2:13–22) and the passion narrative, but also points to their mutually enlightening functions. The temple

---

46. See Juel, *Messiah and Temple*, 188; *pace* Gaston, *No Stone on Another*, 149 n. 1.

47. Chilton, *The Isaiah Targum*, xvii.

48. *Lev. Rab.* 9:6 reads: "Or, the Messianic King whose place is in the north will come and rebuild the Sanctuary which is situated in the south. This is [indicated by] what is written: I have roused up one from the north, and he is come (Isa 41:25)." The English translation is from *Midrash Rabbah: Leviticus*, 113.

49. Juel, *Messiah and Temple*, 196–97; cf. Chester, *Messiah and Exaltation*, 484; Ådna, *Jesu Stellung zum Tempel*, 86–87; *pace* Gaston, *No Stone on Another*, 149.

50. The unnamed feast in John 5:1 is probably not the Passover.

account (esp. John 2:19–22), in which the motif of Jesus' death makes its first unequivocal appearance, provides the hermeneutical key for apprehending the Johannine conception of the cross.[51] In the other direction, the passion narrative's lucid portrait of the crucified Messiah-King illuminates the theological entailments of the temple-cross connection in this account. The Johannine temple scene has textual parallels with the Synoptic Gospels, in which similar reports of Jesus' action or speech appear in the closing rather than the beginning of his public ministry (Matt 21:12–13; 26:61; 27:40; Mark 11:15–19; 14:58; Luke 19:45–48). Yet this Johannine-Synoptics disparity is not directly germane to our investigation, which concentrates on the royal-messianic implications of the Johannine presentation.[52]

Textual Setting and Structure

The Johannine temple episode is located within the "from-Cana-to-Cana" section (John 2:1—4:54), which is framed by two "signs" that Jesus performs (John 2:1–11; 4:43–54).[53] This episode succeeds the accounts of Nathanael's royal-messianic declaration (John 1:49) and Jesus' execution of ἀχρὴν τῶν σημείων at the Cana wedding (John 2:1–12).[54] As mentioned in chapter 1, the Cana "sign" in a sense stands for the preliminary fulfillment of Jesus' promise to his disciples of a greater revelation (cf. John 1:50–51), which will culminate in his crucifixion. The act of Jesus miraculously converting six jars of water into choice wine (John 2:10), within a festive ambiance, evokes the Jewish hopes for the messianic era.[55] In both biblical and extra-biblical Jewish traditions, profuse wine is a motif associated with the eschatological bliss (e.g., Isa 25:6; Jer 31:12; Joel 4:18 [3:18

51. Coloe, *God Dwells with Us*, 84.

52. For a comparison of the Johannine and the Synoptic temple accounts, see Ådna, *Jesu Stellung aus Tempel*, 179–90. Some scholars (e.g., Keener and Witherington) believe that John moves the synoptic materials to the early part of the narrative in order to serve his theological aim. Other scholars (e.g., Morris and Carson) comment that Jesus probably disrupts the temple trade twice. See Keener, *The Gospel of John*, 1:518; Witherington, *John's Wisdom*, 85–86; Morris, *The Gospel according to John*, 167; Carson, *The Gospel according to John*, 177.

53. Moloney, *The Gospel of John*, 63–65.

54. The term ἀχρήν may mean the "first," "primary," or "beginning" of the signs of Jesus. See Salier, *The Rhetorical Impact of the Sēmeia in the Gospel of John*, 49–50.

55. Watson, "Wine," in *DJG* 870–73; Schnackenburg, *The Gospel according to St. John*, 1:338.

Eng.]; Amos 9:13–14; Hos 14:8 [14:7 Eng.]; *Sib. Or.* 3:620–23, 744–49). The image of copious wine appears in Jacob's blessing to Judah in Gen 49:8–12, a text that is read messianically in Second Temple Judaism (cf. 4Q252 V, 1–7; 1QSb V, 29; *Tg. Onq.* Genesis). In *2 Bar.* 29:5–7, the messianic age is characterized by the delightful boon of abundant wine (cf. *1 En.* 10:9). During the first and the second Jewish revolts (66–70 CE, 132–135 CE), which were to some extent incited by royal-messianic ambitions, various symbols pertinent to wine (e.g., vine, grape, and wine cup/pitcher) were minted on the Jewish coins.[56] In view of the "wine" symbol's messianic associations and John's stated intent (John 20:30–31), the Cana "sign" most probably has the function of authenticating Jesus' messiahship. In this "sign," Jesus the Messiah manifests his "glory" (John 2:11).[57] In John 2:4, the reference to the "hour" (ὥρα) of Jesus is a veiled allusion to the cross (cf. John 4:21, 23; 7:30; 8:20; 12:23, 27; 13:1; 17:1). This reference alerts the reader to look forward to the onset of the "hour," which in the Gospel of John often functions as one of the "proleptische Deutungen des Todes Jesu."[58]

The report in John 2:12 of Jesus' brief stay in Capernaum serves as a transition from Jesus' "messianic" sign (John 2:1–11) to his subsequent deeds and words in the temple precincts (John 2:13–22). There is a shift in geographical setting, from a Galilean village to Jerusalem's cultic center, as well as a change in ambiance, from a joyous wedding to a direct confrontation with the Jewish leaders. The literary fabric of this passage can be configured in the form of a diptych: John 2:13–17 and 2:18–22. The first part of the diptych narrates the action of Jesus (vv. 14–15), the speech of Jesus (v. 16), and the remembrance of the disciples (v. 17). The second part narrates the retort of "the Jews" (v. 18),[59] the reply of Jesus (v. 19), the Jewish misunderstanding of Jesus' reply, the evangelist's commentary on Jesus' words, and the remembrance of the disciples (vv. 21–22).[60] In the

---

56. Hengel, *Studies in Early Christology*, 315.

57. Notice that similar messianic motifs concerning the revelation of "glory" are found in *Pss. Sol.* 17:32 and *1 En.* 49:2. See Brown, *The Gospel according to John*, 1:105.

58. Frey, "Die 'theologia crucifixi' des Johannesevangeliums," 197; cf. Schnelle, "Die Tempelreinigung und die Christologie des Johannesevangeliums," 369.

59. In the Gospel of John, the expression "the Jews" often refers to the Jewish leaders. In our study, this expression will appear in quotation marks in order to avoid unnecessary anti-Jewish implications.

60. Beasley-Murray, *John*, 38; Schnackenburg, *The Gospel according to St. John*, 1:344.

Synoptic Gospels, the act of Jesus at the temple (Matt 21:12–13; Mark 11:15–19; Luke 19:45–48) and his statement regarding the temple (Matt 26:61; 27:40; Mark 14:58) are located in separate scenes.[61] The Johannine treatment conjoins together Jesus' temple deeds (John 2:14–16) and words (John 2:19) within a single literary unit, a treatment that invites the examination of what Jesus does and says at the temple in light of each other. In investigating the theological thrust of the temple scene, it is also crucial to take into consideration the Johannine twofold remark of the disciples recalling the Scripture at the end of each part of the diptych (John 2:17, 22).

Jesus' Action at the Temple

As revealed in John 2:14–16, Jesus is furious upon discovering animal traders and merchant bankers doing commercial business in the temple area. Oxen, sheep, and doves are sacrificial animals that are used for various kinds of cultic offerings (cf. Exod 20:24; 22:30; 24:5; Lev 1:3–9; 4:2–21; 12:6–8; 14:22). Money changers provide the basic service of converting the pilgrims' currency to the local Tyrian coinage, which is the officially accepted coinage for the payment of the half-shekel temple tax (cf. *Bek.* 8:7).[62] Archaeological evidence suggests that the agora of the Herodian temple was located in the Royal Stoa, which was a rectangular vestibule along the temple's southern wall abutting the Court of the Gentiles (*Ant.* 15.411–416).[63] It is likely that during the Passover, the commercial activities in the Royal Stoa would have overflowed to the contiguous Court of the Gentiles.[64]

There is a scholarly controversy over whether Jesus' interference with the trading transactions conjures up the signification that the temple is defiled and in need of purification. E. P. Sanders emphasizes that currency exchange and animal trade are necessary for the regular operation of the temple cult. Therefore, the view that reckons these commercial activities as polluting the temple gives the wrong intimation that the

61. Coloe, *God Dwells with Us*, 65–69. Luke does not report Jesus' statement of the temple.

62. Wahlde, "Archaeology and John's Gospel," 549; cf. Kreitzer, "Coinage: Greco-Roman," *DNTB* 220–22; Stoops, "Coinage: Jewish," *DNTB* 222–25.

63. Wahlde, "Archaeology and John's Gospel," 549; Ådna, "Jesus' Symbolic Act in the Temple (Mark 11:15–17)," 462–63; Sanders, *Judaism*, 68.

64. Wahlde, "Archaeology and John's Gospel," 549.

sacrificial system that these activities support is impure.[65] For Sanders, Jesus' protest at the bazaar represents a prophetic omen of the temple's imminent destruction. Bryan criticizes Sanders' proposal but agrees with him that it is erroneous to conceive of Jesus' temple action as purification.[66] In Bryan's opinion, there is no evidence from the Pentateuchal purity codes or Second Temple Jewish literature that advocates the belief that the trading industry pollutes the temple. Instead of this, Jesus' deeds "symbolically call into question the efficacy of the Temple as a guarantee of the privileges of national election."[67]

A few comments are needed. First, if Jesus' action at the temple is emblematic in character, his real target is probably not so much the merchants as the ruling aristocracy who is in charge of the temple's commerce. The probability rises when it is noticed that the complainers against Jesus' disrupting act are not the dealers but the Jewish leaders. This is most evident in the Johannine presentation, in which "the Jews" immediately retort to and interrogate Jesus for his authority in instigating such disruption (John 2:18–20; cf. Mark 11:18; Luke 19:47). Second, if Jesus' actual target is not the merchants, it is mistaken to think that the point at issue is whether or not selling animals or exchanging currency may taint the temple. What is critical is rather the "pure" or "impure" condition of the temple per se. Third, Jonathan Klawans has shown that in the thoughts of the Hebrew Scriptures and some Second Temple Jewish groups, sin (especially idolatry, murder, and adultery) has the capacity of producing moral impurity, which degrades the status of the people, the temple, and the land of Israel.[68] One implication pertaining to our analysis is that the temple can be "morally tainted" by sin and hence requires divine purgation. Fourth, Craig Evans has called attention to the prophetic critique and the later Jewish reprimand of the priestly corruption and mismanagement of the temple (e.g., Isa 1:11; Mic 3:9–12; Hos 4:4–6; 6:6; Jer 7:11; Ezek 22:23–31; Zeph 3:1–8; Zech 14:20–21; Mal 3:1; *Jub.* 23:21; 1QpHab 8:8–12; 9:4–5; 10:1; 12:9–10; *Ps. Sol.* 8:11–13; *T. Lev.* 14:1–6; *T. Mos.* 5:3—6:1; *Ant.* 20.179–81; 20.204–14; *Life* 38–39).[69] Richard Bauckham

---

65. Sanders, *Jesus and Judaism*, 61–76.

66. Bryan, *Jesus and Israel's Traditions of Judgment and Restoration*, 209–10.

67. Ibid., 220.

68. Klawans, *Impurity and Sin in Ancient Judaism*, esp. 21–42; idem, "Moral and Ritual Purity," 266–84.

69. See Evans, "Jesus' Action in the Temple," 255–56.

remarks that *b. Pesaḥ*. 57a contains a pre-70 tradition that bears witness to "the evils of the high priestly families."[70] Of pertinence to John's post-70 CE situation, several late first-century CE Jewish writings blame Israel's sin as the cause of the destruction of Jerusalem and its temple (e.g., *Ap. Abr.* 27:3–7; *4 Ezra* 6:19; 7:72; 8:26–31; 9:32, 16; 14:31; *2 Bar.* 10:18).[71] In view of these inner-Jewish charges against the wrongdoings of the temple officials and Israel in general, it is logical to infer that the temple was regarded as polluted by sin and requiring purging—at least within some Jewish circles in the first century CE. Fifth, the Johannine depiction of Jesus expulsing the traders out of the temple zone summons Zechariah's prophecy that at the end of time all will be holy in Jerusalem and no merchant will be present in the sanctuary (Zech 14:21).[72] If this prophecy has furnished inspirations for this Johannine depiction, the evangelist may conceive of the temple's condition as a reversal of the anticipated holiness in Zechariah's eschatological vision. In addition, John probably wants to communicate the idea that the prophetic vision of a sanctified temple is fulfilled in Jesus, whose action at the temple prepares for the inauguration of the eschaton.[73] Neither the Gospel of John nor any of the other three canonical Gospels quotes Zech 14:21, however. According to Bryan, one reason why Jesus enacts instead of cites Zech 14:21 is that this verse's Hebrew text, if read literally, could give the impression that the Gentiles (נעני = "Canaanites") will be barred from the eschatological temple (cf. Zech 14:21 LXX).[74] In divergence from certain Jewish eschatological or messianic traditions, Jesus the messianic "purifier" does not purge the temple from the Gentiles (cf. *Pss. Sol.* 17:22, 28, 30 [but see *Pss. Sol.* 17:31]; 4Q174 I, 3–4; 11QT [no Court of the Gentiles in the temple's blueprint]). In fact, Jesus' protest is possibly in part against the Jewish establishment of a boisterous bazaar in the Royal Stoa (and the adjacent Court of the

---

70. Bauckham, "Jesus' Demonstration in the Temple," 79.

71. See Evans, *Jesus and His Contemporaries*, 325–26. For *Tg.* Isa 53:5, see Chilton, *The Glory of Israel*, 23.

72. Lincoln, *The Gospel according to Saint John*, 138; Ådna, *Jesu Stellung zum Tempel*, 202–6; Dodd, *The Interpretation of the Fourth Gospel*, 300; *pace* Bultmann's allegation that John 2:16 does not allude to Zech 14:21 (*The Gospel of John*, 124 n. 1).

73. Hiers, "Purification of the Temple," 82–90 (esp. 83, 87). Other relevant OT prophecies include Jer 7:11; Mal 3:1; Isa 56:7.

74. Bryan, *Jesus and Israel's Traditions of Judgment and Restoration*, 223. For different Jewish views of the role of the Gentiles in the eschatological temple, see pp. 199–206.

Gentiles), as the business transactions there inevitably disrupt the worship of the Gentiles, who are prohibited from the temple's inner districts (cf. *Ant.* 15.417).[75]

The views of Jesus' temple action regarding a prophetic portent, an eschatological purification, and Israel's national identity as God's elect are not irreconcilable or mutually exclusive. Given John's perception that the Herodian temple is morally defiled by sin, his presentation of Jesus' temple deeds probably signifies the sanctuary's necessity for purification and restitution. This presentation is highly evocative of the royal-messianic hopes, not only because of its lexical choice of οἶκος for "temple" (John 2:16, 17; cf. 2 Sam 7:5, 6, 7, 13 LXX), but also because "kingship" and "temple" are intertwined notions in the Jewish Scriptures and traditions. David proposed to build the temple; Solomon erected the temple; Hezekiah and Josiah purified the temple; Zerubbabel (though he is not a king but a governor) rebuilt the temple; Judas Maccabaeus cleansed the temple and founded the Hasmonean dynasty; Herod the Great rebuilt the temple; Simon bar Giora (a royal-messianic pretender) surrendered himself to the Romans at the location of the ruined temple; Simon bar Kochba (another royal-messianic aspirant) sought to rebuild the temple.[76] In light of all these instances, Wright is correct in asserting that Jesus' act is an implicit declaration of his royal-messianic jurisdiction of the temple.[77] In John 10:22, the evangelist's specific mention of Hanukkah reveals that he and his audience were familiar with this feast, whose Hasmonean backdrop connects temple consecration and kingship. The ensuing examination of the scriptural quotation in John 2:17 will shed further light on the royal-messianic signification of Jesus' temple action.

The Quotation of Ps 68:10 LXX

In the final verse of the first part of the diptych (John 2:17), the disciples "remember" (ἐμνήσθησαν) one line of Ps 68:10 LXX (69:10 MT; 69:9 Eng.)

---

75. Köstenberger, *John*, 106; Keener, *The Gospel of John*, 1:524.

76. Notice the connection in the books of Haggai, Zechariah, and Malachi between temple building/reform and the beginning of a new era. See Ådna, *Jesu Stellung aus Tempel*, 378–79; Wright, *Jesus and the Victory of God*, 483; Anderson, *Contours of Old Testament Theology*, 195–208; Hiers, "Purification of the Temple," 86. See also Hurowitz, "I Have Built You an Exalted House," 106–25.

77. Wright, *Jesus and the Victory of God*, 490–93.

upon witnessing Jesus' deeds in the temple agora.[78] Another line of Psalm 68 LXX (v. 22; v. 21 Eng.) is alluded to in John 19:28 in the crucifixion scene (cf. the echo of Ps 68:5 LXX [69:5 MT; 69:4 Eng.] in John 15:25), where the verb πληρόω occurs in the introduction to this allusion.. This subsequent reference to Psalm 68 LXX (69 MT and Eng.) strengthens the connection between the temple episode and the passion narrative, a connection that is also suggested in the Passover setting shared by these two accounts. Psalm 68 LXX can be divided into three sections and it moves from "lament" (vv. 2–14b) to "petition" (vv. 14c–30) and to "praise" (vv. 31–37).[79] The poetic text (v. 10) cited in the Johannine temple account is in the "lament" section, where the author mourns of his suffering and implores God for the divine deliverance from the hostile circumstances.[80] As this section indicates, the supplicant is betrayed by his family members (v. 9 [v. 8 Eng.]) and communities (v. 13 [v. 12 Eng.]) and endures hardship because of his zeal for God and the sanctuary (vv. 8–10). In citing this lament psalm, John dexterously establishes a correlation between Jesus and the psalmist as a righteous sufferer—both are ardent for the "house" of God and endure afflictions for his sake. The form of the Johannine quotation comes close to that of Ps 68:10 LXX, except that John alters the verbal tense from the aorist (κατεφάγεν) to the future tense (καταφάγεται).[81] In effect, this verbal change augments this biblical verse to be a prophecy that will be fulfilled in the destiny of Jesus. Thus the Johannine citation in John 2:17 functions as a proleptic announcement of Jesus' imminent death upon the cross, where he "will be consumed" (καταφάγεται) due to his total commitment to the Father. From the Johannine viewpoint, the significance of Jesus' temple act is inseparable from his crucifixion.[82]

The Davidic character of Psalm 68 LXX (69) as established in its superscript (cf. τῷ Δαυιδ; לדוד) should not be overlooked.[83] Psalm 68 LXX

---

78. In the Gospel of John, the motif of the disciples' "remembering" something often pertains to Jesus' death and resurrection (e.g., John 12:16; 15:20; 16:4, 21; except 14:26). See Coloe, *God Dwells with Us*, 75.

79. Hossfeld and Zenger, *Psalms 2*, 172.

80. Tate, *Psalms 51—100*, 192–96.

81. Köstenberger, "John," 432–34; Menken, *Old Testament Quotations in the Fourth Gospel*, 38–39.

82. Brown, *The Gospel According to John*, 1:124.

83. See Daly-Denton, *David in the Fourth Gospel*, 128–29; cf. McWhirter, *The Bridegroom Messiah and the People of God*, 43.

(69) is collected within the Psalter's second book, which closes with the words "the prayers of David the son of Jesse" (Ps 71:20 LXX [72:20 MT and Eng.]). David's wholehearted dedication to constructing a shrine for God is highly esteemed in the biblical traditions (cf. 1 Chronicles 22—28), though it is Solomon who actually erects the temple.[84] Viewed through the prism that that Psalm 68 LXX (69) is a "Davidic" poem, John's citation of this psalm in his finishing description of Jesus' temple act gives a Davidic flavor to this act. This Davidic notion, albeit subtle, strikes a royal-messianic note on the temple pericope and thereby heightens the Johannine assertion that Jesus the Messiah-King brings about the temple's eschatological restoration.

Jesus' Statement and the Evangelist's Commentary

In reaction to Jesus' deeds at the temple market, "the Jews" demand a "sign" (σημεῖον) from Jesus that can prove his authority to interfere with the commerce (John 2:18). "The Jews" do not appear in the first part of the diptych (John 2:13–17), but the conjunction οὖν and the demonstrative pronoun ταῦτα in John 2:18 indicate that their demand is directed to Jesus' earlier act. In this verse, the term "sign" (σημεῖον) recalls the preceding scene of the Cana wedding (John 2:1–11), where Jesus reveals his glory in a messianic "sign" (σημεῖον). In the present scene, Jesus does not rejoin the Jewish request with the performance of a dazzling miracle on the spot. Rather, he replies to "the Jews" with an enigmatic riddle (John 2:19). At this juncture of the story, John employs the term ναός to denote the sanctuary proper (John 2:19, 20, 21), in distinction to the other two terms—ἱερόν and οἶκος—that occur in John 2:14, 15, 16 (2x), and John 2:17 respectively.[85] This fresh terminology prepares for the subsequent redefinition of the "temple" (ναός) in verse 21. Reminiscent of the prophetic exhortations (e.g., Isa 6:9; Amos 4:4), the second-person plural aorist imperative (λύσατε) in John 2:19 carries "prophetic" force in augmenting Jesus' reply as an ironic invitation for "the Jews" to destroy the "temple," that is, the body of Jesus (cf. σώματος in v. 21 is probably an epexegetical

---

84. Jarick, "The Temple of David in the Book of Chronicles," 373–76; cf. Pomykala, "Images of David in Early Judaism," 42.

85. In the Gospel of John, the term ναός is found only in the temple episode. In addition to this scene, the term ἱερόν occurs elsewhere in John 5:14; 7:14, 28; 8:2, 20, 59; 10:23; 11:56; 18:20.

genitive).[86] "The Jews" misapprehend the words of Jesus and think that he is talking about the edifice of Jerusalem's magnificent temple, which Herod the Great began to construct in 20/19 BCE (*Ant.* 15.380). With the Spirit's illuminating aid (cf. John 14:26), the evangelist offers his exposition in John 2:21–22 that the "temple" (ναός) on Jesus' lips refers not to the Herodian temple but to his crucified and resurrected body.

In the earlier sections, we demonstrated that temple restoration (in the sense of renewal/purification/reconstruction) constitutes part of the royal-messianic mission in some OT and later Jewish traditions. No extant Jewish document mentions that the Messiah will demolish the temple. However, several extra-canonical Jewish texts plausibly attest the prediction of the temple's destruction. According to *Lam. Rab.* 1:5, rabbi Zadok began fasting in 30 CE and presaged that disasters would soon come upon Jerusalem. The *Lives of the Prophets* (possibly pre-70 CE) record two premonitions that augur the devastation of the Herodian temple (*Lives* 10:10–11; 12:11). Josephus says that the peasant Jesus, the son of Ananias, pronounced an oracle against Jerusalem during 62–69/70 CE (*J.W.* 6.300–309). This oracle may invoke Jeremiah's prophecy of the Babylonian conquest of Jerusalem (Jer 7:34) and so portend the imminent doom of the city and its temple.[87] On several occasions, Josephus applies the oracles of Jeremiah and Daniel to the Roman trampling of the temple (*Ant.* 10.79, 276).[88] In fact, Josephus purports to have been foretold by God in nightly dreams that Jerusalem will fall into Roman hands (*J.W.* 3.350–54).[89] These Jewish "predictions" of Jerusalem and its temple often model upon the prophetic critique in the biblical traditions, though some of the "predictions" were evidently declared with post-70 CE hindsight. This manner of utilizing the prophetic materials suggests that some Jews in the first century CE considered the Scripture as presaging the derelict fate of the Herodian temple.

In this light, it is not difficult to discern prophetic connotations in the Johannine statement regarding the temple's demolition and reconstruction, particularly in post-70 CE times when the Herodian temple has been flattened. The Johannine exposition of Jesus' words, in evoking the

---

86. Abbott, *Johannine Grammar*, 322 §2439 (v).

87. Evans, *Jesus and His Contemporaries*, 377–78; Bockmuehl, "Why Did Jesus Predict the Destruction of the Temple?" 12–13.

88. Bockmuehl, "Why Did Jesus Predict the Destruction of the Temple?" 13.

89. Evans, *Jesus and His Contemporaries*, 376.

prophetic promise of the eschatological temple, avers that this promise is fulfilled *through* Jesus' crucifixion and resurrection. In this manner, Jesus' death is presented as the indispensable step to the actualization of an ideal temple, which is redefined as Jesus' crucified and risen body. At the same time, John puts forward a powerful argument in support of the crucified Jesus' royal messiahship—Jesus dies in order to accomplish his royal-messianic mission of temple restoration. In the preceding Nathanael scene, the reader is told that Jesus replaces Bethel as the locus of the divine presence (John 1:51). Now s/he comes to know that Jesus is the eschatological temple. This temple theme will be further elaborated in John 4:4–26 (Jesus as the locus of true worship) and John 7:37–38 (Jesus as the source of the living water that flows from Ezekiel's temple), but the basis of the Johannine identification of Jesus as the temple is laid in the temple account in John 2.[90]

In John 2:22, the evangelist comments that after Easter the disciples remember the words that Jesus avers on this occasion, understand the thrust of Jesus' words, and come to believe τῇ γραφῇ καὶ τῷ λόγῳ ὃν εἶπεν ὁ Ἰησοῦς ("the Scripture and the word which Jesus said").[91] The word γραφή ("Scripture") occurs 12 times in the Gospel John and always in singular forms (John 2:22; 7:38, 42; 10:35; 13:18; 17:12; 19:24, 28, 36, 37; 20:9), save the instance in John 5:39 (γραφαί).[92] In John 2:22, this word most likely stands for the entire Scripture and refers specifically to the quotation of Ps 68:10 LXX (69:10 MT; 69:9 Eng.) in John 2:17. It is worth mentioning that each part of the diptych of the temple episode (John 2:17, 22) concludes with double references to the Scripture and the death of Jesus (cf. the cross notion as implied in the verb καταφάγεται in verse 17). In effect, this manner of conclusion avers that the Scripture has predicted Jesus' death. Thus the crucifixion of Jesus does not subvert but paradoxically buttresses his royal-messianic authenticity, because Jesus' death is necessary for the biblical promise of the eschatological temple to be fulfilled.

90. For the temple theme in John 4 and 7, see Hoskins, *Jesus as the Fulfillment of the Temple in the Gospel of John*, 135–45; Beale, *The Temple and the Church's Mission*, 196–200; Schnelle, "Die Tempelreinigung und die Christologie des Johannesevangeliums," 370–71.

91. Moloney says that the conjunction καί in John 2:22 is epexegetical. See "The Gospel of John as Scripture," 464.

92. The Johannine use of the singular form of γραφή may seek to underscore the "unity" of the Scripture as a witness to Jesus. See Hengel, "The Old Testament in the Fourth Gospel," 389.

This construal of the cross's significance in the temple pericope is in line with our observation that the Nathanael episode alludes to Zechariah's hope for the messianic "Branch" (see chapter 3), who will rebuild Zion's temple according to the prophecy of Zech 6:12–13.

Conclusion

We have argued that the Johannine articulation of Jesus' action and speech in the temple account (John 2:13–22) is pregnant of a royal-messianic significance. In light of the intimate connection between temple and kingship in the biblical and post-biblical Jewish traditions, this articulation amounts to an implicit assertion of Jesus' royal jurisdiction of the temple. In redefining the temple as Jesus' crucified and risen body, the evangelist puts forward the powerful claim that Jesus' death is the essential step to the messianic restoration of the temple. Furthermore, the quotation of Psalm 68:10 LXX adds a Davidic flavor to Jesus' ardor for the temple and thereby points to his royal-messianic status. For John, the royal messiahship of Jesus as builder of the eschatological temple is intimately related to his death. Since Jesus' crucifixion is necessary for the eschatological restoration of the temple, his death has the implication of corroborating his royal-messianic validity.

5

God's Kingdom and the Royal Messiahship of Jesus (John 3:1–21)

WE WILL SEEK TO demonstrate that a function of the cross motif in John 3:1–21 is to identify the crucified Jesus as the royal Messiah. As will be shown, this identity of Jesus emerges in the Johannine correlation of the outcome of his death with the expected mission of the royal Messiah in the biblical and extra-biblical Jewish traditions, namely the implementation of God's kingdom (i.e., God's kingly dominion). Since the kingdom of God in John 3:1–21 is expressed in connection with the notion of eternal life, our examination of pertinent Jewish royal-messianic texts will address this notion as necessary. Analysis of this Johannine passage will mainly focus on the assertion in verses 14–15 that the "lifting up" of the Son of Man will result in the conferral of the life of God's kingdom.

The Messiah-King and the Kingdom of God in the OT

Fundamental to the Jewish hope for the kingdom of God is the belief that the God of Israel is the sovereign king of the cosmos. This belief in Yahweh's universal dominance is powerfully expressed in the biblical writings, though the phrase "kingdom of God" occurs in neither the Hebrew nor the Greek Scriptures.[1] Of special interest to our investigation is the Psalter, because it is the most frequently cited biblical book in the Gospel

---

1. In the apocryphal section of the LXX, the kingdom of God is mentioned in Wis 10:10. See Caragounis, "Kingdom of God/Kingdom of Heaven," *DJG* 417–30; Beasley-Murray, *Jesus and the Kingdom of God*, 17–25.

of John. In celebrating the enthronement of God, Psalms 93 (92 LXX), 97 (96 LXX), and 99 (98 LXX) begin with the solemn declaration that Yahweh reigns (יהוה מלך [ὁ κύριος ἐβασίλευσεν] in Pss 93:1 [92:1]; 97:1 [96:1]; 99:1 [98:1]; cf. Ps 96:10 [95:10]).[2] As proclaimed in Ps 47:6–8 (47:7–9 MT; 46:7–9 LXX), God's royal jurisdiction extends to all the earth and all the nations.[3] Within the overarching fabric of God's universal kingship, the Davidic monarch acts as the deity's earthly mediator in presiding over his people. The monarch is not independent of but subordinate to the authority of God, who alone is the supreme king of the whole cosmos (e.g., Pss 47:1–10 MT [46:1–10 LXX; 47:1–9 Eng.]; 95:3 [94:3 LXX]). As part of the preamble (Psalms 1–2) to the Psalter, Psalm 2 offers a window to observe the relationship between sacral and divine kingship in the conception of the Psalter. The opening verses of Psalm 2 give a graphic portrayal of the foreign assault against the Lord and his "anointed" (Ps 2:2, cf. vv. 3–4). The "anointing" signifies that the Davidic ruler enjoys a special status and a unique relationship to God (cf. the king's divine sonship in Ps 2:7).[4] In Ps 2:4, Yahweh appears as the supreme monarch sitting on his heavenly throne. Since the Davidic king represents the deity on earth, the foes of the king are the foes of God and vice versa (cf. Psalms 21 and 110).[5] In rebuking the arrogant nations, the enthroned God reaffirms his installment of the Davidic king and his choice of Zion as the holy city (Ps 2:6; cf. Ps 132:10–18). Since Psalm 2 presents the Davidic monarch as God's vicegerent in the world, the monarch's earthly dominance manifests God's universal jurisdiction—just as the temple on Mount Zion is a token of God's universal presence among his people.[6]

2. Cf. the motif of Yahweh's kingship in 1 Sam 12:12; Isa 33:22; Isa 52:7; Jer 8:19. The throne of Yahweh is mentioned in Isa 6:1; Jer 3:17; 14:21; 17:12; Ezek 43:7 and other passages. See Schreiber, *Gesalbter und König*, 62–65; Anderson, *Contours of Old Testament Theology*, 215; Poulssen, *König und Tempel*, 135.

3. Many canonical psalms proclaim Yahweh's sovereign kingship (e.g., Pss 10:16 [9:37 LXX]; 24:10 [23:10]; 29:10 [28:10]; 146:10 [145:10]), expressed occasionally in terms of his ascension to the throne (e.g., Pss 9:4 [9:5 LXX]; 29:10 [28:10]; 45:6 [44:7]; 47:8 [46:9]; 93:2 [92:2]; cf. Isa 6:1; 66:1; Ezek 1:26).

4. As Schreiber says: "Der gesalbte König ist Repräsentant der Gottesherrschaft und der den Willen Gottes beinhaltenden Tora" (*Gesalbter und König*, 147).

5. Nel, "#4887–8 מלך," *NIDOTE* 2:956–65 (959).

6. Caragounis, "Kingdom of God/Kingdom of Heaven," *DJG* 418–19; Anderson, *Contours of Old Testament Theology*, 199–204; Durham, "The King as 'Messiah' in the Psalms," 426–27; Roberts, "The Old Testament's Contribution to Messianic Expectations," 42; Durham, "The King as 'Messiah' in the Psalms," 426–27.

Such a relationship between the Davidic ruler and God as the sovereign undergirds the biblical affirmations of both human and divine kingship. These affirmations do not efface but rather reinforce each other. Since the Davidic king is regarded as the earthly manifestation of God's universal rule, the Davidic regime's demise in the sixth century BCE logically engendered the hopes of its future restoration that will lead to the actualization of God's dominion in the world. This restoration hope takes root in the biblical traditions about David/Zion as the divinely chosen king/city, particularly those associated with Nathan's oracle which affirms the eternalness of the Davidic kingdom (e.g., 2 Sam 7:3, 16; David's prayer in 2 Sam 7:24, 25, 26, 29; Pss 89:1–4, 19–37 [88:2–5, 20–38 LXX]; 132:11–12 [131:11–12 LXX]). During the late pre-exilic period, Isaiah and Jeremiah prophesized the coming of a future king who would bring about the righteous rule of God (cf. Isa 2:2–3; 9:5–6; 11:3–5; Jer 23:5–8). The exilic and post-exilic prophets likewise looked forward to God raising up an ideal Davidic ruler, who would restore the fortunes of Israel, reinstate the glorious kingdom, and bring peace and salvation to the world (e.g., Ezek 34:25–26; 37:23–24; Zech 3:8–9; 8:20–21; 9:9–10; 14:9).

Among these writings, the books of Isaiah and Daniel require closer scrutiny because they have specific points of contact with the Johannine passage under examination (John 3:1–15): ὑψόω ("lift up" in v. 14; Isa 52:13 LXX), "Son of Man" (vv. 13–14; Dan 7:13–14), and "eternal life" (vv. 15–16; Dan 12:2–3). Pertinent Isaianic texts are the four so-called "Servant songs" (Isa 42:1–9; 49:1–13; 50:4–11; 52:13—53:12), in which the "Servant" (עבד) features prominently (Isa 42:1; 49:3, 5, 6, 7; 50:10; 52:13; 53:11).[7] For the present purpose two questions will be addressed: (1) What is the relationship of the Servant to the kingdom of God? (2) Does the Servant have royal status?

The kingdom or kingship of God is a central motif of Isaiah 40—55 in which the four Servant texts are lodged. Within these chapters, Yahweh

---

7. There is no scholarly consensus on the identity of the "Servant". For a summary of various views, see Rowe, God's Kingdom and God's Son, 71–72. A debated issue is whether the "Servant" is an individual (cf. Isa 53:4–6, 10–12) or a corporate representative of Israel as God's "servant(s)" (e.g., Isa 41:8, 9; 44:1, 2, 21; 45:4; 48:20; 54:17; 56:6; 63:17; 65:8, 9, 13 [3x], 14, 15; 66:14). There are several parallel descriptions between the Servant and Israel, such as that both are referred to as God's "servant(s)" and his "chosen" one(s) (for the "Servant," see Isa 42:1; 49:7; for "Israel," see Isa 41:8, 9; 43:10; 44:1, 2; 45:4; 65:9, 15). Thus the Servant is correlated with Israel. Yet he should be an individual distinct from Israel, in view of his portrayal in Isa 53:4–6, 10–12. See France, "Servant of Yahweh," DJG 745.

is designated three times as the "king" of Jacob/Israel (Isa 41:21; 43:15; 44:6) and the message מלך אלהיך ("Yahweh reigns," or "Yahweh becomes king") is proclaimed as the good tidings of salvation (Isa 52:7; ; cf. יהוה מלך in Pss. 93:1 [92:1 LXX]; 97:1 [96:1 LXX]; 99:1 [98:1 LXX] et al.). In Isa 52:10, the description of God stretching out his holy arm to all the earth is reminiscent of a similar gesture of God in Ezek 20:33, where his outstretched arm signifies his royal authority (cf. the use of the verb מלך) over Israel.[8] Within this context of a strong accent on divine sovereignty, the Servant appears as God's "chosen" agent (Isa 42:1; 49:7) through whom the divine plan will be realized.[9] The ministry of the Servant is consigned first to Israel (Isa 49:5–6a) and then to the nations, eventually bringing the salvation of God to the world (Isa 49:6b; cf. Isa 52:10). The Servant, moreover, will restore the righteous status of God's people by bearing their suffering and sins (Isa 53:4, 6, 12). In executing his divine assignment, the Servant performs an instrumental function in implementing God's redemptive plan and kingly rule.

While the Servant is not designated as "king" in the four Isaianic texts in which he appears, certain features of his portrayal are indicative of royalty. These features include the Servant's exceedingly exalted status (Isa 52:13; cf. the resemblance with Yahweh's enthronement in Isa 6:1), his superiority over kings and nations (Isa 52:15), and the image of his dividing military plunder (Isa 53:12a).[10] In addition, two Servant passages (Isa 42:1–4; 52:13—53:12) emulate the literary form of the "designation or presentation of a king as the one to whom God's promise attaches,"[11] or what Mowinckel calls a "royal initiation oracle" (cf. the royal Psalms 2 and 90).[12] This literary trait of two Servant songs lends credence to the view that discerns a royal shade implicitly present in the depiction of the Isaianic Servant. Whether or not the Isaianic Servant is messianic, it is

---

8. Goldingay and Payne, *Isaiah 40—55*, 2:262.

9. There are biblical precedents of referring to God's agent as his "servant" (e.g., Moses in Deut 34:5 and Jos 1:2, David in 2 Sam 3:18 and 1 Kgs 8:24–26, and the prophets in 1 Kgs 15:29 and 2 Kgs 9:7, 36; 10:10). See Blenkinsopp, *Isaiah 40—55*, 118.

10. Rowe, *God's Kingdom and God's Son*, 77. Rowe discerns a number of similarities between the Isaianic depiction of the Servant and the canonical royal psalms (pp. 74-77).

11. Goldingay and Payne, *Isaiah 40-55*, 2:280.

12. Mowinckel, *He That Cometh*, 190.

sufficient for the present purpose that he acts as God's intermediary and his profile displays royal characteristics.

Turning to the book of Daniel, its apocalyptic outlook envisages the kingdom of God as a transcendent entity. In Daniel 2, there is a strong emphasis on God's sole sovereignty in setting up his kingdom, which will destroy all earthly regimes but perpetuate itself forever (Dan 2:44). This emphasis is apparent in Daniel's interpretation of Nebuchadnezzar's dream (Dan 2:1–45), in which the stone that crushes the metallic statue is cut out of the mountain without hands (Dan 2:34, 45; cf. *4 Ezra* 13:6). Thus, at first glance Daniel 2 seems to rule out the possibility that a messianic mediator will take part in establishing the kingdom of God. Yet in the later vision of Daniel 7, which has parallels with the vision of Daniel 2 (cf. the shared four-kingdom division of history), the "one like a son of man" receives splendid glory, global dominance, and an eternal kingdom from God (Dan 7:13–14). These descriptions reveal that this man-like figure is of the royal rank.

Scholars' opinions diverge on the actual identity of this figure that stands in contrast to the four animals that stand for four kingdoms. On account of the corresponding idea of God's people possessing an everlasting kingdom (Dan 7:18, 22, 27), some scholars believe that the "one like a son of man" is not an individual but simply a corporate symbol of the saints.[13] In this view, the fact that the Son of Man appears in the vision but not in its interpretation, and the people of God do not appear in the vision but in its interpretation, points to a symbolic understanding of this figure. However, the Danielic portrait of the Son of Man differs from that of the saints in that this portrait exhibits the distinctive features of the Son of Man coming with the clouds and receiving worldwide worship. These two features suggest that this man-like figure has a divine association (Dan 7:13–14), which the saints do not seem to possess. In support of the interpretation that the Danielic Son of Man is a particular personage, the "Son of Man" figures in several late Second Temple Jewish documents that make use of Daniel 7 appear as individuals. Benjamin Reynolds draws attention to an additional phrase ἐποίει πόλεμον πρὸς τοὺς ἁγίους in the "little horn" vision of Dan 7:8 LXX, a phrase that is absent from the MT and Theodotian.[14] Since

---

13. E.g., Kazen ("Son of Man as Kingdom Imagery") and Dunn ("'Son of God' as 'Son of Man' in the Dead Sea Scrolls?").

14. Reynolds, "The 'One Like a Son of Man' according to the Old Greek of Daniel

this Greek phrase mentions the saints, it attests a pre-Christian Jewish understanding of this Danielic vision that considers the saints and the Son of Man as distinct characters.[15] In the *Similitudes* and *Fourth Ezra*, which presumably draw on materials of Daniel 7, the messianic Son of Man is evidently an individual. Summing up, the "one like a son of man" in Daniel 7 is in solidarity with the people of God, but he is not simply their collective emblem.[16] The description of the saints possessing God's kingdom (Dan 7:18, 22, 27) may build on the corporate concept that they rule through their representative, namely the Son of Man.

In the eschatological scenario of Dan 12:2–3, the notions of the kingdom of God and the resurrection of the dead are intimately woven together (cf. Dan 12:13).[17] As this scenario indicates, the righteous dead will be raised to everlasting life and the unrighteous dead to eternal condemnation in the last days. The text of Dan 12:2 (ורבים מישני אדמת עפר יקיצו) highly resembles that of Isa 26:19 (הקיצו ורננו שכני עפר; cf. Isa 25:8), which lies within the setting of Israel's national reinstatement (Isaiah 24—27). It is possible that the resurrection language of Isa 26:19 is not simply symbolic of Israel's renewal, but actually speaks of the resurrection of God's people as the initial step to the nation's eschatological restoration (cf. the language of the revivification of the dry bones in Ezek 37:1–14 and that of rejuvenation in Hos 6:2).[18] This being the case, the hope of resurrection to eternal life is linked to the fulfillment of God's kingdom in both of Dan 12:2–3 and Isa 26:19.

In summary, we have discussed the relevant OT materials in the Psalter and the books of Isaiah and Daniel. In the Psalter, Yahweh's universal kingship is a prominent theme and the Davidic ruler often appears as the deity's earthly representative. In the book of Isaiah, the Servant will

---

7, 13–14," 79. Reynolds thinks that the Son of Man of Daniel 7 LXX/OG enjoys royal-messianic status.

15. Ibid., 79.

16. Chester, *Messiah and Exaltation*, 291; Collins, *The Scepter and the Star*, 175–76.

17. In Dan 12:2, the two expressions, ישן ("sleep") and אדמת עפר ("the dust of the earth"), serve as the imageries of death and Sheol respectively. The Hebrew verb קיץ ("awake") figuratively depicts the resurrection of the dead. See Nickelsburg, *Resurrection, Immorality, and Eternal Life in Intertestamental Judaism and Early Christianity*, 30; Osborne, "Resurrection," *DNTB* 931–36; Bauckham, "Life, Death, and the Afterlife in Second Temple Judaism," 80–95; Collins, *Daniel*, 391–98.

18. Nickelsburg, *Resurrection, Immorality, and Eternal Life,* 31–32; contra Collins, *Daniel*, 395.

act as God's instrument to implement his kingly jurisdiction. The Servant is not designated "king" but his profile contains certain royal features. In the book of Daniel, the Son of Man will be God's agent in implementing his everlasting rule and the notions of God's kingdom and eternal life are connected.

The Kingdom of God and the Messiah-King in Late Second Temple Judaism

The idea that the royal Messiah is God's appointed mediator, who will usher in his end-time kingdom, is present in a number of late Second Temple Jewish documents. In third *Sibylline Oracles*, the kingship of God is an eminent theme that recurs frequently.[19] In this book's extant form, the sibyl's vision inaugurates with the scene of God's enthronement on the cherubim (*Sib. Or.* 3:1 2). There is only "one God," who is "the sole ruler" residing in the heavenly abode (*Sib. Or.* 3:11). He governs over the entire cosmos (*Sib. Or.* 3:19), and in the designated time the "most great kingdom of the immortal king [βασιλεία μεγίστη ἀθανάτου βασιλῆος] will become manifest over men" (*Sib. Or.* 3:47–48). Further, the God of Israel is acclaimed as "the great king immortal God" (ἀθανάτοιο θεοῦ μεγάλου βασιλῆος; *Sib. Or.* 3:56), "the great king" (μεγάλου βασιλῆος [*Sib. Or.* 3:499; cf. 3:56]; βασιλῆα μέγαν [*Sib. Or.* 3:560]; μεγάλῳ βασιλῆι [*Sib. Or.* 3:808]), "the Immortal who always rules" (τὸν ἀεὶ μεδέοντα ἀθάνατον; *Sib. Or.* 3:593), "the great immortal king" (*Sib. Or.* 3:617 Eng.; θεῷ μεγάλῳ βασιλῆι in 3:616 Greek), "the Creator, just judge and sole ruler" (κτίστης ὁ δικαιοκρίτης τε μόναρχος; *Sib. Or.* 3:704), and "the immortal king, the great eternal God" (ἀθάνατον βασιλῆα, θεὸν μέγαν ἀέναόν τε; *Sib. Or.* 3:717; cf. 3:784).[20] These lofty expressions lay emphasis on God's supreme dominance over against the futility of idolatry, to which much of the sibyl's censure is directed (cf. *Sib. Or.* 3:545–55, 601–7, 762–66, etc.).

As underlined in third *Sibylline Oracles*, the sovereign God appoints a royal agent to deliver his people: (1) the seventh king (*Sib. Or.* 3:192–93; cf. vv. 318, 608), (2) the king sent by God (most likely Cyrus; *Sib. Or.*

---

19. According to Collins, the eschatology of *Sibylline Oracles* 3 "centers on the expectation of an ideal king or kingdom." See "Sibylline Oracles," *OTP* 1:356.

20. See Schnackenburg, *God's Rule and God's Kingdom*, 46–47. For the English translation of *Sibylline Oracles*, see Collins, "Sibylline Oracles" in vol. 1 of *OTP*. For the Greek text, see Geffcken, *Die Oracula Sibyllina*.

3:286), and (3) the king from the sun/East (*Sib. Or.* 3:652).[21] In chapter 2, we emphasized that these royal figures are probably, or at least potentially, messianic. In the latter two instances, the king is expressly described as God's emissary. The important oracle *Sib. Or.* 3:657–808, which is situated in the document's closing section, speaks of the realization of the eschatological kingdom. As this oracle declares, the kingdom of God will be an earthly entity in this world, and all the nations will bring gifts to God's "house" (presumably the temple) and pledge their allegiance to him alone (*Sib. Or.* 3:773–74; cf. 3:718–19). While this oracle does not mention a messianic figure, the sibyl draws freely on the motifs in Isa 11:1–12 (esp. vv. 6–9) in presenting God's kingdom as the renewal of the earth (*Sib. Or.* 3:767–95).[22] The net impression is that the fulfillment of this Davidic-messianic prophecy is essentially tied to the fulfillment of God's end-time kingdom. This vision of God's kingdom, which is located near the end of the composition (*Sib. Or.* 3:657–808), echoes the early anticipation in *Sib. Or.* 3:46–62 of the dawn of this "great kingdom" (v. 47). The latter text is part of the larger literary unit *Sib. Or.* 3:1–97, which is probably a late addition to the remainder of third *Sibylline Oracles*.[23] Notwithstanding this, this text (*Sib. Or.* 3:46–62) requires consideration because most likely it is of pre-Christian date.[24] According to *Sib. Or.* 3:39, the "holy prince" (ἀγνὸς ἄναξ) overthrows the foreign power in preparation of the manifestation of God's kingdom. Collins thinks that the "prince" could be the Messiah, but more likely God.[25] Undermining this divine identification, God is twice acclaimed as the "immortal king" within the compact section *Sib. Or.* 3:46–62 (vv. 48, 56) and so he seems to be distinct from the "prince."[26]

---

21. Collins, *The Sibylline Oracles of Egyptian Judaism*, 37. See chapter 2 for the debate on the meaning of the phrase ἀπ' ἠελίοιο in *Sib. Or.* 3:652.

22. Oegema, *The Anointed and His People*, 83–85. A messianic exegesis of Isaiah 11 is attested in sundry Jewish texts including 4Q174 frgs. 1–3; 4Q161 frgs. 8–10; 1QSb (1Q28b); *Pss. Sol.* 17:36–37; *1 En.* 49:3; 62:3; *T. Levi* 18:5, 7. See McWhirter, *The Bridegroom Messiah and the People of God*, 41.

23. Collins, "Sibylline Oracles," *OTP* 1:359–60.

24. Collins says that the section *Sib. Or.* 3:46–62 is "dated shortly after the battle of Actium" (ca. 31 BCE). See ibid., 1:360.

25. Collins, "Messianism in the Maccabean Period," 97–109 (107 n. 14). In another article, Collins says that the "prince" may be the Messiah ("The Kingdom of God in the Apocrypha and Pseudepigrapha," 85).

26. Rowe, *God's Kingdom and God's Son*, 104–5. Lanchester says that the "holy prince" is the Messiah (*APOT* 2:379). Geffcken seems to identify the "prince" as the Messiah,

Therefore this section plausibly entails the idea that the messianic king will be God's instrument in instigating the eschatological kingdom. This reading of *Sib. Or.* 3:46–62 is congruous with the ample allusions in *Sib. Or.* 3:657–808 to the Isaianic prophecy, which lends much substance to the sibyl's articulation of this kingdom.

In the *Psalms of Solomon*, God is exalted as the "king over the heavens" (βασιλεὺς ἐπὶ τῶν οὐρανῶν; *Pss. Sol.* 2:30), the "great and righteous king" (μέγας βασιλεὺς καὶ δίκαιος; *Pss. Sol.* 2:32), and the "king" of his people (βασιλεύς; *Pss. Sol.* 5:19; cf. ἐν τῇ βασιλείᾳ σου in 5:18).[27] The seventeenth psalm, in which the messianic king takes center stage, is framed by the dual references to God's eternal kingship at the beginning and closing of this psalm (vv. 1, 46). The kingdom of God is forever over all the nations and it exists perpetually (*Pss. Sol.* 17:3). Nonetheless, the full demonstration of God's kingdom in this world lies in the future and will be actualized through the administration of his chosen regent, who in the author's belief must be of Davidic lineage (*Pss. Sol.* 17:4, 21). When the Davidic Messiah comes, he will expel all the Gentiles from Jerusalem, implement God's universal jurisdiction, and reign as his earthly representative. The Messiah is the "king of Israel" (*Pss. Sol.* 17:42, cf. vv. 4, 21, 32), but he is subject under the sovereign God (*Pss. Sol.* 17:34; cf. the flock is God's [v. 40]).[28] In *Psalms of Solomon* 18, the Messiah appears as the ruler of Israel (v. 5) and God is the creator of the cosmos (v. 10). Of present interest, the hope of eternal life holds a place within the eschatological scheme of the *Psalms*. As envisaged in *Pss. Sol.* 3:11–12, the righteous people of God will rise to "everlasting life" (ἀναστήσονται εἰς ζωὴν αἰώνιον; cf. a similar wording in Dan 12:2–3 LXX; *Pss. Sol.* 13:11; 14:3), but the wicked will be left in Sheol (cf. *Pss. Sol.* 13:11; 14:9–10; 15:12–13; 16:2).[29] This hope is not mentioned in the messianic psalms 17 and 18. Yet for the final redactor or the community behind the *Psalms*, the advent of the Messiah and the

---

in view of the plenty messianic references provided in the footnote at *Sib. Or.* 3:49 (*Die Oracula Sibyllina*, 49).

27. The Syriac versions of *Pss. Sol.* 2:30 have the additional phrase "over all the earth" and render "kings and rulers" as "kingdoms and princes." See Wright, "Psalms of Solomon," *OTP* 2:653–54.

28. Rowe, *God's Kingdom and God's Son*, 106–108; Schreiber, *Gesalbter und Künig*, 164–65; Davenport, "The 'Anointed of the Lord' in Psalms of Solomon 17," 80.

29. Nickelsburg, *Resurrection, Immorality, and Eternal Life*, 163–67; Winninge, *Sinners and the Righteous*, 41–42. Winninge thinks that *Pss. Sol.* 3:12 alludes to Dan 12:2–3.

kingdom that he will inaugurate seem to link with the future blessing of eternal life.

The scrolls at Qumran frequently speak of God in royal or majestic terms.[30] In 1QapGen ar, God is "the king [מלך] of all ages" (II, 4, 7; X, 10) and "the king [מלך] of the hea[ven]s" (II, 14), who "rule[s] all the kings of the earth, to judge them all" (XX, 13).[31] In column IV of 4Q216 (4QJuba), God is hailed as the "king [on Mount Zion]" (מלך; v. 9–10). The mid-first century BCE compositions *Songs of the Sabbath Sacrifice* (4QShirShabba-h [4Q400–407]; 11Q17; Masada 1039–1200) contain copious references to the kingship or kingdom of God.[32] It is important that within Qumran's royal ideology, the royal Messiah plays a role in connection with the kingly rule of God. This connection between messianic and divine kingship gained importance in Qumran's conceptualization, especially after the mid-first century BCE when the Romans took control of the land of Israel. Two scrolls, 4Q161 and 4Q174, associate the coming of the "Branch" (צמח) with the realization of God's royal dominance.[33] In expounding Isa 11:1–5, the author of 4Q161 frgs. 8–10 declares that God will seat the "Branch" on the "[thro]ne of glory," give him a "h[oly] crown" and, according to Geza Vermes' textual reconstruction, put a "scepter" in his hands (III, 20–21; cf. Num 24:17).[34] The Branch will also govern and judge all the peoples (III, 21–22). Brooke is of the opinion that the portrait of the Branch being seated on the throne points to his passive role and immaterial eschatological function.[35] Yet it is more proper to construe this portrait of 4Q161 against the backdrop of the biblical conception that the

---

30. As Brooke notes, the belief of theocracy and divine dominance is pivotal in the framework of Qumran's royal ideology ("Kingship and Messianism in the Dead Sea Scrolls," 436).

31. The Qumran texts and translations are from Martínez and Tigchelaar, *The Dead Sea Scrolls*.

32. E.g, God is referred to as "king of holiest holiness" (4Q400 frg. 1 I, 8), "king of the heavenly beings" (4Q400 frg. 1 II, 7), and "king of all" (4Q401 XIII, 1; 4Q405 XXIV, 3; 11Q17 I, 1). He is envisaged as sitting enthroned in the temple (4Q402 II, 4; 4Q405 frgs. 14–15 I, 7). Many other writings at Qumran celebrate God's sovereign authority (e.g., 1QM XII, 7–8; 4Q521 frg. 2, II, 7). See Rowe, *God's Kingdom and God's Son*, 100–101; Brooke, "Kingship and Messianism in the Dead Sea Scrolls," 440.

33. In 4Q252 and 4Q285, the "Branch" is not related to the inauguration of God's kingdom.

34. Vermes, *The Complete Dead Sea Scrolls in English*, 498.

35. Brooke, "Kingship and Messianism in the Dead Sea Scrolls," 452.

Davidic ruler is subordinate to God as his vicegerent. The writing 4Q174 (frg. 1 I, 3, 5) proclaims God's perpetual reign through the quotation of Exod 15:17–18 (i.e., יָמְלֹךְ עוֹלָם in frg. 1 I, 3, 5), which affirms God's sovereignty in establishing his sanctuary. Earlier analysis has noted that 4Q174 ties this Exodus quotation with the citation of 2 Sam 7:11–14 (frg. 1 I, 7, 10–11'), which speaks of the divine promise of an eternal Davidic dynasty. Thus 4Q174 relates the appearance of the "Branch" to the manifestation of God's kingship and the restoration of the Davidic monarchy.

The damaged text (לעלמא לכא[מ]) of 4Q246 I, 2 probably refers to God, on account of its connotation of everlasting dominance and the fact that the Son of God has not yet come on scene (col. II). This being the case, 4Q246 describes God as the eternal king. As revealed in II, 5–9, the envisaged kingdom will be universal and eternal. The "Son" designation signifies the Messiah's (if the Son of God is messianic) subordinate relationship to "the great God," who is the source of his strength (II, 7; see chapter 3). Thematic similarities between column II of 4Q246 and Daniel 2 and 7—both of these Danielic chapters prophesies the arrival of God's kingdom—suggest that the messianic "Son" will probably act as God's agent in ushering in the end-time kingdom.

The kingship of God is not a prominent feature of the sectarian documents 1QS, 1QSa and CD, in which the Messiah of Israel appears in several eschatological scenes (1QS IX, 11; 1QSa II, 11–20; CD-A XII, 23—XIII, 1; XIV, 18–19; CD-B XIX, 10–11; XIX, 33—XX, 1). No direct address to God as king is found in these documents, but some of them speak of divine glory (כבוד; 1QS X, 9, 12; XI, 20; CD-B XX, 26) or majesty (תפארת; 1QS X, 12; XI, 15). By contrast, the *War Scroll* underscores God's royal authority. This scroll envisions the latter-day combat of the sons of light against the sons of darkness and the army of Belial. In this warfare setting, God's dominion and his sure victory over the evil forces are celebrated (e.g., VI, 6; XII, 7; XII, 8). 1QM also recalls God's past deliverance of the Israelites from the Philistine attack through the young David (XI, 1–2). It is probable that this Davidic reference foreshadows the military conquest of the "Prince," who will be the commander of God's eschatological army (V, 1; see chapter 2). In view of these considerations, the Prince will play a part through martial combat in implementing God's kingly governance, which will lead to everlasting reign to Israel (cf. XII, 16; XIX, 18). Similarly, the Prince of 1QSb V, 20–21 appears the intermediary who will instates the kingdom of God's people (לעול עמו מלכות[ם]). Aside from column V, kingship terminology occurs twice in 1QSb. Both occurrences are in the setting of the blessing of the priesthood (ומלכות in III, 5; מלכות בהיכל in IV, 25–26). The first text is broken after ומלכות and so the exact referent is vague. The second text depicts the high priest serving in the temple of the kingdom. Robert Rowe claims that these three "kingdom" references (1QSb III, 5; IV, 26; V, 21) "may also mean eschatological kingship to be exercised by the Community."[36] This is plausible, but the Prince will probably also exercise governance in light of his portrayal of possessing a "scepter" (1QSb V, 24, 27) and subduing the nations (1QSb V, 28).[37]

A brief remark regarding Qumran's eschatology is its belief in eternal life and the resurrection (e.g., 1QHa XI, 19–23; XIX, 3–14; 1QS IV, 6–9; CD-A III, 20; 4Q181 frg. 1 II, 5–6; 4Q504 frgs. 1–2 VI, 11–16 ["the book of life"]; 4Q521 I, 12; cf. *J. W.* 2.154; *Ant.* 18.18).[38] However, this belief is not dominant in Qumran's eschatology and the scrolls in general show little interest in the subject of death.[39] The community responsible for the *Hodayota* and the *Community Rule* believed that its members are God's eschatological people and have already been participating in the bliss of everlasting life, which will consummate at the time of God's "visitation" (1QS IV, 6, 11, 18–19).[40] No messianic figure appears in 1QHa. According to 1QS IX, 11, the royal Messiah will arrive in the community at the end of time.

In the judgment scene of *1 Enoch* 63, the mighty ones and the kings of earth confess their sins before the Lord of Spirits and acknowledge his

36. Rowe, *God's Kingdom and God's Son*, 103 n. 46.

37. Several other texts at Qumran (if the liberator in question is royal-messianic) may attest the idea that the messianic king will take part in inaugurating God's kingdom. These texts include 4Q369 frg. 1 II, 4–12 (this text envisages a person possessing the land of God forever?), 4Q287 X, 13 (this text alludes to Isa 11:2), 4Q286 frg. 1 II, 2 and frg. 7 I, 5 (this text speaks of the kingship of God), and 4Q458 frg. 2 II, 3–6 (this text speaks of a משיח defeating Israel's enemy and ushering in the kingdom). See the relevant discussions in Chester, *Messiah and Exaltation*; Evans, *Jesus and His Contemporaries*.

38. Nickelsburg, *Resurrection, Immorality, and Eternal Life*, 179–209; Puech, "Messianism, Resurrection, and Eschatology at Qumran and in the New Testament," 246–56.

39. Nickelsburg, *Resurrection, Immorality, and Eternal Life*, 205–6; Collins, *Daniel*, 397–98.

40. Nickelsburg, *Resurrection, Immorality, and Eternal Life*, 205–6; contra Laurin, "The Question of immortality in the Qumran 'Hodayot,'" 344–55. Puech underlines the influence of Daniel 12 on 1QS III-IV, XI and 1QM XIII–XIV ("Messianism, Resurrection, and Eschatology," 250–51).

jurisdiction (*1 En.* 63:1). These earthly authorities acclaim God as "the Lord of kings," "the Lord of the mighty," "the Lord of the rich," "the Lord of glory and the Lord of wisdom" (*1 En.* 63:2)—acclamations that climax in the honorable tribute to God as "the Lord of the kings, and him who reigns over all kings" (*1 En.* 63:4; cf. "the Lord of the kings" in *1 En.* 63:7).[41] In *1 En.* 47:3; 60:2; 71:7, God is referred to as sitting on "the throne of his glory," surrounded by his righteous people and the angelic beings. The majestic God shares his kingly power with the messianic Chosen One or Son of Man (cf. chapter 2), who is seated by God on "the throne of glory" (cf. *1 En.* 45:3; 51:3; 55:4; 61:8; 62:1–3, 5; 69:27–29) and authorized to adjudicate the evil humans and angels (e.g., *1 En.* 45:3–6; 46:4–6; 4:1–6; 55:4; 61:8; 69:27).[42] All the officials of the world will laud the Son of Man, "who rules over all" (*1 En.* 62:6), and will plead for his mercy (*1 En.* 62:9). It is evident that the Messiah in the *Similitudes* is "God's heavenly vice-regent,"[43] who will implement his just rule. As envisioned in this document, "everlasting life" (*1 En.* 37:4; 40:9; 58:3) or "life" (*1 En.* 48:8; 62:16; 67:2) is one of the blessings of the future age that will be ushered in by the Messiah.[44] The triple references in *1 En.* 51:1 to the earth/Sheol/destruction "restoring" what has been entrusted to it[45] on the days when the Chosen One is enthroned (*1 En.* 51:2–3) probably refers to the resurrection of the dead.[46] In *1 En.* 61:5, the day of the Chosen One is linked to the resurrection.[47]

---

41. Rowe, *God's Kingdom and God's Son*, 93–95; Nickelsburg, "Salvation Without and With a Messiah," 56–65. The expression "kingdom of God" is missing from the *Similitudes* and God is explicitly denoted as "king" only in *1 En.* 63:2–4. See Collins, "The Kingdom of God in the Apocrypha and Pseudepigrapha," 89.

42. The text of *1 En.* 62:2 in *OTP* 1:43 adopts a variant that describes God sitting on the throne, instead of God seating the Chosen One on the throne.

43. Nickelsburg, "Salvation Without and With a Messiah," 63.

44. References to eternal life or the resurrection are also present in *1 En.* 10:10; 15:6; 91:10; 92:3–4; 103:3–7; 104:2–5, but without messianic association. See Bauckham, "Life, Death, and the Afterlife in Second Temple Judaism," 93; Puech, "Messianism, Resurrection, and Eschatology," 249.

45. The reference to "earth" is found in two Ethiopic manuscripts (Princeton Ethiopic 3 and EMML 2080). The English translation of *1 En.* 53:1a (*OTP* 1:36) does not entail the notion of the earth restoring the souls in it.

46. Bauckham, "Life, Death, and the Afterlife in Second Temple Judaism," 91; Mowinckel, *He That Cometh*, 399.

47. Mowinckel, *He That Cometh*, 400. Mowinckel seems to suggest that the Messiah of *1 Enoch* will summon forth the dead (cf. *1 En.* 61:5).

In *Fourth Ezra*, God is not directly addressed as king but his "throne" is mentioned once in *4 Ezra* 8:21. It is plausible that the "seat of judgment" in *4 Ezra* 7:33 refers to the heavenly throne of God. Other than these two instances, no other observable reference to God's kingdom/kingship is detected in this apocalypse, excluding chapters 1–2 and 15–16 which are most likely of Christian origin.[48] The eschatological vision of *4 Ezra* 7:28–29 looks forward to a transitory messianic era of 400 years. This era will be succeeded by seven days of primordial silence (*4 Ezra* 7:29–31), the (bodily) resurrection of all the dead people (*4 Ezra* 7:32, 37; cf. Dan 12:2), and God's final judgment (*4 Ezra* 7:32–37; cf. 4:41–43; 5:45; 7:75–101, 113).[49] The souls of the righteous will "enjoy in immortality" (*4 Ezra* 7:97) and "the immortal age to come, in which corruption has passed away" (*4 Ezra* 7:113; cf. 7:13; 8:55; 14:22, 35).[50] As other texts in *Fourth Ezra* reveal, the Davidic Messiah will primarily perform the functions of delivering the remnant of Israel and judging the Romans (*4 Ezra* 11:37—12:1; 12:31–34; 13:3–13; 13:25–52; 14:9). These functions will pave the way for the instatement of the messianic epoch, which is the preliminary phase to the final age. There may be a direct connection between the Messiah and the final resurrection in *4 Ezra* 12:33 ("he will set them living before the judgment seat"). It is of Mowinckel's opinion that this verse envisages the Messiah partaking in raising the dead.[51]

Second Baruch refers to God as the "Majesty" (*2 Bar.* 55:8) and speaks of "the great power of our Ruler" (*2 Bar.* 83:7), God's "reign" or "rule" (*2 Bar.* 21:6; 54:13, 22), and his "throne" (*2 Bar.* 46:4; 51:11; 54:13; 73:1 [God's?]).[52] The visions of chapters 39—40 (cf. the allusions to Daniel 7) anticipate the revelation of the Messiah's "dominion" at the designated time. His royal rule will be universal and "last forever until the world of corruption has ended" (*2 Bar.* 39:7; 40:3).[53] It is possible that the one who sits down "in eternal peace on the throne of the kingdom" (*2 Bar.* 73:1) is

---

48. Metzger, "The Fourth Book of Ezra," *OTP* 1:517–24.

49. Nickelsburg, *Resurrection, Immorality, and Eternal Life*, 171–74.

50. It is possible that the "life" in *4 Ezra* 7:48 refers to the eschatological life (cf. 8:46, 52), in view of this term's contrast with the notions of "death" and "perdition" in the immediate context.

51. Mowinckel, *He That Cometh*, 400. The correct reference is *4 Ezra* 12:33, not *4 Ezra* 13:33 as mentioned in Mowinckel's book.

52. The English translation is from A. F. J. Klijn, "2 Baruch," in *OTP* 1:615–52.

53. Oegema, *The Anointed and His People*, 225.

the Messiah, who has appeared shortly before in 2 Bar. 72:2 (cf. God does not appear in the text between 2 Bar. 72:2 and 73:1). This being the case, the Messiah is depicted as God's vicegerent in his kingdom.

Several passages in *Second Baruch* are pertinent to the Jewish expectation regarding the resurrection of the dead. This expectation may be articulated in the metaphorical language of the treasuries opening up and restoring the souls (2 Bar. 21:23; 30:1–2), the earth/dust giving backing all that in it (2 Bar. 42:8; 50:2) or, more explicitly, the revivification or return of the dead (2 Bar. 49:3–4; 85:15; cf. "the promise of the life" in 57:2). It is noteworthy that in 2 Bar. 30:1–2 the hope of resurrection is overtly connected with the Messiah's "return in glory."[54]

The fifth of the *Sibylline Oracles* sets forth the double assertions of messianic and divine kingship. God's absolute dominion is affirmed in *Sib. Or.* 5:499, where he is overtly designated as "king" (βασιλῆα). Twice the imperishable God is denoted as the "ruler of all" (*Sib. Or.* 5:277, 499); he is "eminent" (*Sib. Or.* 5:285 Eng. [cf. v. 284 in Greek]) and "great" (*Sib. Or.* 5:406). In chapter 2, we mentioned that three oracles in fifth *Sibylline Oracles* (5:155–61, 5:247–85, and 5:414–27) contain plausible royal-messianic references. The future hope of resurrection or eternal life is not mentioned in this writing, whose eschatological outlook is described as pessimistic by Collins.[55] Whereas this Diaspora writing does not relate the Messiah to the realization of the eschatological kingdom, this writing's royal eschatology supports the understanding that the expectation for a royal-messianic figure is congruent with the belief of God as king.

Finally, the "Servant" in *Isaiah Targum* is explicitly identified as the royal Messiah (*Tg.* Isa 43:10; 52:13; 53:10).[56] This targumic writing, whose constituent traditions can be dated to the first century or early second century CE,[57] indicate that the royal-messianic Servant as will rebuild Zion's temple (*Tg.* Isa 53:5; see chapter 4 for the temple-king association)

---

54. Mowinckel, *He That Cometh*, 399–400. Mowinckel notes that the Messiah's "return in glory" refers to his return from heaven to earth, whereas for Charles this means that the Messiah will return to heaven after his reign (*APOT* 2:498). Stone interprets this messianic reference as pointing to the Messiah's death (cf. 4 Ezra 7:28–29). See Stone, *Fourth Ezra*, 209; cf. Beasley-Murray, *Jesus and the Kingdom of God*, 49.

55. Collins, "Sibylline Oracles," *OTP* 1:392.

56. Cf. "my Servant the Messiah" in *Tg.* Zech 3:8; "Branch" = "servant" in Zech 3:8 MT; "my Servant, the Anointed One" in 2 Bar. 70:10. See Chilton, *The Glory of Israel*, 90–91; Juel, *Messianic Exegesis*, 126.

57. Chilton, *The Glory of Israel*, 94–96.

and establish a kingdom (במלכות משחהון; *Tg.* Isa 53:10).[58] However, the targumist transfers the notion of suffering from the Servant to other subjects (compare Isa 53:5, 10 MT and *Tg.*), presumably in order to avoid the absurd idea of a suffering Messiah.[59]

In short, a number of post-biblical Jewish writings contain the notion that the royal Messiah will be God's intermediary in bringing about his everlasting kingdom. This notion is present in third *Sibylline Oracles*, the *Psalms of Solomon*, the DSS, the *Similitudes*, *Fourth Ezra*, *Second Baruch*, and *Isaiah Targum*. Some of these writings (e.g., the *Similitudes* and *Second Baruch*) further connect the Messiah with resurrection or eternal life. The following section will examine the kingship-cross link in John 3:1-21 in light of the Jewish association of the royal Messiah with God's kingdom or everlasting life.

Analysis of John 3:1–21

In John's Gospel, the expression ἡ βασιλεία τοῦ θεοῦ ("kingdom of God"; cf. the "kingdom" of Jesus in John 18:36) occurs twice in the Nicodemus pericope in John 3:1–21 (vv. 3, 5). This pericope contains the first of the three references to the "lifting up" (ὑψόω) of the Son of Man (John 3:14; 8:28; 12:32–34) and the first appearance of "eternal life" (ζωὴ αἰώνιος; John 3:15) in this Gospel. We will analyze the thematic interactions of these three notions—the kingdom of God, the "lifting up" of Jesus, and eternal life—within the immediate context of John 3:1–21, focusing on the implications for the royal-messianic validity of the crucified Jesus.

Textual Setting and Structure

The passage John 3:1–21 records Nicodemus's first appearance in the narrative of the Gospel of John (cf. John 7:45–52; 19:38–42). This passage directly follows the summary report in John 2:23–25 of many people believing in Jesus as an outcome of the astounding "signs" that he performed

---

58. The targumic texts are from Stenning, *The Targum of Isaiah*. Several NT writings interpret the Isaianic Servant in a messianic sense (e.g., Matt 8:17; 1 Pe 2:22–25). See Goldingay and Payne, *Isaiah 40–55*, 2:284–86.

59. For the rabbinic traditions concerning the kingdom of God, see Rowe, *God's Kingdom and God's Son*, 109–12; Schnackenburg, *God's Rule and Kingdom*, 54–62. In the *Testaments of the Twelve Patriarchs*, the hope of resurrection or afterlife is found in *T. Lev.* 18:10–14; *T. Jud.* 25; *T. Ben.* 10:6–10; *T. Zeb.* 10:1–4; *T. Sim.* 6:7. See Collins, *The Apocalyptic Imagination*, 142 n. 103.

during the Passover festival (v. 23). The meeting of Jesus and Nicodemus probably takes place in the precincts of Jerusalem, as there is no textual hint of a change of geographical milieu since John 2:13 (cf. 2:23).[60] At the outset of the present scene (John 3:1), Nicodemus is introduced as ἄνθρωπος ἐκ τῶν Φαρισαίων ("a man from the Pharisees") and ἄρχων τῶν Ἰουδαίων ("a leader of the Jews"). He is referred to as ὁ διδάσκαλος τοῦ Ἰσραήλ ("the teacher of Israel") later in John 3:10. These descriptions of Nicodemus (cf. his greeting of Jesus as "rabbi" in v. 2), together with the scene's locale in Jerusalem, set the dialogue between Jesus and Nicodemus within the Jewish context and point to this context as interpretive clue for construing John's articulation of their encounter.[61]

Since Jesus executed no miracle in Jerusalem prior to John 2:23, some scholars find the statements regarding many "signs" in Jerusalem (John 2:23; 3:2) impossible to reconcile with the references in John 2:11 and 4:54 to the ἀρχή and δεύτερος "signs" of Jesus respectively.[62] Other interpreters believe that certain verses of John 3 were displaced and slotted into their current positions in the story sometime after the Fourth Gospel's completion.[63] Such speculation of textual displacement, however, lacks the support from textual witness and offers little insight in explicating the extant writing. More important, the present location of the Nicodemus pericope and its internal literary arrangement make logical sense in the narrative flow. As Raymond Brown comments, in the Johannine plot the succinct report of John 2:23-25 serves as "the introduction to the Nicodemus scene."[64] Notably, several terms in this report reappear in the opening verses of John 3:1–21: ἄνθρωπος (2:25 [2x]; 3:2), σημεῖα (2:23; 3:2), and the juxtaposition of ἦν and δέ, (2:23; 3:1).[65] It is likely that Nicodemus is one of the spectators who have been amazed by Jesus' miracles during

---

60. Moloney, *The Gospel of John*, 89.

61. Ibid., 89–91.

62. See, e.g., Mendner, "Nikodemus," 293–323. Mendner alleges that only 3:2, 3a, 7b, 9, 10, 12b and 13a are authentic and these verses should originally fall in the narrative of John 7.

63. Schnackenburg claims that John 3:31–36 follow John 3:12 (*The Gospel according to St. John*, 1:360–63). For Bultmann, John 3:31–36 come after John 3:21 (*The Gospel of John*, 131–33, 160 n. 2).

64. Brown, *The Gospel according to John*, 1:137; cf. Köstenberger, *John*, 113; Beasley-Murray, *John*, 45–46; Schnackenburg, *The Gospel according to St. John*, 1:360.

65. See also Köstenberger, *John*, 115; Schnackenburg, *The Gospel according to St. John*, 1:360; Jonge, "Nicodemus and Jesus," 337–59 (esp. 340).

the Passover and have come to believe in him, but their faith is deemed as insufficient. The employment of the first-person plural verb οἴδαμεν and the reappearance of the term σημεῖα in John 3:2 (cf. 2:23) espouse this identification of Nicodemus as one of the people referred to in John 2:23–25. The concluding accent in John 3:19–21 on the necessity of coming out of "darkness" to the light echoes and contrasts with Nicodemus's portrayal at the beginning of the account that he visits Jesus "at night" (John 3:2). It is probable that Jesus' discourse ends at John 3:15 and the section John 3:16–21 unfolds the evangelist's reflection on this discourse.[66] Thus the two sections John 3:1–15 and 3:16–21 are integrally connected in the storyline, a connection that is indicated in their shared motifs (e.g., night/darkness, eternal life) and the use of the conjunction γάρ in verse 16. The structure of John 3:1–21 can be delineated as follows:

A.   3:1–15   The exchanges between Jesus and Nicodemus

     3:1–2a   Introduction of the two protagonists

     3:2b   Nicodemus' first speech (in statement form)

     3:3   Jesus' first discourse: Begetting ἄνωθεν and "seeing" God's kingdom

     3:4   Nicodemus misapprehends Jesus' discourse and utters his second speech (in question form)

     3:5–8   Jesus' second discourse: Begetting ἐξ ὕδατος καὶ πνεύματος and "entering" God's kingdom

     3:9   Nicodemus fails to understand Jesus' discourse and utters his third speech (in question form)

     3:11–15   Jesus' third discourse: The "lifting up" of the Son of Man, faith, and eternal life

B.   3:16–21   The Johannine commentary (or Jesus' continuous discourse): The necessity of faith in Jesus in order to receive eternal life

---

66. Köstenberger, *John*, 114; Bruce, *The Gospel of John*, 89.

Entrance in the Kingdom of God (John 3:3, 5)

In response to Nicodemus' statement (John 3:2), Jesus utters two speeches in John 3:3 and 3:5 about participation in the kingdom of God.[67] As is often noted, the adverb ἄνωθεν, which occurs five times in the Gospel of John, may express the idea of "again" or "from above" (John 3:3, 7, 31; 19:11, 23). Since all three instances of this adverb outside John 3:1–21 connote the sense of "from above" (3:31; 19:11, 23) and given John's overall interest in "vertical dualism" (i.e., the contrast between the heavenly and the earthly spheres), the phrase γεννηθῇ ἄνωθεν in John 3:3 and 3:7 most likely means "born from above."[68] This meaning is tantamount to "born from God" or "born of God," based on the Johannine and the Jewish treatments of "above" or "heaven" as a circumlocution for God (e.g., John 19:11; *1 En.* 6:2; 13:8; *3 En.* 28:9; 1QM 12:5; *Gen. Rab.* 51:3).[69]

For the reader of John's Gospel, s/he has encountered the concept of birth of God in the prologue to this Gospel (John 1:12–13). There the same verb γεννάω occurs for the first time in the Johannine story (18x in total; the second time is in John 3:3), with regard to those who receive the incarnated Logos and believe in his name. These people's new relationship to God is described in familial language; they are the "children of God" (John 1:12) and "have been born of God" (John 1:13).[70] In the Nicodemus episode, the reader is further informed that the children of God are the children of the king and, by implication, will "see" and "enter" God's kingdom (John 3:3, 5).[71] In seeking to relate the Johannine concept of "children of God" (John 1:12; 11:52; cf. "other sheep" in John 10:16) intrinsically to Israel's restoration hopes, Dennis confines the referent of God's children as well as the pertinent "begetting" expressions in John 3 to the restored Israel, at the expense of the Johannine interest in Gentile

---

67. These two speeches display a symmetric structure. See the analyses in Frey, *Die eschatologische Verkündigung in den johannischen Texte*, 249; Burge, *The Anointed Community*, 167–68.

68. Most commentators prefer the meaning "from above." For example, Beasley-Murray, *John*, 45; Ridderbos, *The Gospel according to John*, 123; cf. Büchsel, "ἄνωθεν," *TDNT* 1:378.

69. See more Jewish references in Keener, *The Gospel of John*, 1:539 n. 47.

70. See Watt, *Family of the King*, 376–81; cf. idem, *Salvation in the New Testament*, 122–24.

71. Idem, *Family of the King*, 381.

mission.[72] This confinement is unnecessary and it presumes that the evangelist must have adopted the conventional Jewish identification of God's children as Israel or the remnant of Israel (e.g., *Pss. Sol.* 17:26–27; 1QH XI, 35–36).[73] Despite the Fourth Gospel's Jewish heritage, it is evident that the evangelist has undertaken a redefinition of God's children (John 1:12–13; cf. 1 John 3:1, 2, 10; 5:2) in light of the career, death, and resurrection of Jesus. In divergence from contemporary Jewish thinking, the Johannine criterion of being a member of God's family is not based on ethnicity but faith in Jesus. In John 3:1–21, Jesus' statement (v. 15) and the evangelist's exposition of Jesus' words (vv. 16–21) in unison strike a universal note and indicate clearly that membership of God's family/kingdom extends beyond the nation of Israel (cf. the "world" as the object of God's love and the adjective πᾶς in vv. 15, 16). We will return to the subject of the inclusion of believing Gentiles as God's people (see chapter 6).

Nicodemus's misapprehension of γεννηθῇ ἄνωθεν in the literal sense as physical rebirth (John 3:4) opens up the occasion for Jesus' second discourse in John 3:5 concerning γεννηθῇ ἐξ ὕδατος καὶ πνεύματος. The two anarthrous genitives ὕδατος and πνεύματος share a single preposition (ἐκ) and are tied together by the conjunction καί. This grammatical construction suggests that these two nouns are conceptually unified, or at least interrelated, notions within the immediate contexts.[74] Given John's later explication in John 7:38–39 of "water" as symbolizing the Spirit, the entire phrase γεννηθῇ ἐξ ὕδατος καὶ πνεύματος in John 3:5 probably refers to the Spirit's purifying and rejuvenating power (i.e., καί is epexegetical).[75] The necessity of birth from God is further emphasized in John 3:6–7, where the spiritual nature of those begotten of the Spirit is contrasted with the fleshy nature of those begotten through physical birth. Notice that the earlier scene of John 1:32–34 has spoken of the Spirit descending and remaining on Jesus, who will baptize with the Spirit. In John 7:39, Jesus promises the believers that they will receive the Spirit upon Jesus'

---

72. Dennis, *Jesus' Death and the Gathering of True Israel*, 292–302, 306–11.

73. For the Jewish references, see ibid., 278–84; Keener, *The Gospel of John*, 1:401.

74. Carson, *The Gospel according to John*, 194; Belleville, "Born of Water and Spirit," 125–41. However, Belleville (followed by Carson) believes that the word pneu/ma in John 3:5 refers to God's nature and not to the Holy Spirit (pp. 140–41). See also Burge, *The Anointed Community*, 166, though Burge holds that "water" points to baptism.

75. Keener, *The Gospel of John*, 1:350–51; Jones, *The Symbol of Water in the Gospel of John*, 74. As la Potterie and Lyonnet aptly note, "it is the action of the Spirit, which alone can render us fit (*dunatai*) to 'see' the kingdom." See *The Christian Lives by the Spirit*, 29.

glorification, that is, his death and resurrection as a unified event (cf. John 12:16; 13:31). Since the coming of the Spirit is contingent upon Jesus' crucifixion, his death is the precondition for birth from God through the agency of the Spirit. In other words, the notion of "birth of the Spirit" in John 3 has the function of anticipating the Spirit's impending bestowal, when Jesus the Messiah-King goes to the cross.

Most scholars concur that the prophecy of Ezekiel 36 (esp. vv. 25–27) provides the biblical background of the formulation of γεννηθῇ ἐξ ὕδατος καὶ πνεύματος. As this prophecy declares, Israel is in exile because the people have defiled themselves with idolatrous and murderous sins (Ezek 36:16–19).[76] The dual motifs of "water" and "Spirit" are connected in Ezek 36:25–27, which look forward to the purification of God's people by "clean water" (Ezek 36:25), the renewal of their heart and spirit to obedience, and the divine conferral of "my [God's] Spirit" (Ezek 36:27; cf. "a new spirit" in Ezek 11:19; 18:31; "my Spirit" in Ezek 37:14; 39:29; also cf. Joel 2:28).[77] As a result of the Spirit's activity, the Israelites will return to their land and their covenantal relationship as God's people will be renewed (Ezek 36:24, 28; cf. 37:27). In the subsequent vision of Ezek 37:1–14, the reinstatement of the "house of Israel" (v. 11) is illustrated in symbolic terms of the Spirit (v. 14; cf. "breath" [רוח/πνεῦμα] in vv. 5, 6, 8, 9, 10, 14) revivifying the dry bones in the valley to life (חיה/ζάω or ζωή in vv. 3, 5, 6, 9, 10, 14). The life-giving act of God through the Spirit will lead to the reunification of the divided nation into one people under one Davidic king (Ezek 37:21–25).[78] Thus in Ezekiel's conception the Spirit's cleansing and revitalizing work is the overture to the advent of the Messiah. The twin themes of "water" and "Spirit" are likewise juxtaposed in the Isaianic vision of Israel's national restoration in Isa 44:3–6, where God's "pouring out" his Spirit on Israel is likened to the "pouring out" of water on a dry land and refreshing it accordingly (v. 3).[79] In post-biblical Judaism, a metaphorical use of "water" with respect to the Spirit's consecrating work is present in Qumran's *Rule of the Community* (1QS). As envisaged in 1QS IV, 20–22 (cf. III, 6–9), God will sprinkle over his people "the spirit of truth like lustral water" so as to purge them from the abhorrence of falsehood and the defilement by

---

76. Klawans, *Impurity and Sin in Ancient Judaism*, 30–31.

77. Cooper, *Ezekiel*, 317.

78. Thompson, "The Breath of Life," 72.

79. Ibid., 73.

the unclean spirit. This pre-Christian sectarian scroll looks forward to the eschatological arrival of the Messiah of Israel (IX, 11), though in the surrounding context his appearance is not directly related to the Spirit's bestowal or cleansing work.[80]

The "Lifting Up" of the Son of Man and Eternal Life (John 3:14–15)

The motif of the "lifting up" of the Son of Man surfaces three times in the Gospel of John and the first time this motif appears is in John 3:14 (cf. 8:28; 12:32–34). In both of John 3:14 and 12:34, the verb δεῖ occurs to heighten the idea of the divine necessity that the Son of Man must be "lifted up."[81] In John 1:51, the reader has been told that the Son of Man is a heavenly figure that connects God and human. In his reply to Nathanael's royal-messianic extolment, Jesus promises him and other disciples that they will witness a revelation far greater than what their ancestor, Jacob, saw at Bethel. In chapter 3, we argued that this promise concerning the Son of Man functions as a literary prolepsis in anticipating the splendid display of the divine glory in Jesus' death. The description of the "lifting up" of the Son of Man (John 3:14) likewise points in the direction of the cross. The presence of the cross notion in this description of John 3 is only subtle. Yet it will be more conspicuous as the Johannine story unfolds in John 8:28 and especially in John 12:32–33, where the evangelist reveals that "lifting up" is a veiled expression of the manner of Jesus' death, namely crucifixion (cf. John 18:32).[82] In short, in the Johannine conceptualization the promised revelation of John 1:51 will culminate in the moment when Jesus the Son of Man is "lifted up" on the cross.[83]

For John, the "lifting up" of Jesus (i.e., his death) will result in the divine conferral of eternal life (John 3:15–16; cf. 6:27 [the Son of Man and eternal life]). The term ζωή ("life") occurs a total of 36 times in John's

---

80. In *Jub.* 1:22–25, God promises Moses that he will "create for them [his people] a holy spirit" and "cleanse them" (1:23). As a result, God's people will be called his "sons" (1:25). While this text conjoins the themes of the Spirit, divine purification, and the children of God, the envisioned scenario differs from that of John 3 in that the author of *Jubilees* confers the status of God's children only on Israel. The English translation is from Wintermute, "Jubilees," *OTP* 2:35–142.

81. Brown, *The Gospel according to John*, 1:146.

82. Smith, *The Theology of the Gospel of John*, 119, 132.

83. Moloney, *The Gospel of John*, 95.

Gospel, of which 17 are in the combination ζωή αἰώνιος ("eternal life").[84] The first time this expression surfaces in the Gospel story is in John 3:15 (cf. 3:16; ζωή in John 1:4), which comes after two Johannine references to the "kingdom of God" (John 3:3, 5). The conjunction ἵνα in John 3:15 indicates that the dispensing of eternal life is the intended purpose or outcome of Jesus' death. In the context of the Nicodemus pericope, the phrase ζωή αἰώνιος is parallel to the preceding ἡ βασιλεία τοῦ θεοῦ. This change of terminology reveals that "eternal life" for John is the life of this "kingdom."[85] While in Jewish belief eternal life is one of the eschatological blessings in the world to come, the evangelist avers that one can have a foretaste of this life in the present age.[86] This is possible because the one who embodies life (John 1:5; 5:26; 11:25; 14:6) has come into the world to bring life to all who believe (John 3:15–16; 6:33, 51, 63; 10:10). However, the full consummation of eternal life is still in the future when the final resurrection will take place (John 5:28–29; 6:40).

It is generally agreed that the Johannine reference in John 3:14 to Moses "lifting up" (ὑψόω) the serpent in the wilderness summons the biblical incident of Num 21:8–9.[87] In this passage, God commands Moses to make a bronze serpent and put it on a "standard" (נֵס; σημεῖον) so that the rebellious Israelites bitten by poisonous snakes "will live" (חָיָה; ζήσεται) when they gaze upon this "lifted-up" serpent. In an analogous way, the "lifting up" (ὑψωθῆναι) of Jesus as the Son of Man has salvific significance in effecting the bestowal of "life" on God's people—the Israelites in Num 21:8–9 but πᾶς ὁ πιστεύων ("everyone who believes") according to John 3:15. Nonetheless, Jesus surpasses the "lifted-up" serpent because the life that he mediates has no end. Since the Johannine term σημεῖον is laden with theological overtones, the allusion to Moses' bronze serpent on a σημεῖον (Num 21:8 LXX) probably connotes the idea that the "lifting up"

---

84. (1) ζωή: John 1:4 [2x]; 3:15, 16, 36 [2x]; 4:14, 36; 5:24 [2x], 26 [2x], 29, 39, 40; 6:27, 33, 35, 40, 47, 48, 51, 53, 54, 63, 68; 8:12; 10:10, 28; 11:25; 12:25, 50; 14:6; 17:2, 3; 20:31. (2) ζωή αἰώνιος: John 3:15, 16, 36; 4:14, 36; 5:24, 39; 6:27, 40, 47, 54, 68; 10:28; 12:25, 50; 17:2, 3.

85. Similar thematic shifts between "[eternal] life" and the "kingdom of God/ heaven" are found in Mark 9 (vv. 43, 45, 47) and Matthew 19 (vv. 16, 17; cf. vv. 23, 24, 29).

86. For the Johannine concept of eternal life, see Frey, *Die johanneische Eschatologie*, 254–70; Ladd, *A Theology of the New Testament*, 290–95.

87. E.g., Lincoln, *The Gospel according to Saint John*, 153; Brown, *The Gospel according to John*, 1:133; Dodd, *The Interpretation of the Fourth Gospel*, 306.

of Jesus is a σημεῖον ("sign").[88] If this idea is operative in John 3:14–15, the Fourth Gospel's stated purpose (20:30–31) invites the consideration of the "lifting up" statement in light of the Johannine concern with the validity of Jesus' messiahship (cf. the shared themes of "life," "faith," and "Son of God" in John 3:15–18 and 20:31).

The term ὑψόω bears a double entendre in Johannine treatment in communicating the twin notions of exaltation and crucifixion (cf. ὑψόω as exaltation in Acts 2:33; 5:31), by which the Son returns to his heavenly Father.[89] Most scholars believe that the dignified image of the "Servant" in Isa 52:13 LXX provides the background of John's use of this verb, on account of his articulation of Jesus' death as his "glorification" (δοξάζω; cf. John 7:39; 12:16; 12:23; 13:31).[90] In Isa 52:13 LXX, the two future passive indicative verbs ὑψωθήσεται and δοξασθήσεται are juxtaposed in the description of God's vindication of the suffering Servant. The evangelist picks up and interprets this verse, which commences the section of Isa 52:13—53:12, as a "summary statement" that points to "the whole sequence of humiliation, suffering, death, and vindication beyond death which chapter 53 describes."[91] Just as the Isaianic Servant is exalted through his suffering, Jesus is "lifted up" to a lofty and glorified status through his crucifixion.[92] Moreover, the Septuagintal connection of the noun δόξα or the verb δοξάζω with the notion of divine salvation adds substance to the Johannine assertion that the "lifting up" of Jesus to glory will result in the conferral of eternal life.[93] If the variant ὁ ἐκλεκτός in John 1:34 is original (see chapter 3), the linkage between Jesus and the Isaianic Servant has been set up from the onset of the Gospel story. At any rate, the Johannine expression "the lifting up of the Son of Man" (John 3:14; 8:28; 12:32–34) combines the dual images of the Danielic Son of Man and the Isaianic Servant into a single portrait of Jesus. Dennis proposes that the

---

88. Keener, *The Gospel of John*, 1:565.

89. See Evans, *Word and Glory*, 180; Dennis, *Jesus' Death and the Gathering of True Israel*, 325; Nicholson, *Death as Departure*, esp. 141–44, 163. Evans says that "the manner of his [Jesus'] death, that is, being lifted up the cross, becomes part of the apologetic itself."

90. E.g., Williams, "Isaiah in John's Gospel," 114–15.

91. Bauckham, *Jesus and the God of Israel*, 47.

92. Ibid.

93. For the salvific overtone of the terms δόξα and δοξάζω in the LXX, see Troxel, *LXX-Isaiah as Translation and Interpretation*, 130–32.

depiction of the royal-messianic Son of Man in *1 En.* 48:2–6 alludes to the image of the Servant in Isa 42:1–7 (cf. Isa 49:6; Son of Man = Messiah in *1 En.* 48:10), on the basis of the Son of Man's designation as the "Chosen One" and his role as the light to the nations.[94] If this proposal is correct, John's messianic integration of the Danielic Son of Man with the Isaianic servant should have been conceivable in first-century CE Judaism.

The last occurrence of the term ζωή ("life") in the Gospel of John is in its purpose statement (20:31), or to borrow Zimmernann's terminology, in one of Johannine "paratexts."[95] This statement announces that belief in Jesus as the χριστός, the Son of God, is necessary for receiving "life" (i.e., eternal life). The concept that faith in God's "messianic" Son will lead to life resonates with the promise of John 3:16 (cf. 3:14–15), where John elaborates on Jesus' words and explains that faith in God's Son will lead to everlasting life. While the epithet χριστός is absent from John 3:1–21, the overt messianic overtone linked to ζωή in the Gospel's purpose statement espouses the construal that the promise about "eternal life" in John 3 concerns Jesus' messianic status. In the earlier sections, we noted that in the thoughts of certain biblical and post-biblical Jewish texts, the royal Messiah will function as God's agent in establishing his end-time kingdom or implementing his kingly rule. Within some Jewish circles, the advent of the royal Messiah is further tied to the hope of the final resurrection and/or eternal life. In light of the OT and late Second Temple Jewish instances regarding the Messiah-King's connection with the eschatological kingdom or life, the articulation of Jesus' death in John 3:1–21 most likely seeks to evoke the future hope for the kingdom of God. For it is through the "lifting up" of Jesus as the Son of Man that makes the life of this kingdom available. All those who believe in the crucified Jesus will "see" and "enter" the kingdom of God (John 3:3, 5) or, in other words, will participate in "eternal life." In Johannine vernacular, these people are the "children of God" (John 1:12–13) and have been born "from above" and "of water and spirit [the Spirit]" (John 3:3, 5). In summary, the narrative of John 3:1–21 seeks to elicit faith in the crucified Jesus as Israel's Messiah-King. This narrative achieves this royal-messianic purpose by

94. Dennis, "The 'Lifting Up of the Son of Man' and the Dethroning of the 'Ruler of This World,'" 688; cf. Nickelsburg, "Salvation Without and With a Messiah," 59–60. Nickelsburg says that the two messianic epithets "Chosen One" and "Righteous One" in the *Similitudes* are derived from the Isaianic portrait of the "suffering servant" (p. 58)

95. Zimmermann, "Intratextuality and Intertextuality in the Gospel of John," 123.

asserting that life in God's eternal kingdom is conferred on everyone who believes in the crucified Jesus, whose death is the divinely ordained means by which the eschatological life is made available in the present age.[96]

Conclusion

We have examined the thematic-conceptual interplay between Jesus' messianic kingship and death in the Nicodemus account (John 3:1–21). Although this account does not explicitly designate Jesus as king or Messiah, the assertion that Jesus' death (= "lifting up") will lead to the conferral of the life in God's kingdom resonates with the Jewish hope concerning the Messiah-King's participation in implementing God's kingly dominion. Because the Gospel of John frequently makes references to the Psalter and because the intertwined motifs "lifting up," "Son of Man," and "eternal life" in the Nicodemus passage have noticeable parallels with Isaiah and Daniel, our discussion of OT texts focused primarily on the relevant notions in these three biblical documents. The examination of pertinent late Second Temple Jewish writings indicated that the royal Messiah's arrival often links with the inauguration of God's kingdom and occasionally with the final resurrection; in some cases, the Messiah is the agent through whom God's end-time kingdom is ushered in. Against this Jewish royal-messianic background, we closely scrutinized the notions in John 3:1–21 pertaining to entrance in the kingdom of God, the "lifting up" of Jesus, and the dispensing of eternal life. We also called attention to the way in which the cross motif functions to validate the Johannine identification of the crucified Jesus as Israel's Messiah-King. This function is performed in the powerful assertion that the eschatological life in God's kingdom is made available *through* the "lifting up" of Jesus, that is, crucifixion.

---

96. Dennis provides a lengthy discussion of the apologetic function of the lift-giving effect of Jesus' death. See *Jesus' Death and the Gathering of True Israel*, 328–29.

6

Israel's Unification
and the Royal Messiahship of Jesus
(John 10:14–18)

THE "ONE FLOCK, ONE shepherd" motif in John 10:14–18 is pertinent to the Jewish eschatological hope for "the regathering of Israel," which David Aune comments is "one of the central themes of post-exilic Jewish eschatology."[1] This eschatological theme has attracted much scholarly attention, partly due to N. T. Wright's controversial thesis that most Second Temple Jews conceived themselves of being in exile and awaiting its end.[2] In the field of Johannine research, Andrew Brunson and John Dennis's studies from varied perspectives have examined the evangelist's treatment of the Jewish restoration hopes for Israel's gathering.[3] Their studies are enlightening but do not probe the implications for the crucified Jesus' royal messiahship, a subject that clearly stands at the heart of John's Gospel (cf. 20:31). We will seek to address this neglected area by scrutinizing the royal-messianic connotations in the shepherd discourse in John 10 that emerge from the thematic interplay between Jesus' death and Israel's unification. Wayne Meeks rejects a messianic reading of this

---

1. Aune, "From the Idealized Past to the Imaginary Future," 158. Sanders notes that the variegated expressions of Second Temple Jewish eschatology share "the general hope for the restoration of the people of Israel." See Sanders, *Judaism*, 294, cf. 289.

2. Wright, *Jesus and the Victory of God*, esp. 126–27, 203–4; idem, *The New Testament and the People of God*, esp. 268–72, 299–301.

3. Brunson, *Psalm 118 in the Gospel of John*, 63–69, 163–66; Dennis, *Jesus' Death and the Gathering of True Israel*, 187–209.

discourse and claims that John's depiction of Jesus as the good shepherd is decisively shaped by the Mosaic traditions.[4] Ruben Zimmermann, David Ball, and other scholars analyze Jesus' shepherd-portrait in John 10:1–21 against the backdrop of the Jewish conception of God as Israel's shepherd and consequently lay stress on this portrait's divine connotations.[5] It is gratuitous to assume that the evangelist cannot draw on and combine sundry shepherd-pictures in the OT in order to present Jesus as the shepherd *par excellence*. We will focus on the royal-messianic implication of John's articulation of the shepherd's death, especially in its relation to the "one flock, one shepherd" motif in John 10:16.[6] An excursus at the end of this chapter will briefly look at several other Gospel passages in which the notions of Jesus' death/kingship and Israel's unification/gathering are connected.

Israel's Unification under a Davidic (Shepherd) King in the OT

In the biblical tradition, shepherd imageries frequently occur in the context of the prophetic hopes for the unification of Israel under an ideal Davidic king. The book of Micah contains a prophecy in Mic 5:1–3 (5:2–4 Eng.) of one who will arise from Bethlehem to be "ruler in Israel" (v. 1).[7] This future ruler is subordinate to Yahweh, as the two terms לי (the suffix refers to Yahweh) in Mic 5:1 and אלהיו ("his God") in Mic 5:3 indicate. The geographical reference "Bethlehem Ephrathah" (Mic 5:2 Eng.; 5:1 MT) conjures up the tradition regarding David's provenance from Bethlehem (cf. 1 Sam 16:18; 17:12, 58), thus pointing to the ruler's Davidic pedigree.[8]

---

4. Meeks, *The Prophet-King*, 307–13.

5. Zimmermann, "Jesus im Bild Gottes," 81–116 (esp. 107–9); idem, *Christologie der Bilder im Johannesevangelium*, 332–44; Ball, "*I Am*" *in John's Gospel*, 224–32.

6. Given our specific interest in royal messianism, we will not discuss the OT and Second Temple Jewish texts that apply the shepherd metaphor to God (e.g., Gen 49:24; Pss 23:1–4; 80:1 [79:1 LXX]; Isa 40:11; Ezek 34:11–17; *Sir.* 18:13; *1 En.* 89:18), Moses (e.g., *L.A.B.* [*Pseudo-Philo*] 19:3; *Tg. Ps.-J.* on Gen 40:12 ["three shepherds" = Moses, Aaron, and Miriam]; cf. Ps 77:20; Isa 63:11), Cyrus (Isa 44:28), or other figures unless these texts are pertinent to our investigation.

7. Barker and Bailer, *Micah, Nahum, Habakkuk, Zephaniah*, 97.

8. Cf. Ps 132:6; Ruth 4:11; 1 Chr 2:24, 50–51; 4:4. The word "Ephrathah" probably denotes a clan, the region in which Bethlehem is located, or Bethlehem itself. At any rate, this word highlights the ruler's Davidic origin. See Anderson and Freedman, *Micah*, 463; Barker and Bailer, *Micah, Nahum, Habakkuk, Zephaniah*, 96.

Similarly, the verb יצא and the expressions מקדם and מימי עולם in Mic 5:1 evoke the Davidic dynasty promise and thereby accentuate the ruler's "ancient" tie with the imperial house of David.[9] Micah speaks of the ruler as משל instead of מלך, probably because this latter title has just been applied to Yahweh (Mic 4:9, cf. 4:7).[10] In Mic 5:3 (5:4 Eng.), the Davidic ruler appears as a "shepherd" (רעה; ποιμαίνω). The MT does not specify the object of this third-person Qal perfect verb רעה, but the LXX interprets its object as τὸ ποίμνιον αὐτοῦ. This Greek phrase reveals the translator's understanding that the Davidic ruler is Yahweh's under-shepherd; in this sense, God's sheep can be described as the ruler's.

The notion of the reinstatement of "former dominion" in Mic 4:8, which resides in the context concerning Yahweh's kingship (Mic 4:7–9), most likely anticipates the advent of the Davidic משל (Mic 5:1). For Micah, this royal figure will function as Yahweh's vehicle in restoring his kingly rule in Zion. As envisioned in Mic 4:6, Yahweh will "assemble" (אסף and קבץ; συνάγω and εἰσδέχομαι) the dispersed Israelites and govern over his renewed people. These two Hebrew/Greek verbs are also juxtaposed in Mic 2:12 MT/LXX pertaining to Yahweh's act of "gathering" the remnant of Israel as his sheep. While no human mediator appears in Mic 2:12 and 4:6, the oracle of Mic 5:2 (5:3 Eng.) explicitly connects the coming of the Davidic ruler with the "return" of the "remnant of his brothers" to the "children of Israel." The third-person masculine singular suffix of אחיו in Mic 5:2 (i.e., "*his* brothers" in Mic 5:3 Eng.) most probably refers to this ruler, who is depicted as in solidarity with God's people. The promise of "return" presupposes the exilic state of the Israelites (cf. Mic 2:12–13; 4:6–7), whose dispersion will end upon the divine intervention to bring them back to the land and raise up a ruler from David's line.

In Mic 5:4 (MT), shepherd vocabulary (רעה) resurfaces in the setting of the Davidic ruler's military combat against the Assyrians.[11] On account of this lexical usage, Anderson and Freedman propose that the preceding

---

9. Notice the use of יצא in 2 Sam 7:12; Isa 11:1; Jer 30:21, בימי in Neh 12:46, and כימי עולם in Amos 9:11. See Chae, *Jesus as the Eschatological Davidic Shepherd*, 36; Wolff, *Micah*, 144.

10. In Mic 6:5, the term מלך is used of the king of Moab. Thus Micah does not apply this title exclusively to Yahweh. The designation of the Davidic ruler as משל probably serves to stress his subordinate role as Yahweh's agent. See Barker and Bailer, *Micah, Nahum, Habakkuk, Zephaniah*, 97; Wolff, *Micah*, 144, 146.

11. McKane, *The Book of Micah*, 149.

occurrence of this term (רעה) in Mic 5:3 likewise pertains to the ruler's martial power.[12] This interpretation is plausible, but it is perhaps structurally more appropriate to relate Mic 5:3 to verse 2 (which concerns Israel's future unification) rather than to verse 4 (which concerns militant combat). The reason this seems more appropriate is that the Hebrew construct והיה at the outset of Mic 5:4 clearly signals the beginning of a new unit, although the pronoun הו there refers back to the ruler in Mic 5:1–3. As envisaged in Mic 5:3 (5:4 Eng.), the Davidic shepherd-ruler's jurisdiction is not curtailed within the land of Israel but extends to "the end of the earth" (אפסי־ארץ).[13]

The prophetic message of Jer 23:1–4 indicts the Judean leaders as disloyal shepherds and announces that Yahweh, as the divine shepherd, will care for his own sheep (cf. sheep = "my [God's] people" [מי; τὸν λαόν μου] in v. 2). These unfaithful shepherds have done "evil deeds" (v. 2)—they "destroy" (v. 1), "scatter" (vv. 1, 2), "disperse" (v. 2), and do not "take care of" (v. 2) the flock of God. In order to rescue his afflicted sheep, Yahweh will "gather" (קבץ; εἰσδέχομαι) the "remnant of his flock" (את־שארית צאני; κατάλοιπος τοῦ λαοῦ μου; cf. "flock" = λαός) from all the nations and "bring [them] back" to their pasture, that is, the promised land (Jer 23:3).[14] In view of parallel expressions in the book of Genesis, the statement that this remnant "will be fruitful and multiply" (ופרו ורבו; καὶ αὐξηθήσονται καὶ πληθυνθήσονται; Jer 23:3; cf. Jer 3:16; Ezek 36:11) probably serves to liken Yahweh's eschatological act of restoring his people to a new creation.[15] Aside from Jeremiah 23, the oracle of Jer 31:8–10 speaks of Yahweh "like a shepherd" (כרעה; ὡς ὁ βόσων; v. 10) gathering the northerners and escorting them back to Zion. The shepherd metaphor surfaces in Jer 10:21; 25:34–36; 50:6 with regard to the divine arraignment against the misrule of the evil shepherds, specifically, the chief of the flock (Jer 25:34–36). In

---

12. Anderson and Freeman, *Micah*, 469.

13. The Hebrew phrase, אפסי־ארץ, occurs in Pss 2:8; 72:8; Zech 9:10 to affirm the universality of the Davidic rule. See Wolff, *Micah*, 146.

14. In the book of Jeremiah, the idea that a remnant of God's people will survive in exile and return to their land is present in Jer 24:4–7; 29:10–14; 31:7–9; 44:11–14, 27–28; 50:19–20. Similar notions are found in other prophetic books such as Isaiah (1:9; 4:3; 7:3; 10:20–23; 11:1–9; 37:4, 31–32) and Micah (2:12; 4:6–7; 5:6–7 [5:7–8 Eng.]; 7:18). See Lundbom, *Jeremiah 21–36*, 168.

15. E.g., Gen 1:22, 28; 8:17; 9:1, 7. See ibid., 168–69; Laniak, *Shepherds After My Own Heart*, 137.

Jer 10:21 and 50:6 (cf. 23:1–4), these shepherds are impeached of dispersing the sheep of God (i.e., Israel's exile).[16]

Following the oracle of Jer 23:1–4, in which Yahweh rebukes the wicked shepherds and announces his shepherding mission, the prophecy of Jer 23:5–6 predicts the future appearance of an ideal Davidic king. In verse 5, God promises that he will raise up for David a "righteous Branch" (cf. Jer 33:14–16 MT [absent from the LXX]; Zech 3:8; 6:12) who will execute "justice and righteousness in the land" (cf. Isa 32:1a). The compound expression מלך ומלך (καὶ βασιλεύσει βασιλεύς) in Jer 23:5 is made up of two cognate words and serves to highlight this figure's royal dignity. In Jer 23:6, "Judah" and "Israel" probably stand for the southern and the northern monarchies which will be federated as one nation, over which the new David will preside.[17] This national hope resounds in the ensuing oracle of Jer 23:8, which presages that the northerners will return to and dwell in their own land. Such hope is also echoed in the eschatological visions of Jer 3:6–18 and 30:1–11, although the former text does not mention a Davidic royal figure. As the prophet declares, the renewed people will serve "Yahweh their God and David their king [דוד מלכם]" (Jer 30:9). This declaration is followed by Yahweh's assurance that he will rescue the exiles from the land of their captivity (Jer 30:10–11).[18] In agreement with Micah's use of the shepherd imagery, Jeremiah portrays Yahweh as Israel's shepherd congregating his scattered people from the nations. Jeremiah also presents the new David as Yahweh's viceroy, who will govern over the restored Israel. While the shepherd image is not applied to the Davidic "Branch," his function apparently links with Yahweh's shepherding task, which will result in Israel's unification.

In the interrelated visions of Ezekiel 34 and 37, Yahweh appears as the compassionate shepherd searching for and assembling his sheep. The divine shepherd, moreover, installs a Davidic shepherd-king over the reinstated flock (Ezek 34:23–24; 37:22–25; cf. Jer 23:1–8).[19] The oracle in

16. Allen, *Jeremiah*, 131; Bracke, *Jeremiah 30—52 and Lamentations*, 145–47.

17. Cf. Jer 3:11, 18; 31:31; 33:14. See Lundbom, *Jeremiah 21—36*, 176; contra Allen's claim that "Judah" and "Israel" in Jer 23:6 are "synonymous parallels" (*Jeremiah*, 259).

18. Bracke, *Jeremiah 30—52 and Lamentations*, 2–5.

19. These visions are lodged in the literary section (Ezekiel 34—48) regarding the prophecies of the restoration of Israel. Most interpreters concur that Ezekiel 33 sums up the prophetic message of judgment in the preceding chapters and it commences a series of oracles regarding Israel's future redemption. See Renz, *The Rhetorical Function*

Ezek 34:1–10 accuses the "shepherds of Israel" (= the Jewish leaders; cf. v. 1) of dereliction of their duty. These unfaithful shepherds feed themselves instead of the sheep (Ezek 34:2–3, 8); they do not heal the sick, strengthen the weak, or seek the lost (Ezek 34:4, 8). "Because there is no [good] shepherd" (מבלי רעה; διὰ τὸ μὴ εἶναι ποιμένας; Ezek 34:5; cf. v. 6), God's sheep wander and "are dispersed" (2] פוץx in Ezek 34:5; 1x in Ezek 34:6]; διασπείρω [1x in Ezek 34:5; 2x in Ezek 34:6]) in the whole earth. For Ezekiel, the sheep's destitute situation is the direct consequence of lack of a (good) shepherd. The prophet's remedy is that the wicked shepherds must be removed and Yahweh must assume the role as the shepherd of his people (Ezek 34:11–16, 22). In Ezek 34:12-16, Yahweh avers that he will "search for" (v. 12; cf. v. 15) his sheep, "bring [them] out" (v. 13) and "gather" (v. 13) them from the nations. Furthermore, he will "bring [them] into" (v. 13) their land, "shepherd" (רעה; βόσκω; vv. 12, 13, 15; cf. v. 31) them, and "bring back" (v. 16) the strayed sheep.

As with the oracles in Micah 5 and Jeremiah 23, Ezekiel's proclamation of Yahweh gathering his sheep is closely followed by the prophecy of a Davidic shepherd-king (a Davidic king in Jeremiah 23). This figure first appears in Ezek 34:23–24, subsequent to the oracle in verse 22 of Yahweh undertaking his shepherding mission to rescue his flock. By contrast to two kingdoms of Judah and Israel, God will establish "one shepherd" (רעה אחד; poime/na e3na; Ezek 34:23) over the renewed flock. The adjective אחד ("one") highlights the "uniqueness" of this shepherd, who will be Yahweh's *only* under-shepherd.[20] This figure will be God's "servant David" (עבדי דויד; τὸν δοῦλόν μου Δαυιδ; Ezek 34:23, 24 [without the term δοῦλος in v. 24])[21] and "prince" (נשיא; ἄρχων; Ezek 34:24) among the Israelites.[22]

---

of the Book of Ezekiel, 101–3; Cooper, *Ezekiel*, 291–92. A number of scholars note that the shepherd language in Ezekiel 34 and 37 draws on Jer 23:1–8. See Blenkinsopp, *Ezekiel*, 155–56; Zimmerli, *Ezekiel 2*, 218.

20. Zimmerli, *Ezekiel 2*, 218; cf. Chae, *Jesus as the Eschatological Davidic Shepherd*, 70.

21. David is often denoted as God's "servant" in the OT (e.g., 2 Sam 3:18; 1 Kgs 8:24–26; 11:34, 36, 38; 2 Kgs 8:19; Pss 36:1; 78:70). See Greenberg, *Ezekiel 21–37*, 702.

22. The shift in terminology from "king" to "prince" does not necessarily imply that the prophet plays down the expected figure's royal status. In 1 Kgs 11:34, God says that he will make Solomon a "prince" (נשיא) for David's sake. See Block, "Bringing back David," 175–76; Pomykala, *The Davidic Dynasty Tradition in Early Judaism*, 28.

The second time the Davidic shepherd-king appears in the book of Ezekiel is in the prophecy of Ezek 37:24–25.[23] This prophecy succeeds the vision in Ezek 37:15–23, where two sticks of wood are conjoined into one piece. The wooden sticks symbolize the divided houses of Judah and Israel, which will be reunited into one nation.[24] Reminiscent of the prophetic message in Ezek 34:22–23, the oracle of Ezek 37:21–25 declares that the Davidic shepherd-king will administer in the reconstituted nation. Contrary to Claus Westermann's claim that this royal prophecy's recurrence in Ezek 37:24–25 "is awkward and serves no real purpose,"[25] its reiteration in Ezekiel 37 functions as a literary device by heightening the crucial idea of "one king, one nation." As revealed in Ezek 37:21, God will "gather" the scattered Israelites from among the nations and "bring" them back to their land. These activities (gathering and bringing) are akin to Yahweh's shepherding tasks as delineated in Ezekiel 34, despite the absence of the term רעה in Ezekiel 37. Upon reinstating the divided monarchies as "one nation" (גוי אחד; ἔθνος ἕν; Ezek 37:22), Yahweh will set up his "servant" (עבד; δοῦλος; Ezek 37:24, 25) David as "one king" (מלך אחד; ἄρχων εἷς; Ezek 37:22; cf. Ezek 37:24) and "one shepherd" (רועה עחד; ποιμὴν εἷς; Ezek 37:24) over his people. Echoing the vision in Ezek 34:24, the new David will be "prince" (נשיא; ἄρχων; Ezek 37:25) amidst the Israelites forever.

The portrayals of the Davidic shepherd-king in Ezekiel 34 and 37 are coherent and equally illuminating. Whereas the figure's kingly status comes to the fore only in Ezek 37:22 and 37:24 (מלך; ἄρχων in the LXX),[26] his ruling function is implied in his description as "over them [the sheep]" (עליהם; ἐπ' αὐτούς) in the earlier oracle of Ezek 34:23–24 (cf. עליהם in Ezek 37:24; albeit ἐν μέσῳ αὐτῶν in the LXX).[27] The assertion that the Davidic king is "*one* shepherd" (Ezek 34:23; 37:24) does not contradict

23. As Thomas Renz remarks, the dual references to this Davidic figure at the beginning and closing of Ezek 37:24–25 form an *inclusio* (v. 24a, b and v. 25c) and accentuate his association with Israel's renewed allegiance to Yahweh (vv. 24c–25b). See *The Rhetorical Function of the Book of Ezekiel*, 116 n. 145.

24. Cooper, *Ezekiel*, 326–28. The importance of the theme of Israel's reunification is evident in its dual occurrences in Ezek 37:22. See Westermann, *Prophetic Oracles of Salvation in the Old Testament*, 175.

25. Westermann, *Prophetic Oracles of Salvation in the Old Testament*, 174.

26. For the tendency in the LXX of translating Klm as a!rxwn, see Freund, "From Kings to Archons," 58–72.

27. Chae, *Jesus as the Eschatological Davidic Shepherd*, 67.

Yahweh's role as the shepherd of Israel (Ezek 34:25; cf. 34:1–10, 16, 17–22, 31).[28] Analogous to the biblical concept that the Davidic monarch reigns as Yahweh's vicegerent (see chapter 5), Ezekiel's anticipated Davidic figure functions as the deity's representative in shepherding his flock.[29] The designation of the new David as "servant" (Ezek 34:23, 24; 37:24, 25) suggests that he is subject to Yahweh, who is Israel's chief shepherd-king. As the Davidic shepherd-king discharges his "shepherding" duty, God's people will obey his decrees and reside in peace and security in the land (Ezek 34:25–29; 37:24–26). Furthermore, the temple will be restored (Ezek 37:25–27; cf. Ezekiel 40–48) and the whole world will come to acknowledge that Yahweh is God (Ezek 37:28; cf. v. 23).

In shepherding terms, the prophecies in Zechariah 9–14 proclaim Yahweh's eschatological acts of deliverance among his people. Zechariah 9 contains two interrelated oracles regarding Yahweh's reinstatement of the land (Zech 9:1–8) and the people of Israel (Zech 9:11–17). These two oracles enclose the prophecy of Zech 9:9–10, which speaks of the future advent of a "king" (מלך; βασιλεύς) in Jerusalem. As Meyers and Meyers note, this prophecy's central location in Zechariah 9 indicates that this royal figure's arrival is "the lynchpin of the restored land and people."[30] Most likely, the "king" of Zech 9:9–10 refers back to the Davidic Branch, who has appeared as the temple-builder and the inaugurator of a new era of peace and righteousness (Zech 3:8; 6:12). In Zech 9:9, the king is described as "righteous" (cf. 2 Sam 23:3; Jer 23:5–6; 33:14–16 MT), "having salvation,"[31] and "humble." After Yahweh removes warfare from the land of Ephraim and Jerusalem[32] (cf. a similar picture in Ps 46:9),[33] the king will offer "peace" (Zech 9:10; cf. Ps 72:7 [71:7 LXX]; Isa 9:5–6 [9:6–7 Eng.]) to all nations and rule "from sea to sea and from the [Euphrates] river to the ends of the earth" (Zech 9:10; cf. Ps 72:8 [71:8 LXX]; Mic

---

28. Zimmerli, *Ezekiel 2*, 218.

29. Renz, *The Rhetorical Function of the Book of Ezekiel*, 107.

30. Meyers and Meyers, *Zechariah 9–14*, 169.

31. In the MT, the Nifal participle נושׁע conveys the meaning that the king "is saved" by God. By contrast, the reading in the LXX refers to the king as "one who brings salvation" (σῴζων).

32. In the LXX, it is not Yahweh but the king who removes the chariots and horses. For a comparison between Zech 9:9–10 MT and LXX, see Kooij, "The Septuagint of Zechariah as Witness to an Early Interpretation of the Book," 57–58.

33. Collins, "The Literary Contexts of Zechariah 9:9," 39.

5:3–4 [5:4–5 Eng.]).[34] The juxtaposition of "Ephraim" and "Jerusalem" may signify the prophetic hope for the nation's reunification.[35] While the king of Zech 9:9–10 is not explicitly denoted as a shepherd, he will probably act as God's agent in overseeing his restored people, who are likened to God's "flock" (כעאן עמו; ὡς πρόβατα λαὸν αὐτοῦ) near the end of Zechariah 9 (v. 16).

The shepherd metaphor surfaces recurrently in the oracles of Zechariah 10–13 (esp. 10:2–3, 8–10; 11:4–17; 13:7–9), in which Yahweh reproaches the disloyal shepherds and takes action to salvage his sheep. Akin to the prophetic utterance in Ezek 34:5, Zechariah asserts that God's flock are oppressed and scattered for absence of a (good) shepherd (כי־אין רעה; Zech 10:2).[36] In Ezekiel 34 and 37, the prophetic solution is that Yahweh undertakes a shepherding mission to deliver his sheep and establish a Davidic shepherd-king over the flock. Zechariah's antidote is similar. The prophet anticipates Yahweh as the shepherd rescuing his sheep and establishing a Davidic ruler over the restored people (Zech 9:9–10, 16). In addition, the oracle of Zech 10:3–12 declares that Yahweh will use the "house of Judah" as his instrument to "save" (v. 6) the "house of Joseph," that is, the northern tribes of Israel.[37] God will "gather" (vv. 8, 10) the scattered Israelites and "bring [them] back" (v. 10; cf. vv. 9–12) to the land. The return of the northerners to Zion will finally realize Israel's longed-for hope for the nation's reunification.

It is plausible that the prophecy of Zech 10:4 envisages the new David as playing a part in the liberation of the northern Israelites, whose return to Zion is an essential step to the nation's restoration. This prophecy mentions four things that will "together" (יחדו) come from the house of Judah—"cornerstone" (פנה), "tent peg" (יתד), "battle bow" (קשת מלחמה), and "overseer/ruler" (נוגש). Their shared verb יצא (ἐξέρχομαι) and the fourfold prepositional construct ממנו (ἐξ αὐτοῦ/) draw attention to the source of these things, namely "the house of Judah" (v. 3). For the

---

34. Duguid, "Messianic Themes in Zechariah 9–14," 266–67. Meyers and Meyers note that in the MT the verb משל ("to rule"; Zech 9:10) is applied only to Davidic kings (David, Solomon, and Hezekiah). See Meyers and Meyers, *Zechariah 9–14*, 136.

35. Peterson, *Zechariah 9-14 and Malachi*, 59.

36. In the LXX, διότι οὐκ ἦν ἴασις ("healing"). See Conrad, *Zechariah*, 168.

37. According to Gen 48:8–22, "Joseph" represents the tribes of Ephraim and Manasseh. These two tribes eventually became the "nucleus" of the northern kingdom. See Blenkinsopp, *Ezekiel*, 175.

present purpose the first and the second things, "cornerstone" and "tent peg," require comment. The term פנה literally means the "corner" of an architectural building and may be used to denote a "cornerstone" (e.g., Jer 51:26; Job 38:6; Ps 118:22; Isa 28:16) or, in a figurative sense, a "chief" (e.g., Judg 20:2; 1 Sam 14:38; Isa 19:13). The latter usage bears a royal overtone.[38] The other term, יתד ("tent peg"), likewise may symbolize a leader and thus have regal implications. Such a symbolic sense is conveyed in Isa 22:15–25 (esp. v. 23), where the Jewish official Eliakim is described as "a tent peg" (יתד) fastened in a secure place and "a throne of glory" to his father's house.[39] It is possible the "cornerstone" and the "tent peg" in Zech 10:4 represent the future Davidic מלך (= צמח "Branch" in Zech 3:8; 6:12), whose advent is announced in Zech 9:9–10.[40] The likelihood that Zech 10:4 links with this royal prophecy increases when it is noticed that the "battle bow," which is the third thing from the house of Judah, is mentioned in Zech 9:10 concerning the mission of this מלך.[41] In fact, the "battle bow" in Zech 10:4 may point to this royal figure, given the (emblematic) meaning of the other three related things ("cornerstone," "tent peg," and "ruler").[42] Simply put, the arrival of the Davidic king (Zech 9:9–10) is tied to Israel's unification and the renewal of God's "flock" (cf. Zech 9:16).[43]

38. Meyers and Meyers, *Zechariah 9—14*, 200; Duguid, "Messianic Themes in Zechariah 9—14," 271–72; cf. Conrad, *Zechariah*, 167, although Conrad does not address the messianic implication.

39. Meyers and Meyers, *Zechariah 9—14*, 200; Duguid, "Messianic Themes in Zechariah 9—14," 271–72.

40. In the *Targum*, the "cornerstone" and "tent peg" in Zech 10:4 are interpreted as "king" and "Messiah" respectively.

41. Duguid, "Messianic Themes in Zechariah 9—14," 272.

42. Peterson, *Zechariah 9—14 and Malachi*, 74.

43. Other shepherd terminologies in the book of Zechariah are mainly located in Zech 11:4–17 and Zech 13:7–9. The first text depicts two shepherds, one good (11:4–14) and one bad (11:15–17). The good shepherd represents Yahweh, who cares for his sheep but they detest him (v. 8). In Zech 11:15–17, Yahweh says that he will raise up a "foolish" (v. 15) and "worthless" (v. 17) shepherd who deserts the sheep but he will be punished. In Zech 13:7–9, the motif of the "smitten shepherd" reappears but this time it is applied to a ruler. As an outcome of the striking of the shepherd, the flock will wander and be scattered. One third of God's people will survive in the land, whereas two thirds will be killed in battles or carried in exile. Yet the striking of the shepherd will result in the preservation of a remnant in the land, where Yahweh will reign (Zech 14:9, 16).

Summing up, Micah, Jeremiah, Ezekiel, and Zechariah envisage Yahweh as the shepherd assembling his wandering sheep, bringing them back to their land, and establishing a perfect Davidic ruler over the restituted flock. Micah and Ezekiel expressly describe the Davidic ruler as Yahweh's appointed shepherd, who will tend his flock on the divine behalf. In the oracles of Jeremiah and Zechariah, shepherd terminology is applied to God but not the new David. However, some of these prophetic oracles interlace God's shepherding activities with the promise of an ideal Davidic king, who will preside over the reunited nation. The prophecy of Zech 10:4 probably insinuates that the Davidic king will be Yahweh's vehicle in bringing the exilic northerners back to Zion and reinstating the nation of Israel. The motif of Israel's reunification under a perfect David is present in a number of biblical texts including Hos 2:2 (1:11 Eng.); 3:4–5; Isa 8:23–9.1 (9:1 2 Eng.); 11·10–16, despite the absence of shepherd vocabulary in them. Broadly speaking, the prophetic portrayals of the Davidic (shepherd) king not only entail the notion of this figure's Davidic lineage but also emphasize his embodiment of the qualities of the idealized David (e.g., righteousness and universal dominance). In his study of the prophetic articulations of the eschatological David, Yuzuru Miura remarks that the prophets tend to put the accent on the typological rather than the genealogical aspect of Davidic messianism.[44] Recognition of this biblical tendency may help discern the Davidic-typological elements that are subtly at work in John's depiction of Jesus as the good shepherd, who is never identified as David's descendant in the Gospel of John.

The Messiah-King, Shepherd Imagery, and Israel's Gathering/Unification in Late Second Temple Judaism

In a number of late Second Temple Jewish writings, the royal Messiah is connected with the realization of Israel's eschatological confederation or unification. The late first-century BCE *Psalms of Solomon* 17 envisions the Davidic shepherd-king gathering the dispersed of Israel and ruling over God's restored people. In *Pss. Sol.* 17:5–20, the author laments the Roman devastation of Jerusalem and the sinners' assail against his community. In order to "save their lives from evil" (v. 17), the pious ones escape from the city and wander in foreign lands (vv. 16–20).[45] The predicament of

44. Miura, *David in Luke-Acts*, 30–32.

45. See Winninge, *Sinners and the Righteous*, 101; Schüpphaus, *Die Psalmen Salomos*, 68–69.

God's people being in exile mounts to a crescendo in verse 21, where the psalmist cries out for the divine intervention to set up a "son of David" on the throne (cf. the allusions to 2 Sam 7:14–16 in *Pss. Sol.* 17:4). From the authorial perspective, the return of the scattered Israelites to their homeland and the nation's reinstatement hinge upon the arrival of this Davidic figure. The Davidic Messiah "will gather a holy people" (συνάξει λαὸν ἅγιον; *Pss. Sol.* 17:26) and "lead [them] in righteousness" (*Pss. Sol.* 17:26) after expelling the unrighteous Gentiles and Jews from Jerusalem (*Pss. Sol.* 17:22–25). He "will distribute" (καταμερίσει) the Israelites in the land "according to their tribes" (*Pss. Sol.* 17:28) and reconstitute the twelve tribes of Israel as one nation. While *Pss. Sol.* 17:22–25 (cf. 17:30b) speak of the Messiah purging Jerusalem from the Gentiles, the subsequent vision of *Pss. Sol.* 17:31 reveals that the (converted) Gentiles will be the Messiah's conduit in bringing the strayed Israelites back to Zion. These returnees will be the "gifts" (v. 31) that the Gentiles offer to the God of Israel. As Gene Davenport remarks, this vision in verse 31 invokes the prophecy of Isa 66:18–21 (cf. Isa 49:22; 60:4, 9) and probably anticipates the Gentiles as the "major instruments in the reconstruction of the nation."[46] Therefore, some Gentiles will be admitted into the Messiah's kingdom and "serve him under his yoke" (17:30a). In view of the Gentiles' positive role in the vision of *Pss. Sol.* 17:30–31, the referent of the plural pronoun αὐτούς in verse 32 may include the Gentiles, along with the pious Jews, as members of the messianic kingdom.[47] This reading is supported by the grammatical observation that ἔθνη is the subject of the infinitive ἰδεῖν (2x) in the immediately prior verse 31. If this judgment is correct, the genitival phrase λαοῦ μεγάλου ("of a great people") in *Pss. Sol.* 17:36 probably has the converted Gentiles in view and points to their eschatological incorporation as God's people.

Kenneth Atkinson observes that Ezek 34:23 is one of the scriptural "intertexts" that undergird the shepherd-portrayal of the royal Messiah in *Pss. Sol.* 17:40.[48] In this latter passage, the Messiah's restorative function

---

46. Davenport, "The 'Anointed of the Lord' in Psalms of Solomon 17," 75; cf. Schreiber, *Gesalbter und König*, 174–75; Mowinckel, *He That Cometh*, 316–17; Schürer, *The History of the Jewish People in the Age of Jesus Christ*, 2:530.

47. Davenport, "The 'Anointed of the Lord' in Psalms of Solomon 17," 76; cf. Pomykala, *The Davidic Dynasty Tradition in Early Judaism*, 164.

48. Atkinson, *An Intertextual Study of the Psalms of Solomon*, 356. Atkinson also mentions that Mic 5:4 LXX; Isa 40:11 LXX; Jer 23:4; Ezek 34:15 are other scriptural intertexts of *Pss. Sol.* 17:40.

is expressly described in "shepherding" terms. The expression ἐν τῇ νομῇ αὐτῶν in verse 40 resonates with similar Greek phrases in Jer 23:3 LXX (εἰς τὴν νομὴν αὐτῶν; cf. Jer 23:1) and Ezek 34:14 LXX (ἐν νομῇ ἀγαθῇ and ἐν νομῇ πίονι). These phrases are lodged within the prophetic setting of Yahweh bringing his exilic people back to the (pasture) land.[49] Another expression, ἀπ' ἄκρου τῆς γῆς, in *Pss. Sol.* 17:31 regarding the Messiah's universal kingship is reminiscent of the phrase of ἕως ἄκρων τῆς γῆς in Mic 5:3 LXX, which proclaims the Davidic shepherd-ruler's worldwide dominance.[50] Given these scriptural allusions and the psalmist's portrait of the Messiah gathering the scattered Israelites (*Pss. Sol.* 17:26–39; esp. vv. 26, 28, 31), it is reasonable to infer that part of the Messiah's "shepherding" function (*Pss. Sol.* 17:40) is to gather the dispersed of Israel. Although in the biblical traditions Yahweh is the shepherd who assembles the sheep, the royal Messiah of *Psalms of Solomon* 17 performs this task. Yet the psalmist makes clear that the sheep do not belong to the Messiah but are the Lord's (*Pss. Sol.* 17:40). On account of the inclusion of the Gentiles in *Pss. Sol.* 17:30–32, 34 and 36, the referent of the ποίμνη in verse 40—and by extension, the four plural pronouns αὐτοῖς/αὐτούς in *Pss. Sol.* 17:40–41—probably encompasses the reverent Gentiles.[51] This being the case, the author of *Psalms of Solomon* 17 envisages that the Davidic Messiah will be the eschatological shepherd of God's renewed flock, which is constitutive both of the Jewish and non-Jewish people.[52]

At Qumran, the royal Messiah is not depicted in the figure of a shepherd. Two scrolls, however, are potentially pertinent to this analysis. The late second-century BCE scroll 4Q504 (4QDibHama) is a collection of prayers for liturgical use on certain days of the week. In 4Q504 frgs. 1–2, IV, 5–14, the writer affirms God's commitment to his "covenant" with David (v. 6), who is "like a shepherd, a prince over your [God's] people"

---

49. The term νομή ("pasture") does not occur in the Greek texts of Micah and Zechariah. See Willitts, *Matthew's Messianic Shepherd-King*, 81. Aside from Jer 23:3 and Ezek 34:14, the depiction of the "Servant" in Isa 49:9 is a possible background of *Pss. Sol.* 17:40 (pp. 81–82).

50. Chae, *Jesus as the Eschatological Davidic Shepherd*, 124.

51. Ibid.; Willitts, *Matthew's Messianic Shepherd-King*, 88–89.

52. In addition to the seventeenth psalm, the motif of Israel's gathering is present in *Psalms of Solomon* 8 and 11. See Elliot, *The Survivors of Israel*, 558 n. 112; Schüpphaus, *Die Psalmen Salomos*, 55–56, esp. n. 219–24.

(כרעי נגיר על עמכה; v. 7).[53] David will sit "on the throne of Israel forever" (vv. 7–8a) and all the nations will bring their treasures to God so as to glorify his people, city, and temple (vv. 11–12). There is no ostensible indication that the textual setting of 4Q504 is future or eschatological, but this writing "introduces titles for David (Shepherd and, especially, Prince) that have [a] very obvious potential messianic resonance."[54] Kenneth Pomykala claims that these Davidic references provide only "an example of divine blessing" in the past, "not a statement of a continuing expectation for a davidic messianic figure."[55] Yet even Pomykala acknowledges that these references can be interpreted along the lines of "corporate personality" and hence may refer to "a typologically new David."[56] In fact, biblical precedents of such a typological signification of "David" are found in sundry prophetic passages including Hos 3:5; Jer 23:5; 30:9; Ezek 34:23–24; 37:24–25.[57] If a futuristic reading of 4Q504, frgs. 1–2, IV is at least partly correct, this text plausibly witness to pre-Christian Qumran expectation for a Davidic shepherd-king.

The second Qumran text is CD-B XIX, 7–14, which Johannes Zimmermann describes as "Zechariah-Ezekiel-Midrash."[58] Both messianic references and shepherd imageries are found in this text. In lines 7–9a, there is contain a quotation from Zech 13:7 regarding the striking of the shepherd and the scattering of the flock. In line 9b, "the poor ones of the flock" in Zech 11:11 are identified as "those who revere him [God]." These "poor ones" are the faithful remnant of Israel, who will escape the final judgment in "the age of the visitation" (XIX, 10a). Those who entered the "covenant" but fail to keep its precepts will be "delivered up to the sword," when the Messiah(s) of Aaron and Israel arrive (XIX, 10b, 13–14). It is possible that, in CD-B XIX, the smitten shepherd of Zech 13:7 is interpreted as representing God's evil adversary, who will be destroyed upon the advent of the Messiah(s).[59] At any rate, the appearance

53. The Qumran text and the English translation are from Martínez and Tigchelaar, *The Dead Sea Scrolls*.

54. Chester, *Messiah and Exaltation*, 250.

55. Pomykala, *The Davidic Dynasty Tradition in Early Judaism*, 178.

56. Ibid., 175 n. 16.

57. Pomykala, "Images of David in Early Judaism," 36; idem, *The Davidic Dynasty Tradition in Early Judaism*, 175.

58. Zimmermann, *Messianische Texte aus Qumran*, 43.

59. Chae, *Jesus as the Eschatological Davidic Shepherd*, 149–51.

of the Messiah of Israel is tied to the reconstitution of God's people, although the Messiah is not described as the shepherd of "the poor ones of the flock."

The late first-century CE apocalypse *Second Baruch* makes several references to the exilic ten (1:2) or nine and a half tribes (62:5; 77:17, 19; 78:1) of Israel's northern kingdom as well as the remaining two (1:2) or two and a half tribes (63:3; 64:5) of the southern kingdom. According to Aune, the gathering of the exiles is referred to explicitly or implicitly in *2 Bar.* 40:2; 77:6; 78:7; 84:2; 85:3–5.[60] This notion makes its first appearance in connection with the Messiah, who will "preserve the remnant of my [God's] people, gathered in the place that I [God] have chosen" (*2 Bar.* 40:2).[61] In *2 Bar.* 77:6; 84:2; 85:3–5, Israel's confederation in the land is preconditioned upon the nation's obedience and observance of the law. The remaining reference in *2 Bar.* 78:7 affirms that the merciful God will "assemble all those again who were dispersed."[62] On the whole, the writer of *Second Baruch* looks forward to God reinstating the people of Israel in the Jewish land. The Messiah's mission pertains to Israel's restoration, but his exact role in this national program is unclear.

In *Fourth Ezra*, the Messiah takes a significant part in the amalgamation of Israel's northern tribes with their kinsmen in Jerusalem and Judea.[63] In the sixth vision in *4 Ezra* 13, the messianic "man" (= God's "son" in *4 Ezra* 13:32, 52)[64] carves out a great mountain and gathers a peaceable multitude upon annihilating all of his pagan adversaries (vv. 1–13). The interpretation of this vision (*4 Ezra* 13:21–58) reveals that the "mountain" stands for the replenished Zion (cf. *4 Ezra* 7:26; 10:20–28, 42, 44–54) and the "peaceable multitude" represents the ten (or nine and a half) tribes that were "led away from their own land into captivity in the days of King Hoshea, whom Shalmaneser the king of Assyrians led captive" (*4 Ezra* 13:40; cf. 2 Kgs 17:1–6).[65] Thus the Israelite exiles were not

---

60. Aune, "From the Idealized Past to the Immediate Future," 161.

61. The English translation of *2 Bar.* 40:2 is from ibid., 162.

62. The English translation is from A. F. J. Klijn, "2 Baruch," in *OTP* 1:615–52.

63. The Jewish portion of extant *Fourth Ezra* (i.e., *4 Ezra* 3—14) lacks shepherd vocabulary. The reference in *4 Ezra* 2:34 to the eschatological "shepherd" is of Christian origin. For this Christian treatment of the "shepherd," see Chae, *Jesus as the Eschatological Davidic Shepherd*, 157–60.

64. See chapter 3 for "son" rather than "servant" as the preferred reading.

65. Metzger gives "ten" as the number of the lost tribes (*OTP* 1:517–59). Stone, how-

perished or "lost" in foreign regions during the Assyrian deportations in the eight century BCE. Rather, the deportees migrated from the nations and crossed over the Euphrates river to take lodging in "another land," where "mankind had never lived" (4 Ezra 13:40–43; cf. Ant. 11.133).[66] In this remote "land," they are able to keep the commandments in the Torah and wait for the last times, when they will be brought back to the land of Palestine (4 Ezra 13:42–46). Reminiscent of the Exodus miracle in Josh 3:14–16 and the eschatological vision of Isa 11:11–16, God will stop the channels of the Euphrates river so that the ten (or nine and a half) tribes may walk through the dried riverbed and return home (4 Ezra 13:47).[67] It is uncertain whether all of the northern returnees will be saved in the messianic era.[68] As 4 Ezra 13:13 unfolds, some of the people who come to the Messiah are "joyful," while others are "sorrowful," "bound," or "bringing others as offerings." The first group most probably refers to the returning Israelites who will participate in the eschatological bliss and "rejoice" (cf. 4 Ezra 7:28; 12:34). While the "sorrowful" and the "bound" ones may denote only the Gentiles who will approach the Messiah for the final judgment, these two groups may encompass the disobedient northerners. It is possible that some people from the fourth group are reverent Gentiles, through whom the exiles will be led back to Zion (cf. Isa 66:20).

In 4 Ezra 13:48–50, the author turns the attention to the fate of the Jewish inhabitants in the vicinity of Palestine. Verse 48 affirms that those "who are found within my [God's] holy borders shall be saved." Although the Messiah is not mentioned in 4 Ezra 13:48–51, he will probably be the agent of the "Most High" in "defend[ing] the people who remain" in the Jewish land (v. 49b). The reason is that the statement "he destroys the multitude of the nations that are gathered together" in the immediately preceding verse 49a evidently refers to the Messiah's defeat of his foes (cf. 4 Ezra 13:5, 8–11, 33–38).[69] In light of this, the Messiah's restorative

---

ever, prefers the variant "nine and one half" that is attested in the Syriac, Arabic 1, and two Ethiopic witnesses (cf. 2 Bar. 77:17, 19; 78:1). See Stone, Fourth Ezra, 404.

66. Ibid., 404.

67. For the Isaianic reference, see Fuller, The Restoration of Israel, 82; Elliot, The Survivors of Israel, 510.

68. Elliot, The Survivors of Israel, 509; Stone, Fourth Ezra, 397.

69. This messianic identification of the perpetrator in the phrase, "defend the people who remain [in the land of Israel]" (4 Ezra 13:49b), comports with the earlier vision in 4 Ezra 12:34. As this vision anticipates, the lion-Messiah "will deliver in mercy the remnant

mission concerns not only the gathering of the exilic ten tribes and their confederation with the remaining two tribes, but also the protection of the Palestinian Jews who survive the Roman invasion of Jerusalem in 70 CE. Nonetheless, only a "small" number of Palestinian Jews will be saved (cf. *4 Ezra* 6:25; 7:27, 45–61; 12:34).[70]

Finally, the messianic king in several *Targumim* plays a role in the eschatological restoration and unification of Israel. Of particular importance is *Isaiah Targum*, whose underlying traditions might have been in circulation during the first century CE.[71] Bruce Chilton comments that גלותא ("exile") is "a central term of reference within the Isaiah Targum."[72] In this targumic writing, the notion of Israel in exile surfaces recurrently.[73] In *Tg.* Isa 28:6, the advent of the royal Messiah is directly connected with the return of the scattered Israelites "in peace to their houses," presumably their homeland in Palestine. In Craig Evans' assessment, this targumic reading displays a flavor of the early Roman period, thereby lending support to the view that the royal Messiah is associated with the realization of a unified Israel during the late first century CE.[74] In *Tg.* Isa 53:8, the "Servant," identified as the Messiah earlier in *Tg.* Isa 52:13 (cf. *Tg.* Isa 42:1; 43:10), is depicted as bringing back the wandering Israelites. If Chilton's judgment that the fourth "Servant" song in *Tg.* Isa 52:13—53:12 took shape during the period 70–135 CE is accurate,[75] *Tg.* Isa 53:8 may provide first-century CE Jewish evidence of the connection between the messianic king and Israel's end of dispersion. In the *Targumim* to Micah and Jeremiah, the Davidic (shepherd) king is overtly identified as the Messiah.[76] In *Tg.* Mic 5:3, the Hebrew term וישבו ("and they shall remain") in the MT is interpreted as "and they shall be gathered in from the midst

---

of my [God's] people, those who have been saved throughout my [God's] borders" (cf. *4 Ezra* 9:8). See Hogan, *Theologies in Conflict in 4 Ezra*, 194.

70. Fuller, *The Restoration of Israel*, 82.

71. Chilton, *The Glory of Israel*, 94–96.

72. Idem, "Salvific Exile in the Isaiah Targum," 239.

73. E.g., *Tg.* Isa 6:13; 8:18; 27:6; 28:2, 6, 13, 19, 25; 35:6, 10; 42:7; 43:6, 14; 46:11; 51:11; 54:7, 15; 66:9. See Evans, "Jesus and the Continuing Exile of Israel," 89.

74. Ibid.

75. Chilton, *The Glory of Israel*, 97, 110–11; cf. Evans, "Jesus and the Continuing Exile of Israel," 89.

76. Cf. *Tg.* Mic 5:1–3; *Tg.* Jer 23:5 [cf. 30:9]; cf. *Tg.* Zech 3:8; 6:12; 10:4; *Tg.* Hos 14:8. See Manns, "Traditions targumiques en Jean 10, 1–30," 145–55. The word "Messiah" is absent from *Targum* to Ezekiel.

of their Dispersions."[77] In this interpretation, the Messiah-King's appearance is explicitly tied to the fulfillment of the hope for Israel's eschatological gathering. Unlike *Isaiah Targum*, it is difficult to ascertain the extent to which these targumic references are relevant to the royal-messianic beliefs in first-century CE Judaism.[78]

In brief, the advent of the royal Messiah is connected with Israel's eschatological confederation or unification in several late Second Temple Jewish documents. These include the *Psalms of Solomon*, the DSS, *Second Baruch*, *Fourth Ezra* and several *Targumim*. Of special importance is *Psalms of Solomon* 17, which employs shepherding terminology to depict the Davidic Messiah and probably anticipates the inclusion of converted Gentiles as God's people. The next section will investigate the kingship-cross interplay in John 10 in light of the Jewish royal-messianic connection with Israel's unification.

Analysis of John 10:14–18

Textual Setting and Structure (John 10:1–21)

In the narrative sequence of the Fourth Gospel, the shepherd discourse in John 10:1–21 directly succeeds the story of the man born blind in John 9 and precedes the exchange between Jesus and the Jewish leaders in John 10:22–41. No indication in John 10:1–21 signals a change in the audience or the geographical or temporal setting from the scene of John 9. On the one hand, the mention of Jesus' miraculous healing of the blind man at the end of this discourse (v. 21) recalls this "sign," which Jesus performs in the previous chapter.[79] On the other hand, the shepherd discourse is inextricably tied to the ensuing passage of John 10:22–41, in which the

---

77. Levey, *The Messiah*, 93.

78. Several passages in the *Testaments of the Twelve Patriarchs* speak of a future king from the tribe of Judah and link his appearance with Israel's eschatological gathering and unification Although the Jewish *Vorlage* of the *Testaments* was probably composed during the second century BCE, it is notoriously difficult to determine the original Jewish elements due to possible Christian interpolations. Some of the pertinent passages are *T. Jud.* 24:1–4; *T. Dan* 5:7–13; *T. Naph.* 8:1–3; *T. Sim.* 7:1–3; *T. Benj.* 3:8. For discussions of these texts, see Jonge, "The Future of Israel in the Testaments of the Twelve Patriarchs," 196–211; VanderKam, "Exile in Jewish Apocalyptic Literature," 89–109 (see pp. 100–103 concerning the *Testament of Levi* 16—17).

79. For the literary connection between John 9 and 10 and the internal coherence of John 10, see Zimmermann, *Christologie der Bilder im Johannesevangelium*, 243–50; Rand, "A Syntactical and Narratological Reading of John 10 in Coherence with Chapter 9," 94–115.

sheep metaphor and the promise concerning "eternal life" both appear again (cf. the occurrences of "sheep" in John 10:4, 26–27; "life" in John 10:10; "eternal life" in John 10:28).[80] While this passage is set in the context of the feast of Dedication, which is about 1–3 months after the event in John 10:1–21 (and the miracle in John 9), these shared themes between John 10:1–21 and 10:22–41 suggest that the evangelist intends the reader to glance at Jesus' discourse concerning the shepherd and the sheep (vv. 1–21) and his subsequent conversation with "the Jews" (vv. 22–41) in light of each other.[81] As will become patent, the shepherd discourse's narrative linkage with the pericopae John 9:1–41 and 10:22–41 is helpful in illuminating the messianic connotation in this discourse.

The literary structure of John 10:1–21 can be broadly outlined as follows:[82]

10:1–5	The introduction of the main characters in the παροιμία (v. 6): the sheep, the thief and the robber, and the shepherd
10:6	The incomprehension of "the Jews" on the παροιμία
10:7–18	The elaboration of the παροιμία
10:7–10	The elaboration concerning Jesus as the gate
10:11–18	The elaboration concerning Jesus as the good shepherd
10:11–13	The good shepherd in contrast to the hireling
10:14–18	*The good shepherd and his "one flock"*
10:19–21	The Jewish reactions to Jesus' discourse

All five of the allusions to Jesus' death—τίθημι τὴν ψυχήν (vv. 11, 15, 17, 18 [2x]; cf. 1 John 3:16)—in the shepherd discourse reside in the literary section John 10:11–18. This section can be partitioned into two smaller units (vv. 11–13 and vv. 14–18), based on the twin occurrences

---

80. Brown, *The Gospel according to John*, 1:406. The sheep of Jesus will receive the eschatological gift of eternal life which, according to John 3:14–15, is made available through the "lifting up" of Jesus as the Son of Man. See our analysis in chapter 5.

81. Busse, "Open Questions on John 10," 9.

82. Despite minor differences, most of the proposals of the literary structure of John 10:1–21 are akin to the one as delineated in this section. See, e.g., Ball, "I Am" in John's *Gospel*, 94; Carson, *The Gospel according to John*, 380–90; Brown, *The Gospel according to John*, 1:391–400; Kiefer, *Die Hirtenrede*, 20–21.

of the expression "I am the good shepherd" in verses 11 and 14. Four of these five references to the cross are clustered in the second unit, namely John 10:14–18 (vv. 15, 17 and 18 [2x]), where the motif "one flock, one shepherd" is situated (v. 16). The two references in John 10:17 and 10:18b occur in conjunction with an allusion to Jesus' resurrection, i.e., λαμβάνω τὴν ψυχήν. The following diagram delineates the thematic progression within John 10:14–18:

(10:11	Jesus' first self-identification as the good shepherd "laying down" his life for the sheep [# 1])
10:14a	Jesus' second self-identification as the good shepherd
10:14b–15a	The knowledge between Jesus and his sheep as analogous to the knowledge between the Father and Jesus
10:15b	Jesus "laying down" his life for the sheep (# 2; cf. # 1 in v. 11)
10:16	*Jesus gathering "other sheep" and establishing "one flock" under "one shepherd"*
10:17a	The Father's love for Jesus
10:17b	Jesus "laying down" his life (# 3) + "taking [it] up" (# 1)
10:18a	Jesus "laying down" his life (# 4)
10:18b	Jesus "laying down" his life (# 5) + "taking [it] up" (# 2)
10:18c	The Father's command to Jesus

It is apparent from this diagram that the notion of the creation of a unified flock under a single shepherd (v. 16) stands at the center of John 10:14–18. This notion, moreover, is surrounded by repeated references to the death and resurrection of Jesus.

Jesus as the Royal-Messianic Shepherd

Scholars have reached a consensus that, despite the absence of an OT citation in the shepherd discourse, the Johannine portrait of Jesus as the good shepherd is deeply rooted in the Jewish Scriptures.[83] Bultmann and Meeks

---

83. E.g., Zimmermann, "Jesus im Bild Gottes"; Deeley, "Ezekiel's Shepherd and John's Jesus," 252–64.

allege that the Christological portrait in John 10 lacks messianic features.[84] Contrary to this allegation, we will demonstrate that the Johannine presentation of Jesus as the good shepherd is essentially royal-messianic, at least within the literary milieu of John 10:14–18.

As noted earlier, the Johannine shepherd discourse is sandwiched between the stories of Jesus healing a blind man (John 9:1–41) and his conflict with "the Jews" (John 10:22–41). Significantly, the motif of Jesus' messiahship comes to the fore in both of these stories. In John 9:22, the evangelist remarks that the parents of the man born blind fear for "the Jews," who have agreed to expulse anyone from the synagogue who confess Jesus as the "Christ." In John 10:24, "the Jews" approach and interrogate Jesus as to whether he is the "Christ." This question leads directly to Jesus' rejoinder in John 10:25–30, where he declares that "the Jews" are not his sheep (v. 26). The reappearance of the sheep imagery gives the narrative impression that the Jewish question regarding Jesus' messiahship concerns his self-designation as the good shepherd, in spite of the temporal gap between the incidents in John 10:1–21 and 10:22–41.[85] Given that the eminent motif of Jesus' messiahship surrounds the shepherd discourse, the shepherd-portrayal of John 10:1–21 would hardly lack a messianic connotation. This construal of the shepherd discourse accords with John's summary statement, which focuses on Jesus' messianic status (20:31).

Several features of the account John 10:1–21 indicate its connection with the passion narrative, where Jesus dies as the king of Israel.[86] First, the fivefold description of Jesus laying down his life in John 10:11–18 is proleptic of his crucifixion. Second, the recurrent motif of hearing Jesus' voice in John 10 re-emerges in John 18:36–37 in the trial scene.[87] In John 10:3–4, the sheep "hear" (ἀκούω) and recognize the "voice" (φωνή) of the shepherd and follow him (cf. v. 8). This motif surfaces again in John 10:16, as the "other sheep" will "hear" (ἀκούω) Jesus' "voice" (φωνή) and become part of his flock. In John 18:36–37, the notion of "hearing" (ἀκούω) Jesus'

---

84. Meeks, *The Prophet-King*, 308; Bultmann, *The Gospel of John*, 367.

85. The absence of the term χριστός (or Μεσσίας) in John 10:1–21 can be explained by the fact that this passage is largely made up of Jesus' monologue and he tends to avoid an overt messianic self-identification.

86. See Meeks, *The Prophet-King*, 66–68, 311–13, although he thinks that these features indicate John's interest in depicting Jesus as the new Moses rather than the Messiah.

87. Ibid., 66–67.

"voice" (φωνή) is intrinsically bound up with his kingship (cf. βασιλεία [3x] in v. 36 and βασιλεύς in v. 37). Jesus' statement that everyone who is of the truth "hears his voice" (i.e., the voice of the king) corresponds to his earlier saying in John 10 that the sheep "hear the shepherd's voice." Moreover, both of the shepherd discourse and the passion narrative comprise the term ληστής ("robber"), which is found nowhere else in the Fourth Gospel.[88] Unlike the good shepherd who brings life to the sheep, the ληστής comes to steal, kill, and destroy (10:1–10; vv. 1, 8). In John 18:40, the evangelist provides the aside that Barabbas is a ληστής. Thus "the Jews," in choosing a ληστής in favor of Jesus, show themselves to be not of Jesus' flock. Fourth, Jesus' declaration in John 10:18 that he has the "authority" (ἐξουσία) to lay down his life and take it again reverberates and contrasts Pilate's claim in John 19:10 that he has the "authority" (ἐξουσία) to release or crucify Jesus (cf. the parallel structure ἐξουσία ἔχω . . . καὶ ἐξουσία ἔχω . . .).[89] In concerted efforts, these four features shared by the shepherd discourse and the passion story connect these two passages and enhance the Johannine identification of the messianic shepherd as the crucified king.

It is generally agreed that the fundamental ideas of John's portrayal of Jesus as εἷς ποιμήν ("one shepherd"; 10:16) originate from Ezekiel's prophecy concerning the Davidic shepherd-king.[90] In Ezek 34:23 and 37:24, the new David is denoted as רעה אחד. In the LXX, the adjective אחד is translated as ἕνα (accusative) in Ezek 34:23 and εἷς (nominative) in Ezek 37:24. While these two verses are essentially related, the Johannine employment of the nominative form (εἷς ποιμήν) resonates particularly with the vision of Ezek 37:24, where the same form is used (ποιμὴν εἷς). Since the eschatological Davidic shepherd is designated as "one king" (מלך אחד; cf. ראש אחד in Hos 2:2) in Ezekiel 37 (v. 22) but not in Ezekiel 34, John's terminological choice may hint at his special interest in the good shepherd's royal status. Such Johannine interest is very probable, as the biblical hope for the Davidic shepherd-king leading God's flock is featured prominently not only in Ezekiel 34 and 37 but also in Micah 5, Jeremiah 23, and Zechariah 9 (though the latter two passages do not explicitly denote the king as shepherd). The fact that this hope pervaded

88. Ibid., 67–68.
89. Köstenberger, *John*, 308.
90. Zimmermann, "Jesus im Bild Gottes," 108.

during the late Second Temple age suggests that John's royal-messianic use of the shepherd image was intelligible within the milieu of first-century CE Judaism. In the context of Ezekiel 37, the installment of the Davidic shepherd-king closely links with the national hope for the unification of Israel's southern and northern kingdoms (Ezek 37:1–20), which will join together to become "one nation" under "one king" (Ezek 37:21–22). In light of this joining, the Johannine "one flock, one shepherd" statement most likely summons the Jewish hope of Israel's restoration and unification under the new David.

While the Scripture depicts God as Israel's principal shepherd and the evangelist expressly underlines Jesus' oneness with the Father (cf. John 10:30), a main thrust of the good shepherd portrait in John 10:14–18—pecifically, εἷς ποιμήν in verse 16—should be messianic. Throughout the Johannine shepherd discourse, the Father is mentioned three times and exclusively in John 10:14–18 (vv. 15, 17, 18). There is little doubt that the unity between Jesus and the Father is a crucial theme of this section (vv. 15, 17, 18). Yet the Father remains a character in distinction to Jesus and is never explicitly portrayed in shepherding terms. Rather, Jesus is presented as the *only* (εἷς) shepherd of the flock. In Ezekiel 34 and 37, the adjective אחד/ἕνα/εἷς is applied to the Davidic king but not to Yahweh.[91] If the Christological designation εἷς ποιμήν (John 10:16) seeks to invoke the eschatological vision of Ezekiel 37, the fact that the only *explicit* shepherd-figure in this vision is the new David espouses our view that this Christological designation is essentially royal-messianic, albeit pregnant of the divine connotation. Further, despite the absence of Jesus' Davidic pedigree from John's Gospel, it is likely that his shepherd-depiction is typologically modeled upon the Davidic shepherd-king as envisaged in Ezekiel and other prophetic books.[92] This is especially likely given the Johannine utilization of the prophetic materials about the eschatological Davidic shepherd-king as well as the prophets' predisposition in stressing the king's embodiment of Davidic-typological features (see the earlier sections).

---

91. Bauckham, *Jesus and the God of Israel*, 105.

92. Daly-Denton, *David in the Fourth Gospel*, 309–14; Köstenberger "Jesus as the Good Shepherd Who Will Also Bring Other Sheep (John 10:16)," 77, 81–82.

The Shepherd "Lays Down" His Life "for" the Sheep

The death of the good shepherd is formulated in figurative terms of τίθημι τὴν ψυχήν (John 10:11, 15, 17, 18 [2x]). Of the 18 occurrences of the verb τίθημι in the Gospel of John, eight convey the idea of death: five times in regard to Jesus' death for his sheep (John 10:11, 15, 17, 18 [2x]), twice in regard to Peter's death for Jesus (John 13:37, 38), and once in regard to one's death for his/her friend (John 15:13). This usage of τίθημι with reference to someone's death is absent from this term's 32 instances in the Synoptic Gospels (11x in Matthew, 5x in Mark, and 16x in Luke). In contemporary Greek literature and the LXX, the word τίθημι often connotes the meaning of "taking a risk rather than full sacrifice of life."[93] Instead of this word, the conventional terms for expressing the notion of offering up one's life are ἐκπνέω, ἀφίημι, προβάλλω, προτείνω, and δίδωμι.[94] The term δίδωμι is used in Mark 10:45 (cf. Matt 20:28), where Jesus as the Son of Man avers that he comes to "give his life" (δοῦναι τὴν ψυχὴν αὐτοῦ) as a ransom for others. In spite of varied terminologies, Joachim Jeremias is right to note that the Johannine τίθημι τὴν ψυχήν μου is parallel to the Markan δίδωμι τὴν ψυχὴν αὐτοῦ—both phrases refer to Jesus' self-sacrifice of his life.[95]

Why does John speak of Jesus' death as τίθημι τὴν ψυχήν? One plausible explanation is that this expression's usual meaning of "risking one's life" fits the symbolic ambiance of the shepherd discourse, in which the shepherd imperils his life in order to protect the sheep from the wolf. More significantly, John may want to conjure up the image of the Servant in Isaiah 53, as the formulation τίθημι τὴν ψυχήν corresponds to the Hebrew phrase אם־תשים אשם נפשו in Isa 53:10.[96] In this case, the word τίθημι matches the term שׂים. In the Isaianic context, Isa 53:10 belongs to the fourth Servant passage (Isa 52:13—53:12) which speaks of the Servant suffering on behalf of God's people in order to reinstate their righteous status. While most of John's scriptural quotations are in alignment with the texts in the LXX, the peculiar expression τίθημι τὴν ψυχήν directly alludes to the Hebrew text in Isa 53:10. This is probably because

93. Maurer, "τίθημι," in *TDNT* 8:155–56; idem, "παρατίθημι," in *TDNT* 8:162. Maurer mentions the use of παρατίθημι in Homer's *Odyssey* (2:237; 3:74; 9:255) and the LXX (e.g., Judg 12:13; 1 Sam 19:5; 28:21; Job 13:14).

94. Idem, "τίθημι," in *TDNT* 8:155.

95. Jeremias, "παῖς θεοῦ," in *TDNT* 5:654–717 (5:708, 710). See also Maurer, "τίθημι," in *TDNT* 8:155–56.

96. Jeremias, "παῖς θεοῦ," in *TDNT* 5:710; Maurer, "τίθημι," in *TDNT* 8:156.

the nominative ἡ ψυχὴ ὑμῶν in Isa 53:10 LXX (ἐὰν δῶτε περὶ ἁμαρτίας ἡ ψυχὴ ὑμῶν ὄψεται σπέρμα μακρόβιον) seems to be the subject of the verb ὄψεται and so this verse gives the impression that the Servant presents a sin offering, rather than his soul being presented as an offering. Although the Isaianic Servant does not appear in the figure of a shepherd (cf. the Servant as a lamb and a sheep in Isa 53:7), the shared appropriation of the sheep metaphor to God's people (Isa 53:6) may provide a link between Isaiah's fourth Servant song and Jesus' discourse on the shepherd and the sheep. In chapter 5, we mentioned that John's construction of Jesus' death as being "lifted up" on the cross (3:14; 8:28; 12:32–34) alludes to the Servant's exalted and glorified portrayal in Isa 52:13 LXX, which is part of the fourth Servant passage (Isa 52:13—53:12). In light of this Servant allusion (cf. John 1:29), it is very likely that the Johannine notion τίθημι τὴν ψυχήν makes use of the constituents in this Servant passage again, i.e., Isa 53:10. Unlike the "lifted up" expression, which augments Jesus' crucifixion as his exaltation and glorification, the "laying down" formula confers a sacrificial connotation on the cross.

Allusions to Isaiah's Servant are also in play in the ὑπέρ-formula in John 10:11 and 10:15, where the object for whom the good shepherd lays down his life is specified.[97] According to Maurer, "the ὑπέρ formula is a rendering of the Hebrew אָשָׁם" in Isa 53:10.[98] Nine of the 13 occurrences of the preposition ὑπέρ in John's Gospel are employed to express Jesus' death "for" the world (6:51), the sheep (10:11, 15), the people (11:50; 18:14), the nation (11:51, 52), the disciples (17:19), and in a proverbial setting, the friend (15:13).[99] Some scholars claim that the Johannine presentation of Jesus' death, the good shepherd's death in particular, lacks a sacrificial overtone.[100] Yet if Isaiah's Servant portrait lies behind the description of Jesus "laying down" his life "for" the sheep, the logical inference is that the shepherd's death is conceived of as a genuine sacrifice for the sheep.[101] In brief, John integrates the biblical portrayals of the Davidic shepherd-king

---

97. Obielosi, *Servant of God in John*, 240–41; Beutler, "Two Ways of Gathering," 403.

98. Maurer, "τίθημι," in *TDNT* 8:156.

99. See Frey, "Edler Tod–Wirksamer Tod-Stellvertrender Tod–Heilschaffender Tod," 82–90.

100. These scholars include Käsemann, Forestell, la Potterie, Painter, and Müller. See the relevant discussion in chapter 1.

101. Lindars, "The Passion in the Fourth Gospel," 73.

and the Servant in order to accentuate Jesus' death as the royal-messianic shepherd's sacrifice on behalf of his sheep.

The Gathering of "Other Sheep" and the Establishment of "One Flock" (John 10:16)

In the context of John 10:14–18, multiple allusions to Jesus' death (vv. 15, 17, 18 [2x]) encircle the critical assertion in verse 16 regarding Jesus assembling "other sheep" not of the present fold and establishing "one flock" under himself as the good shepherd.[102] This structural encirclement strongly suggests that the creation of Jesus' flock directly relates to his death (and resurrection [vv. 17–18]), despite the cross motif's absence from John 10:16. The exact nature of this relationship is not spelled out in John 10:14–18, but it may be deduced from the pertinent pericope of John 11:51–52. In this pericope, the evangelist interprets Caiaphas's words as an ironic prophecy that the death of Jesus will result in the longed-for gathering and unification of God's scattered children (see the excursus below). Given the biblical analogy of God's people as his sheep or flock,[103] the corollary is that Jesus' constitution of a unified flock (John 10:16) would be the *upshot* of his death as the royal-messianic shepherd. In other words, Jesus as the royal Messiah fulfills his shepherding mission *by means of* his death. It is possible that Isaiah's portrayal of the Servant gathering Jacob and Israel to Yahweh (Isa 49:5) has provided the biblical basis of John's connection of Jesus' death with the unification of God's (renewed) flock or people,[104] though this Isaianic text is outside the fourth Servant song which has furnished inspirations for the Johannine idea τίθημι τὴν ψυχὴν ὑπέρ. At any rate, the cross motif in the shepherd discourse corroborates the royal-messianic identity of the crucified Jesus by asserting that the shepherd's death is essential and instrumental to the assembly of "other sheep" and the establishment of "one flock"—a flock that recognizes the voice of Jesus as the messianic shepherd-king.

What is the referent of the "other sheep"? Most commentators believe that the "other sheep" stand for the believing Gentiles or at least include

---

102. The verb δεῖ in John 10:16 suggests that Jesus' shepherding mission of gathering the "other sheep" is part of the divine plan.

103. In the LXX, e.g., Num 27:17; Pss 7:52; 74:1; 77:52; Jer 23:1; Mic 2:12; 5:3; Isa 40:11; Ezek 34:2, 3, 5, 6, 8, 10, 11, 12, 15, 22, 31; Zech 9:16; 10:3.

104. Obielosi, *Servant of God in John*, 242 (mainly concerning John 11:52).

the Gentiles, who will be incorporated into the messianic flock.[105] Several scholars reject this interpretation. Among them is John A. T. Robinson, who claims that the "other sheep" in John 10:16 "are not the Gentiles . . . but the Jews of the Dispersion."[106] John Dennis argues that the "other sheep" symbolize the "dispersed Israelites," who will be confederated with Jesus' "existing sheep in the historic land of Israel."[107] For J. Louis Martyn, the "other sheep" represent the Jewish Christians (outside the Johannine community) who are persecuted due to the enforcement of the *Birkat-ha-Minim* in the synagogues and are in need of being gathered.[108] Despite some differences in their standpoints, these scholars share the belief that Johannine thinking does not involve the Gentile mission and so the "other sheep" in John 10:16 could not refer to the Gentiles.

It is unlikely, however, that the referent of the "other sheep" (and by implication, the "one flock") is bounded by the racial boundary of Israel. Such limitation is not in tune with the universalistic tenor that pervades John's Gospel[109]—Jesus' mission field is the world (3:16–17; 16:28); he is the savior and the light of the world (4:42; 1:9; 8:12); his death will draw πάντας to himself (12:32).[110] Rather than representing a specific group of people, it is more probable that "the referent, those who were to become the 'sheep,' were still unknown."[111] In verse 16, the two future indicative verbs ἀκούσουσιν and γενήσονται hint at that the "other sheep" symbolize all of those who will come to faith upon Jesus' death and resurrection.[112] While sheep or flock is a stock metaphor of Israel in the OT and

105. E.g., Keener, *The Gospel of John*, 1:818–20; Brown, *The Gospel according to John*, 1:396.

106. Robinson, *Twelve New Testament Studies*, 121.

107. Dennis, *Jesus' Death and the Gathering of True Israel*, 300, see pp. 293–302. For Dennis, the "sheep" in John 10:15 stand for the believing Palestinian Jews.

108. Martyn, "A Gentile Mission that Replaced an Earlier Jewish Mission?" 124–44 (esp. 128–30).

109. Klink , *The Sheep of the Fold*, 230–36. For the mission theme in the Gospel of John, see Köstenberger, *The Missions of Jesus and the Disciples according to the Fourth Gospel*, esp. 133–38.

110. The variant πάντα (neuter) is supported by 𝔓66 a* D it vg et al. According to Metzger, the weight of the external evidence of the masculine πάντας (adopted in NA27) is stronger than that of πάντα, which "suggests ideas of cosmic redemption." See Metzger, *A Textual Commentary on the Greek New Testament*, 202.

111. Klink, *The Sheep of the Fold*, 232.

112. Kiefer, *Die Hirtenrede*, 73. Kiefer notes that John 10:1–5 and 10:16 speak of two

post-biblical Judaism, it is unnecessary to assume that John must have adopted this metaphor's wholesale Jewish nuances without any modification. More probable, "the old image of the gathering of the scattered Israelites is taken up into the universal perspective of all those chosen by God."[113] In fact, *Psalms of Solomon* 17 in all likelihood bears witness to a pre-Christian, Jewish redefinition of God's "flock" as entailing the reverent Gentiles (see the earlier section). One should not underestimate the evangelist's capability of reinterpreting the traditional Jewish symbols in light of the career, death, and resurrection of Jesus. As early as the prologue to the Gospel, John has redefined the concept of the "children of God" as encompassing everyone who believes in Jesus (1:12). The metaphor of the vine and the branches in John 15:1–17, which has several parallels with the shepherd discourse, likewise suggests a new definition of "Israel" that traverses racial lines.[114] Within the context of John 10, the ideas of the shepherd's death and the Messiah assembling his sheep evidently go beyond the traditional beliefs about the Davidic shepherd-king. If the Johannine expression τίθημι τὴν ψυχὴν ὑπέρ really draws upon the Isaianic portrait of the suffering Servant, his mission as "a light to the nations" in order to bring salvation to the whole world (Isa 49:6; cf. Isa 49:7, 22–23) undermines the view that Jesus' sheep are confined to the Jewish people. Moreover, the interpretation that asserts that John broadens the racial boundary of the messianic flock beyond Israel accords well with the biblical ideas concerning the Davidic shepherd-king's worldwide dominance (e.g., Zech 9:10; Mic 5:3–4 [5:4–5 Eng.]; cf. Ps 72:8 [71:8 LXX]) and the nations' eschatological ingathering in Zion (e.g., Isa 56:8; 66:18; Jer 3:17).[115]

Conclusion

Our examination of the kingship-cross entailments in the shepherd discourse in John 10 centered especially on the cross motif's interplay with the "one flock, one shepherd" notion in John 10:14–18. In order to illumi-

---

phases in Jesus' work, i.e., "eine ortsgebundene während seines irdischen Lebens und eine unbeschränkte nach der Erhöhung."

113. Schnackenburg, *The Gospel according to St. John*, 2:350.

114. For the parallel features between John 10:1–21 and 15:1–17, see O'Grady, "Good Shepherd and the Vine and the Branches," 86–89.

115. Beutler, "Two Ways of Gathering," 404.

nate this notion's royal-messianic overtone, we conducted a survey of the relevant OT and post-biblical Jewish texts in which a future, royal figure links with the themes of shepherd/sheep and Israel's eschatological assembly or unification. The Johannine theme of "one flock, one shepherd" was then considered against the backdrop of the Jewish associations of royal messianism, shepherd imagery, and Israel's gathering/unification. At stake in this consideration was how the motif of Jesus' death interacts with this shepherding theme to depict the crucified Jesus as the messianic shepherd-king promised in the Scripture. The Johannine portrayal of Jesus as "one shepherd" over "one flock" draws its substance on the scriptural traditions (especially Ezek 37:24) regarding Israel's future hopes for the installment of a Davidic (shepherd) king over the restored Israel. The idea of the good shepherd's sacrificial death for his sheep is probably derived from the Isaianic depiction of the Servant, whose suffering on behalf of Israel brings about its renewal. While utilizing the traditional symbols, the evangelist redefines God's "flock" as constitutive both of Jews and Gentiles, who "hear" Jesus' voice as the messianic shepherd-king. From the Johannine perspective, the good shepherd's death is instrumental to the realization of the biblical hope for Israel's unification under the eschatological Davidic shepherd-king. In this manner, Jesus' death turns out to strengthen rather than subvert his legitimacy as the Messiah-King promised in the Scripture.

The following excursus will reinforce our construal of the kingship-cross link in the shepherd discourse by underlining the connection between Jesus' kingship or death and Israel's gathering/unification in three other passages of the Fourth Gospel, namely John 6:1–15; 11:46–53; 12:30–36. While these passages lack a patent shepherd terminology, within the Gospel's framework they join forces with the Christological portrait in John 10 to identify the crucified Jesus as the messianic shepherd-king, whose death will lead to the establishment of a unified people of God.

⁓ Excursus: The Interplay between Israel's Gathering/Unification and Jesus' Kingship/Death in John 6:1–15; 11:46–53; 12:30–36

At several key places in John's Gospel, the future hope for Israel's eschatological assembling and unification is implicitly evoked and connected with Jesus' kingship or death. Though lacking an explicit shepherd vocabulary, a number of passages (John 6:1–15; 11:46–53; 12:30–36) play a part in the Johannine identification of the crucified Jesus as the Messiah-King over the unified Israel.

The pericope of Jesus feeding a multitude in Galilee (John 6:1–15) contains the second occurrence of the term βασιλεύς (v. 15) in the Gospel.[116] Wayne Meeks and John Lierman argue that this royal title in John 6:15 refers to Jesus as the Mosaic king (cf. Deut 18:15–18), on account of this pericope's rich allusions to the Exodus traditions and this title's apposition with the designation προφήτης in verse 14.[117] Richard Bauckham, however, emphasizes that Moses is rarely acclaimed as "king" in the canonical and extra-canonical Jewish writings (apart from Philo's works). Bauckham notes that the evangelist clearly distinguishes between the Messiah and the prophet like Moses in John 1:20–21 and 7:40–41.[118] For the unlearned mass in the first century CE, these two eschatological figures were possibly amalgamated and not sharply differentiated. On the other hand, the evangelist may employ the term βασιλεύς at the closing of John 6:1-15 "in order to link this passage with the theme of true and false understandings of Jesus' kingship."[119] In John 6:12–14, the graphic description of the disciples "gathering" (συνάγω) the leftover and filling "twelve" baskets probably conjures up the Jewish hopes for the restoration of Israel's twelve tribes.[120] In the popular expectation, this hope will be actualized when the Davidic kingdom is reinstated and the Israelites are liberated from foreign oppression. Jesus' refusal to succumb to the peo-

---

116. For the biblical motif of plentiful foods in the messianic age, see Isa 25:6; 55:1–2. In *2 Bar.* 29:8, "manna" is an eschatological gift.

117. Meeks, *The Prophet-King*, 87–99; Lierman, "The Mosaic Pattern of John's Christology," 221–22.

118. Bauckham, "Messianism according to the Gospel of John," 50–51.

119. Ibid., 51.

120. Dennis, *Jesus' Death and the Gathering of True Israel*, 194–96; Cf. Köstenberger, *John*, 203; Meeks, *The Prophet-King*, 96, 98.

ple's wish (v. 15a) reveals that his royal mission does not involve political revolutions. The passage John 6:1–15 may entail a prolepsis of Jesus' death because the phrase ἵνα μήτι ἀπόληται in verse 12 can relate to eternal life (John 6:39–40; cf. μὴ ἀπολέσω in v. 39), which is a gift of salvation as an outcome of Jesus giving his flesh (i.e., his death; 6:51).[121] If this figurative reading of John 6:12 is accepted, the motifs of Israel's gathering, Jesus' kingship, and his death are interwoven in John 6:1–15.

The convention of the Sanhedrin in John 11:46–53 marks a critical juncture in the Johannine plot. In this scene, the Jewish leaders contrive to arrest and kill Jesus. In verses 51–52, the evangelist elaborates on Caiaphas's statement and offers his post-resurrectional insight that Jesus not only dies "for" (ὑπέρ) the nation but ἵνα καὶ τὰ τέκνα τοῦ θεοῦ τὰ διεσκοπισμένα συναγάγῃ εἰς ἕν. This ἵνα clause (v. 52b) indicates the purpose or result of Jesus' death, namely the gathering of God's dispersed children. While the "scattered children of God" generally refer to Diaspora Jews in Second Temple Jewish thought, John's treatment of the concepts of the "children of God" (1:12), "born of God" (1:13), "born of the Spirit" (3:5), and the Messiah's "sheep/flock" (10:16) suggests that the referent of God's scattered children in John 11:52 includes Gentile believers.[122] In John 11:48, the "place" to which the Jewish leaders attach importance most likely is the temple, which will be replaced by Jesus' body upon his crucifixion and resurrection (see chapter 4). In view of Jesus' statement at the temple (John 2:19–22), the reference to the gathering of the Gentiles (John 11:52) amounts to an implicit declaration that the biblical expectation for the Gentile pilgrimage to the temple (cf. Isa 2:12; 56:7; Zech 14:16) will be actualized in the crucified and risen Jesus as the eschatological temple.[123] In John 11:52, the language of "gathering" (συνάγω) and "oneness" (εἷς) recalls Jesus' speech in John 10:16, which announces that Jesus as the royal-messianic shepherd will "gather" (ἄγω) other sheep outside the present fold and establish "one" (εἷς) flock. Therefore, both of John 11:51–52 and 10:16 summon the Jewish restoration hope for Israel's

---

121. Dennis, *Jesus' Death and the Gathering of True Israel*, 196–200. Dennis's analysis builds upon Meeks, *The Prophet-King*, 87–99.

122. Note that "the Jews" are arraigned as the children of the devil, despite their physical lineage from Abraham (John 8:44). See Keener, *The Gospel of John*, 1:819; Köstenberger, *The Missions of Jesus and the Disciples according to the Fourth Gospel*, 166; Brown, *The Gospel according to John*, 1:442–43.

123. Brown, *The Gospel according to John*, 1:443.

gathering and unification in order to heighten Jesus' death as the decisive event that leads to the realization of this hope.

The episode of John 12:20–36 follows directly the account of Jesus' royal arrival in Jerusalem (John 12:9–19; see chapter 7). This episode opens with the mention of some Ἕλληνες visiting Jesus (v. 20) and Jesus' solemn announcement that the "hour" of his glorification has arrived (vv. 23, 27). Robinson, Martyn, and Dennis allege that the Ἕλληνες (John 12:20; cf. 7:35) are Greek-speaking Jews or Gentile proselytes and so their presence in the Gospel of John on no account suggests the evangelist's interest in Gentile mission.[124] Yet it is doubtful that the Ἕλληνες are Hellenized Jews, for in this case the term Ἑλληνιστής (cf. Acts 6:1) would have been employed.[125] The Ἕλληνες in John 12:20 (cf. 7:35) are probably Gentile adherents of Judaism, i.e., God-fearers.[126] Notwithstanding their affiliation with Judaism, the appearance of the Ἕλληνες in the Gospel is telling of the Johannine concern about the inclusion of the Gentiles into the messianic community. In John 12:32, Jesus announces that upon his being "lifted up" from the earth (cf. 3:14; 8:28), he will "draw" (ἑλκύω) "all people" (πάντας) to himself.[127] The adjective πάντας stresses the universal significance (cf. the Ἕλληνες) of this salvific "drawing," which is an outcome of the death of Jesus.[128] This announcement in John 12:32 resonates with Jesus' proverbial saying in John 12:24, where a seed's "death" will bear much fruit (cf. the similar ἐάν-construction in these two verses). On account of this textual connection, the "fruit" may symbolize the people who will be "drawn" to the crucified Jesus (cf. the Father "drawing" [ἑλκύω] people to Jesus in John 6:44). Although the term ἄγω (John 10:16) or συνάγω (John 6:12–14; 11:52) is not used in John 12:32, the thrust of Jesus "drawing" all

---

124. Robinson, *Twelve New Testament Studies*, 120; Martyn, "A Gentile Mission That Replaced an Earlier Jewish Mission?" 127–28, 131–33; Dennis, *Jesus' Death and the Gathering of True Israel*, 306–7.

125. Cf. Mark 7:26. See Witherington, *John's Wisdom*, 223; Carson, *The Gospel according to John*, 436.

126. Keener, *The Gospel of John*, 2:871; Witherington, *John's Wisdom*, 223; Frey, "Heiden-Greichen-Gooteskinder," 251–64; Carson, *The Gospel according to John*, 436; cf. Williams, "Isaiah in John's Gospel," 114.

127. Reynolds construes this "lifting up" saying in John 12:32 as implicitly referring to Jesus as the Son of Man and calls attention to similar ideas in *Fourth Ezra* (the Son of Man assembling a peaceful multitude) and the Synoptics (the gathering of the elect). See *The Apocalyptic Son of Man in the Gospel of John*, 200.

128. Dennis, *Jesus' Death and the Gathering of True Israel*, 204.

people to himself is in tune with that of Jesus "gathering" around himself a messianic community that has no ethnic boundary.[129] In the Johannine anticipation, the hallmark of this multiethnic community will be "unity" (cf. John 17:11, 21, 22, 23).

129. Ibid., 203–5, though Dennis denies the Johannine interest in Gentile mission.

7

Scriptural Witness and the Royal Messiahship of Jesus (John 12:12–19)

THE EPISODE OF JESUS' entry into Jerusalem (John 12:12–19) contains the second occurrence of the royal epithet "king of Israel" (v. 13; cf. 1:49) in the Gospel of John. In this episode, the kingship theme surfaces in association with an allusion to Jesus' death and resurrection (v. 16). Two scriptural texts are cited in John 12:13 and 12:15, namely Ps 118:26 (Ps 117:26 LXX) and Zech 9:9 respectively. The latter text in particular predicts the future arrival of a king in Zion. We will argue that the cross motif as articulated in John 12:12–19 bolsters the Johannine claim that the crucified Jesus is the Messiah-King. As will be seen, this claim is buttressed by the fact that Jesus' death will effect the revelation of the Scripture's deeper meaning concerning the Messiah.

Textual Setting and Structure

The Johannine account of Jesus' entrance into Jerusalem resides within the setting of the final stage of his public career, during the third and final Passover feast in John's Gospel (cf. 11:55–57; 12:1, 12). In the Gospel sequence, this incident takes place the day after Mary has anointed Jesus in Bethany (John 12:1–11; cf. 12:12) and precedes the visitation of some Ἕλληνες (John 12:20–21), Jesus' announcement of the dawn of his "hour" (John 12:22–27), and his further dialogue with the bystanders (John 12:28–36). As Jesus' public ministry is drawing to its close, the evangelist repeatedly calls the reader's attention to Jesus' imminent death—the μύρον as symbolic of Jesus' forthcoming burial (John 12:7; cf. 19:38–42), the glorification of Jesus (John 12:16, 23), the onset of his "hour" (John 12:23, 27), the "death" (ἀποθνήσκω) of a grain of wheat (John 12:24), the maxim of dying in order to live (John 12:25), and Jesus' prediction of his being "lifted up" (John 12:32–34).[1] The prominence of the cross motif within the surrounding context of John 12:12–19 not only looks forward to Jesus' crucifixion, but also strengthens the connection between Jesus' death and his venerable status as "king of Israel" (John 12:13, 16).

Among the four Gospels, only the Johannine account of Jesus' entry into Jerusalem is framed by the references to the "sign" of Jesus raising Lazarus from the dead (John 12:9–11, 17–19; cf. 11:1–44). As indicated in John 12:9–11, a large crowd of "the Jews" comes to Bethany to see Jesus and the revivified Lazarus (cf. John 12:1–2). Since many Jews believed in Jesus on account of this miracle, the chief priests decide that they must kill Lazarus in addition to Jesus (cf. John 11:57). In the closing of this account (John 12:17–18), the evangelist remarks that "the Jews" who were at Lazarus's tomb and witnessed Jesus resurrecting Lazarus give their testimonies to this "sign." As a result of these testimonies, a multitude of people joyously welcomes Jesus into the Jewish capital. In view of John's composition aim (John 20:30–31), the twofold recollection of the Lazarus "sign" in John 12:9–11 and 12:17–18 serve to heighten the messianic connotation that is entailed in Jesus' royal advent in Jerusalem.[2]

The narrative progression in John 12:12–19 runs as follows: (1) Jesus' approach to Jerusalem (v. 12), (2) the crowd's action and acclamation of Jesus (v. 13), (3) Jesus' response to the crowd (v. 14a), (4) the Johannine explication of Jesus' response (vv. 14b–15), (5) the disciples' incomprehension and post-Easter comprehension (v. 16), (6) the recollection of Lazarus's resurrection (vv. 17–18), and (7) the retort of the Pharisees (v. 19). In unfolding the people's extolment of Jesus and his reaction to them, John draws upon the biblical materials in Ps 118:25–26 (Ps 117:25–26 LXX) and Zech 9:9. The entire scene of Jesus' royal entry into Jerusalem closes with the Pharisees' despondent statement in John 12:19c that ironically proclaims Jesus' rising popularity. While being uttered on the

---

1. Schnelle, "Cross and Resurrection in the Gospel of John," 140–41.

2. The references to the Lazarus "sign" look forward to the death and resurrection of Jesus. For this anticipatory function, see Zimmermann, "The Narrative Hermeneutics of John 11," 75–101.

enemies' lips, this statement's universalistic drift foreshadows the approach of the Ἕλληνες to Jesus (John 12:20–21) as well as the climatic pronouncement of Jesus' worldwide kingship in the crucifixion narrative (John 19:19–20).[3]

The Crowd's Reception of Jesus (John 12:13)

In John 12:13, the festal people perpetrate three actions to give homage to Jesus: (1) they take (and presumably wave) palm branches (v. 13a), (2) come to meet him (v. 13b), and (3) shout a royal acclamation (v. 13c). This verse evidently shines the spotlight on the acclamation, in view of the space allocation of these actions (5 words in v. 13a, 5 words in v. 13b, and 13/14 words in v.13c).[4] In addition, the tense choice of the verbal actions—ἔλαβον (aorist), ἐξῆλθον (aorist), and ἐκραύγαζον (imperfect)—intimates the Johannine intention to underline the words of the elated people. Of the six occurrences of the verb κραυγάζω in the Gospel of John (11:43; 12:13; 18:40; 19:6, 12, 15), only the instance in 12:13 is a non-aorist form.[5] Given the Johannine tendency of employing this verb's aorist tense (cf. the aorist forms of the cognate verb κράζω in John 7:28, 37; 12:44) and the fact that the imperfect tense is more heavily marked than the aorist tense,[6] the imperfect ἐκραύγαζον (following two aorist indicative verbs) in John 12:13c performs the narrative function of accentuating the crowd's proclamation, which hails Jesus as the king of Israel.

The reference to "the palm branches" (τὰ βαΐα τῶν φοινίκων) in John 12:13 is unique to the Johannine description of the crowd's reception of Jesus into Jerusalem.[7] In the Synoptic traditions, the jubilant people cut out leafy branches on their way to meet Jesus, but the kind of foliage is not specified (Mark 11:8; Matt 21:8). Since either one of the words, βαΐον

---

3. Schnackenburg, *The Gospel according to St. John*, 2:378.

4. The authenticity of the conjunction καί in John 12:13c is uncertain. This word is present in ℵ*.2 B L Q W Ψ 579 bo, but is missing from many manuscripts including 𝔓66 1 ℵ A D K Θ f1 f13 sa ac2 pbo bomss and the Majority Text. In Nestle-Aland 27, this conjunction is placed within brackets.

5. The variant ἐκραύγασαν in 𝔓66 and B* is probably the outcome of the scribal attempt to gear to the preceding two aorist indicative verbs or to the Johannine tendency of using the aorist tense of κραυγάζω.

6. Porter, *Verbal Aspect in the Greek of the New Testament with Reference to Tense and Mood*, 178–81.

7. For the availability of palm branches in Jerusalem, see Brunson, *Psalm 118 in the Gospel of John*, 219–21.

and φοῖνιξ, is sufficient to denote the branch of a palm tree, some scholars think that the terminological combination of τὰ βαΐα τῶν φοινίκων in John 12:13 is pleonastic and awkward.[8] Yet rather than being redundant, this terminology may seek to draw attention to the greenery itself (i.e., palm) and thereby to underscore the symbolic significance of the "palm branches."[9]

There is evidence that the palm had gradually gained associations with Israel's nationalistic hopes since the Maccabean revolution during the second century BCE.[10] The rare term βαΐον in John 12:13 is a *hapax legomenon* in the NT and occurs only in 1 Macc 13:51 and Song 7:8 (Symmachus's version) in the Septuagint.[11] As the former passage indicates, upon Simon Maccabeus expelling the Syrians from the citadel of Jerusalem (which abutted the temple), he made his entry into it with the accompaniment of praises, "palm branches" (βαΐων), and hymns to celebrate the Jewish triumph over the enemies (ca. 141/142 BCE). "Palms" (φοῖνιξ) were also brought by the Jews into the consecrated temple in 164 BCE, when Simon's brother Judas Maccabeus rededicated the sanctuary which had been profaned by the Seleucid ruler Antiochus IV Epiphanes (2 Macc 10:7; cf. 1 Macc 1:59; *Ant.* 12.320–321). This national incident led to the constitution of the Feast of Dedication, which John refers to in his story of Jesus (John 10:22). In view of this festal reference, the evangelist is familiar with the prominent exploitation of the palm in the Maccabean history and this foliage's possible nationalistic implications. Further, the palm most likely had become a national emblem of Israel by the end of the first century CE. This is suggestive in the Romans' choice of the palm as symbolizing their military victory over the Jews.[12] It is also notable that sundry images of the palm, together with the words ציון לגאלת ("for the redemption of Zion") or לגאלת ("for the redemption"), were minted on the Jewish coins during the time (or in commemoration) of Simon Maccabaeus (141–135 BCE) and the two Jewish revolts against Rome

---

8. E .g., Brown, *The Gospel according to John*, 1:456; Barrett, *The Gospel according to St. John*, 417; Hoskyns, *The Fourth Gospel*, 421.

9. Hill, "τὰ βαΐα τῶν φοινίκων (John 12:13)," 133–35. However, Hill's proposal that this Greek phrase alludes to the phoenix myth is unconvincing.

10. Farmer, "The Palm Branches in John 12, 13," 62–66.

11. The Symmachus reference is from Hoskyns, *The Fourth Gospel*, 421.

12. Farmer, "The Palm Branches in John 12, 13," 64.

(66–70 and 132–135 CE).[13] The palm is a token of victory in the escha-tological vision of *T. Naph.* 5:4, where Levi receives "twelve branches of palm" (βαΐα φοινίκων δώδεκα; cf. Judah's twelve rays) at his exaltation.[14] It is declared in *Lev. Rab.* 30, ". . . the one who takes the palm branch in his hand" is "the victor." In the same text, "[b]ut when Israel goes forth from before the Holy One, blessed be he, with their palm branches and their citrons in their hands, we know that it is Israel that are the victors."[15] In the early Christian traditions, "palms" (φοίνικες) appear in a heavenly scene where the redeemed sing praises to God and the Lamb (Rev 7:9). In light of these "palm" examples, the Johannine portrayal of the people waving the palm branches signifies their welcome of Jesus as a royal liberator who will bring political success to Israel (cf. the multitude's political agenda in John 6:15–16).[16] From the evangelist's viewpoint, however, Jesus' ultimate enemies are not the Romans but the evil forces. His crucifixion and resur-rection will achieve victory over death and "the ruler of this world" (John 12:31).[17]

Some scholars propose that the Greek phrase εἰς ὑπάντησιν in 12:13b displays a political tint and functions to enhance the crowd's salutation of Jesus as a national deliverer.[18] Bill Salier says that John's presentation of Jesus' entry into Jerusalem "resembles the [Greco-Roman] ceremony of *adventus.*"[19] According to Brown, the expression εἰς ὑπάντησιν often occurs "to describe the joyful reception of Hellenistic sovereigns into a

---

13. Wirgin and Mandel, *The History of Coins and Symbols in Ancient Israel*, 114–61 (esp. the references to the palm branches and *lulab* on pp. 147–57); Farmer, "The Palm Branches in John 12, 13," 63.

14. Hollander and Jonge, *The Testaments of the Twelve Patriarchs*, 310–11.

15. The English translation is from Neusner, *Leviticus Rabbah*, 4:140; cf. Schnackenburg, *The Gospel according to St. John*, 2:524 n. 35.

16. Most commentators agree that the "palm branches" in John 12:13 are indicative of political-nationalistic connotations. E.g., Keener, *The Gospel of John*, 2:869; Witherington, *John's Wisdom*, 221; Carson, *The Gospel according to John*, 432; contra Brunson, *Psalm 118 in the Gospel of John*, 215–23.

17. Given that "palm" is a symbol of life in antiquity, the Johannine mention of this greenery may serve the function of anticipating Jesus' resurrection and his triumph over death. See Brunson, *Psalm 118 in the Gospel of John*, 216–17, 221–23; Hill, "τὰ βαΐα τῶν φοινίκων (John 12:13)," 133–35.

18. In the LXX, the expression εἰς ὑπάντησιν occurs once in Judg 11:34 pertaining to Jephthah's daughter coming "to meet" him (Köstenberger, *John*, 369).

19. Salier, "Jesus, the Emperor, and the Gospel according to John," 296.

city," such as the arrival of Attalus III at Pergamum and Titus at Antioch.[20] Coakley puts forward further Greco-Roman and Jewish instances which utilize similar expressions to depict the people or officials of a city lauding a renowned or military leader at his advent.[21] By contrast, Brunson criticizes the view that the crowd in John 12:12–19 entertains any political thought and he underlines the non-political use of εἰς ὑπάντησιν αὐτῷ in Matt 8:28 and 8:34 as counter-examples.[22] Yet these two Matthean texts concern the approach of two demoniacs and the gardeners to Jesus and so have little in common with the royal scene of John 12:12–19. If the cultural milieu of the ancient audience (in Ephesus) is taken into consideration, the Johannine portrayal of the multitude coming "to meet" Jesus as king would plausibly have resonated with the audience's experiences regarding the visitation of royal dignitaries in the city.[23] This does not, however, mean that the evangelist models Jesus' entrance into the Jewish capital upon the figure of a Greco-Roman ruler or personage. The quotations of Ps 118:25–26 (John 12:13c) and Zech 9:9 (John 12:15) apparently point in the direction of a Jewish background. Moreover, John's account lacks certain features that are characteristic of the Greco-Roman entry narratives, such as the failure of the city's authorities to greet Jesus (cf. the Pharisees' complaint in 12:19).[24]

As commented earlier, the Johannine description of the crowd's reception of Jesus puts the accent on the euphoric exclamation in John 12:13c. The cry ὡσαννά ("Hosanna") and the statement εὐλογημένος ὁ ἐρχόμενος ἐν ὀνόματι κυρίου are derived from Ps 118:25 (117:25 LXX) and Ps 118:26 (117:26 LXX) respectively. Psalm 118 is the concluding poem of the "Egyptian Hallel" (Psalms 113—118) sung at various eminent festivals such as the Tabernacles, the Hanukkah, and especially the Passover (cf. *m. Pesaḥ* 5:7; 9:3; 10:7; *m. Sukkah* 3:9).[25] The speaker in this

20. Brown, *The Gospel according to John*, 1:461–62; cf. Köstenberger, *John*, 369; Morris, *The Gospel according to John*, 518 n. 39.

21. E.g., Brasidas at Scione, Apelles at Corinth, Antiochus at Boeotia, Jonathan Maccabeus at Ashkalon, and Cicero at Rome. See Coakley, "Jesus' Messianic Entry into Jerusalem (John 12:12–19 Par.)," 471–72.

22. Brunson, *Psalm 118 in the Gospel of John*, 193–94 n. 36.

23. For the imperial influences in ancient Ephesus, see Carter, *John and Empire*, 52–64; Tilborg, *Reading John in Ephesus*.

24. For Luke's parallel passage, see Kinman, *Jesus' Entry into Jerusalem*, 25–47, 173–75.

25. Knobel, "Hallel," 296.

psalm celebrates Yahweh's victory and deliverance (cf. vv. 13, 18) and calls for the whole assembly to praise the God of Israel.[26] Since Psalm 118 mentions the "gate" of Yahweh (v. 20; cf. v. 19) and exhibits liturgical elements (e.g., God's "house" in v. 26 and "sacrifices" and "the horns of the altar" in v. 27), it is believed that the pilgrims or priests chant this poem when going into the temple.[27] In several rabbinic and NT writings, Psalm 118 is interpreted with reference to the Messiah (e.g., b. Pesah. 117; Midr. Ps 118:22; Matt 21:42; Mark 12:10–11; Luke 20:17; Acts 4:11; Eph 2:20; 1 Pe 2:4–7).[28]

The term ὡσαννά is a phonetic transliteration of the Hebrew הושיעה נא (or the Aramaic הושע נא in Ps 118:25, which is translated literally as σῶσον δή in Ps 117:25 LXX. Aside from Psalm 118, the Hiphil imperative הושיעה is found in various OT passages regarding petitions addressed to kings.[29] Among the 198 occurrences of the verb ישע in the MT, Ps 118:26 contains the only instance of the juxtaposition of this verb's imperatival form with the interjection נא. In the original context of this poem, the cry is an imploration to Yahweh for the divine bestowal of salvation and prosperity.[30] Yet "Hosanna" had likely lost its beseeching sense and become a customary cry of praise or greeting by the end of the first century CE.[31] It is documented in the Mishnah that during the seven-day festival of the Tabernacles, the priests would go around the altar of burnt offering, joyously flutter the lulab (made of willow, myrtle, and palm branches), and repeatedly shout "Hosanna" (m. Sukkah 3:9; 4:5; cf. b. Sukkah 43b).[32] While the rabbinic writings are of relatively late date, these liturgical practices would have been generally observed at the temple before it was demolished by the Romans in 70 CE.[33] Within the NT and later Christian writings, ὡσαννά is clearly an utterance of praise in Mark 11:10 and Matt 21:9, 15 and it has taken on the laudatory denotation by the time of the

---

26. Schaefer, Psalms, 288–91.

27. Kraus, Psalms 60–150, 395.

28. Köstenberger, "John," 471.

29. E.g., 2 Sam 14:4; 2 Kgs 6:26. See Keener, The Gospel of John, 2:869.

30. Kraus, Psalms 60—150, 398.

31. Lohse, "ὡσαννά," TDNT 9:682–84; Fitzmyer, "Aramaic Evidence Affecting the Interpretation of Hosanna in the New Testament," 114–15; Köstenberger, John, 369–70; Beasley-Murray, John, 210.

32. Lohse, "ὡσαννά," TDNT 9:682. The lulab is occasionally referred to as hosannas (הושענא). See b. Sukkah 37a–b.

33. Ibid.

Didache (cf. Ὡσαννὰ τῷ θεῷ Δαυίδ in *Did.* 10:6).[34] Brunson, however, claims that no extant evidence proves that the term "Hosanna" has lost its original supplicatory meaning, and such meaning is present in John's use of this term in his entry account.[35] For Brunson, the evangelist employs this term in order to evoke the ideas in Ps 118:25 regarding Yahweh's sovereignty in "saving" his people and regarding the subtle connection between Yahweh's kingship and the (Davidic) ruler's.[36] Of course, these ideas in Psalm 118 are compatible with the Christology of the Fourth Gospel, which acknowledges Jesus as the "Savior of the world" (John 4:42) and asserts his unity with the Father (John 10:30). Whether the term ὡσαννά carried an imploring element in first-century CE Judaism, it is nonetheless unlikely that John wants to bring this out in his entry narrative—especially because he provides no Greek translation of this Semitic term. Most scholars concur that the Gospel's intended audience was unfamiliar with the Semitic language, given the fact that the evangelist often gives the Greek equivalents when utilizing Semitic words (e.g., John 1:41; 4:25; 9:7). Yet the word ὡσαννά in John 12:13 is a transliteration, not a translation (similarly, Matt 21:9, 15 and Mark 11:9–10). This suggests that John (likewise, Matthew and Mark) simply treats this word as a conventional acclamation without a beseeching signification, for otherwise he would have supplied the Greek translation or quoted directly from Ps 117:25 LXX (i.e., σῶσον δή).[37] In any case, the cry "Hosanna" in John 12:13 functions to enhance the intertextual connection between the story of Jesus' arrival in Jerusalem and Psalm 118 and to prepare for the immediately ensuing citation from Ps 118:26.

The laudatory words εὐλογημένος ὁ ἐρχόμενος ἐν ὀνόματι κυρίου in John 12:13 originate from Ps 118:26a (Ps 117:26a LXX). The Johannine phrasing is identical to the Septuagintal reading, which accurately translates the Hebrew text ברוך הבא בשם יהוה. Yet, deviating from the content of this Hebrew or Greek text in which the blessing is generically bestowed upon every pilgrim, the evangelist tapers the recipient to a particular in-

---

34. Fitzmyer, "Aramaic Evidence Affecting the Interpretation of *Hosanna* in the New Testament," 114. The Greek text of *Didache* is from *LCL*, vol. 24.

35. Brunson, *Psalm 118 in the Gospel of John*, 206.

36. Ibid., 210–14, cf. 213.

37. For the citation of Ps 118:25–26 in Mark 11:9–10, see Subramanian, *The Synoptic Gospels and the Psalms as Prophecy*, 49.

dividual, namely Jesus. As a result, Ps 118:26a becomes a prophecy that foretells Jesus' royal advent in Jerusalem.[38]

These words in John 12:13 should be interpreted within the broader context of the Johannine depiction of Jesus as "the coming one," though in the present pericope they are part of an OT quotation. In John's Gospel, various characters speak of Jesus as "one who is to come" (in different formulations of ὁ ἐρχόμενος): (1) John the Baptist (John 1:15, 27, 30), (2) the Samaritan woman (John 4:25; cf. Jesus' self-divulgence as the "Messiah" in v. 26), (3) a crowd (John 6:14), and (4) Martha (John 11:27). These instances are pregnant of a messianic importance, save the case in John 6:14. It deserves notice that the epithet Μεσσίας/Χριστός occurs in both of John 4:25 and 11:27 and is parallel to ὁ ἐρχόμενος in the latter text. Martha's messianic confession (John 11:27) is particularly relevant to this analysis, because it takes place shortly before the episode of John 12:12–19 and is in the setting of the Lazarus "sign," which frames this episode (cf. John 12:9–11, 17–19). In addition to the references above, sundry forms of ὁ ἐρχόμενος surface four times in John 7:25–44, where the inhabitants of Jerusalem debate among themselves on Jesus' messianic credentials (vv. 27, 31, 41, 42). On the basis of all these textual instances, the designation ὁ ἐρχόμενος on the lips of the crowd (John 12:13) in all probability functions as a messianic title (cf. Matt 11:3; Luke 19:38). This is all the more probable in view of the specific identification of "the coming one" as "the king of Israel» and the succeeding citation of Zech 9:9, which foretells the advent of a future king in Zion.

By contrast to Matthew and Mark, the Johannine entry account does not relate Jesus to David.[39] The lack of a Davidic reference in this account may be partly explained by John's overall emphasis on Jesus' provenance from above. As early as the prologue, the true light is described as "coming [ἐρχόμενος] in the world" (John 1:9). While elaborating on the Baptist's witness to Jesus, the evangelist remarks that "the one who comes [ἐρχόμενος] from above" and "the one who comes [ἐρχόμενος] from heaven" is above all" (John 3:31). In John 5:42, Jesus responds to the challenge of "the Jews" and avers, "I have come [ἐλήλυθα] in the name of my Father" (John 5:43). Similar ideas concerning Jesus' origin from the heaven or the Father surface in a number of other Gospel passages, albeit without the term ἔρχομαι

---

38. For the quotation of Psalm 118 in Mark 11:9–11, see ibid., 51.

39. Cf. "Son of David" (Matt 21:9, 15) and "the coming kingdom of our father David" (Mark 11:10).

(e.g., John 3:16, 34; 7:29; 8;23; 12:45; 13:16). Some of these passages in particular speak of Jesus as being sent by the Father. Given John's strong interest in Jesus' heavenly origin, the statement of Jesus "coming in the name of the Lord" in the Psalm 118 quotation in John 12:13 is tantamount to asserting that he comes from God.[40] Since Jesus' heavenly provenance is implied in this quotation, it is unsurprising that the evangelist does not explicitly bring forth the Davidic hope in the entry story.

The epithet ὁ βασιλεὺς τοῦ Ἰσραήλ in John 12:13c is missing from Psalm 117 LXX (118 MT) and the parallels in the Synoptic Gospels (Matt 21:9, 15; Mark 11:9-10; but βασιλεύς in Luke 19:38). If the conjunction καί in this verse is authentic, its function is probably epexegetical in identifying the "one who comes in the name of the Lord" with "the king of Israel."[41] This regal appellation (albeit without the definite article ὁ) has surfaced in the early part of the narrative, where Nathanael extols Jesus as the Son of God and the king of Israel (John 1:49). In light of this, the evangelist adroitly opens and closes his narrative of Jesus' public ministry with the twofold assertion of Jesus' identity as the king of Israel (John 1:49; 12:13). The fact that the "king of Israel" title in both of these verses is closely followed by a reference to Jesus' death (John 1:51; 12:16) is indicative of the cross's crucial place in the scheme of Johannine royal messianism. We emphasized that Nathanael's titular confession represents his acknowledgement of Jesus' royal-messianic status (see chapter 3). This initial occurrence of the "king of Israel" epithet (John 1:49) clearly sets a messianic tone for its reappearance in John 12:13, where another character (an exulted crowd) in the Gospel uses this epithet again to profess the belief in Jesus as the Messiah-King. In both cases, Jesus does not reject the royal-messianic acclaim but hints at the need for its refinement.

Jesus' Reaction and the Quotation of Zech 9:9 (John 12:14–15)

In response to the laudation of the festive crowd, Jesus finds a donkey, sits on it, and presumably enters Jerusalem riding on this animal (John 12:14a). The quotation formula καθώς ἐστιν γεγραμμένον is found only

---

40. Daly-Denton, *David in the Fourth Gospel*, 183. She remarks that David is referred to as "coming in the name of the Lord" in 1 Sam 17:45 (p. 185).

41. Köstenberger, "John," 471.

twice in John 6:31 and 12:14b in the Fourth Gospel.[42] It is a scholarly consensus that the prophecy of Zech 9:9 lies behind this Johannine citation in John 12:15, although its textual form deviates from the MT and the LXX in a number of areas. It seems that several elements of Zech 9:9 are omitted or altered in order to better adapt this biblical text within the setting of Jesus' royal arrival in Jerusalem.[43] For example, (1) the second half of the address to "the daughter of Jerusalem" is absent from John's quotation; (2) the term ‏לך‎/σου is missing; (3) the king's description is abbreviated to contain only the feature of his arrival on a donkey; (4) the phrase ‏גילי מאד‎/χαῖρε σφόδρα is replaced by μὴ φοβοῦ (cf. Isa 40:9; Zep 3:16); (5) rather than "mounting" (‏רכב‎/ἐπιβαίνω) the donkey, Jesus "sits" (κάθημαι) on it; and (6) the final two words (πῶλον ὄνου) in John 12:15 do not match the text of either Zech 9:9 MT or LXX. In view of these textual variations, John probably leaves out the elements that are not of his theological interest, but retains those that he regards as the most vital and making certain changes in order to more perceptibly bring out the biblical import of the entry event.

We noted in chapter 6 that the oracle of Zech 9:9–10 heralds the future coming of a "king," who most probably harks back to the Davidic "Branch" in Zech 3:8 and 6:12. This oracle is sandwiched between two prophetic visions concerning the eschatological restitution of the land and the people of Israel (Zech 9:1–8 and 9:11–17). In Zech 9:9, the royal figure is described as righteous, humble, and most crucial for the present discussion, riding on a donkey. As declared in Zech 9:10, Yahweh will remove warfare from the Jewish land and this king will offer peace to all nations and enjoy universal dominance. The quotation in John 12:14b–15 apparently identifies Jesus as Zechariah's anticipated "king" (Zech 9:9–10), whose appearance in Zion intrinsically links with the realization of Jewish eschatological hopes. In the Johannine treatment, the act of Jesus riding a donkey into Jerusalem is a deliberate enactment of this royal prophecy. The phrase "your king is coming" in the Zechariah quotation reverberates with the crowd's proclamation of Jesus as "the coming one" and "the king of Israel" (John 12:13). The shared terms (βασιλεύς and ἔρχομαι) between John 12:13 and 12:15 in effect tie together the prophecies of Ps 118:26 and

42. Menken, *Old Testament Quotations in the Fourth Gospel*, 81.

43. For the differences between John's Zechariah quotation and Zech 9:9 MT and LXX, see Köstenberger, "John," 473; Menken, *Old Testament Quotations in the Fourth Gospel*, 79–80.

Zech 9:9, to which these two Johannine verses make reference. Simply put, Jesus' entry into Jerusalem is presented as simultaneously fulfilling these two scriptural prophecies.

In the Synoptic Gospels, the reference to Jesus mounting a donkey or the citation from Zech 9:9 occurs prior to the people's exhilarated acclamation at Jesus' coming (Matt 21:1–11; Mark 11:1–11; Luke 19:28–38). Only John's Gospel places the donkey reference and the quotation immediately after the crowd's reception of Jesus. This literary arrangement gives the impression that Jesus' action of riding on a donkey represents his response to the crowd's accolade. By contrast to the Synoptics, John does not report the process of the disciples obtaining an ass in a village for Jesus. In a terse description, Jesus finds a "donkey's colt" (πῶλον ὄνου) and "sits" (κάθημαι) on it. These two incidents' importance in John's report is evident in the quotation of Zech 9:9, which omits a number of characteristics of the awaited king but retains the feature of his coming on a donkey.

In line with the vision of Zech 9:9, Jesus as the king of Israel arrives in Jerusalem riding on a "donkey."[44] Aside from this prophetic text, donkeys or asses are occasionally associated with royal or dignified figures in the biblical traditions. In 2 Sam 13:29, the sons of David mount on their mules when they attempt to flee from Absalom, who conspires to usurp the throne. According to 2 Sam 16:2, David and his family members ride on the asses that Ziba, the servant of Mephibosheth (Saul's grandson), bring to them during their flight from Absalom. In his final combat, Absalom traverses on a mule in the battle field (2 Sam 18:9). Upon David's return to Jerusalem, Mephibosheth tells him that he formerly planned to ride on an ass to meet the king (2 Sam 19:26). At his coronation, Solomon rides on David's mule during a royal procession to Gihon (1 Kgs 1:38–44). In the pre-monarchic times, the esteemed leaders of Israel (Judg 5:9–10) and the descendants of two judges (Jair and Abdon; Judg 10:3–4; 12:14) rode on donkeys.[45] Although these personages are not "kings," their association with donkey indicates that in Jewish thinking this kind of animal is fitting as a means of transport for dignified figures. A passage that merits consideration is Gen 49:11 LXX (τὸν πῶλον τῆς ὄνου αὐτοῦ), which contains the

---

44. Menken, *Old Testament Quotations in the Gospel of John*, 91–95; cf. Köstenberger, "John," 472–73.

45. Thirty sons of Jair rode on 30 asses (Judg 10:3–4) and Abdon's 40 sons and 30 grandsons rode on 70 asses (Judg 12:14).

only concurrence of πῶλος and ὄνος in the Greek Scriptures. These two words are found at the end of the Zechariah citation in John 12:15, but do not match the reading of Zech 9:9 LXX. In the context of Gen 49:10–11, the portrait of Judah holding the scepter and the ruler's staff is prophetic of his royal progeny (cf. 1 Chr 5:2; Ps 78:67–68). Hence the use of πῶλος and ὄνος in Gen 49:11 LXX has a regal connection.[46] It is plausible that John's formulation of the Zechariah citation obtains lexical inspirations from this text in order to highlight Jesus' royal status. In any case, the donkey reference in John 12:14–15 is not an inconsequential detail in the story but rather points to the kingly identity of Jesus, of whom Zech 9:9 prophesies.

Earlier discussion has mentioned that John's citation of Zech 9:9 diverges from the MT/LXX in that the king appears in the gesture of "sitting" on (κάθημαι) not "mounting" (רכב/ἐπιβαίνω) the donkey. Maarten Menken believes that the "sitting" gesticulation in the Johannine entry scene is telling of Jesus' "royal dignity."[47] Menken calls attention to the biblical precedents of translating רכב as κάθημαι (Isa 19:1) or its cognate terms (e.g., ἐπικάθημαι in 2 Sam [2 Kgs LXX] 16:2; ἐπικαθίζω in 1 Kgs [3 Kgs LXX] 1:38, 44) and to the scriptural references to God or the king "sitting" on the throne.[48] Specifically, the passage 1 Kgs 1:38–44, which has received attention, articulates Solomon's "sitting" on the mule as symbolic of his forthcoming "sitting" upon the throne of Israel. This passage follows the narrative of the aged David affirming to Bathsheba that Solomon will succeed him to be king and "sit" on his throne (cf. 1 Kgs 1:13, 17, 20, 24, 27, 30, 35, 46, 48). David instructs that Solomon should "sit" (ἐπικαθίζω in 3 Kgs 1:38, 44 LXX but ἐπιβιβάζω in 3 Kgs 1:33 LXX; cf. רכב in 1 Kgs 1:33, 38, 44) on David's mule and be escorted to Gihon, where the coronation ceremony will take place. While the portrayal of a king sitting on a mule in 1 Kgs 1:38–44 corresponds to John's entry account, the fact that Solomon

---

46. Menken, *Old Testament Quotations in the Gospel of John*, 94–95.

47. Ibid., 93; Schuchard, *Scripture Within Scripture*, 81–82.

48. In the LXX, e.g., Solomon "sits" (κάθημαι/καθίζω) on the throne (1 Kgs [3 Kgs LXX] 1:13, 17, 20, 24, 27, 30, 35, 46, 48; 2:12, 19); God "sits" (ἐπικαθίζω) on the cherubim (2 Sam 22:11); God "sits" (καθίζω) on the mount of assembly and the highest mountains (Isa 14:13); God "sits" (κάθημαι) on the cloud (Isa 19:1). See Menken, *Old Testament Quotations in the Gospel of John*, 92–93; Schuchard, *Scripture Within Scripture*, 81.

rides the mule to Gihon, rather than to enter Jerusalem, indicates that this passage is not the principal background of this Gospel account.[49]

An OT text that escapes scholars' notice but is perhaps relevant to our inquiry is Zech 6:12–13. If the book of Zechariah is read as a unified whole, the promised king of Zech 9:9 most probably refers back to the Davidic "Branch" who has appeared in Zech 3:8–10 and 6:12–13. As envisaged in Zech 6:13, the Branch will rebuild Zion's temple and "sit" (καθίζω; רשׁי) on the throne. Given John's copious references to this prophetic book in general (see chapter 3) and the Gospel's allusions of Zech 3:10 in John 1:48 (cf. 1:50) and of Zech 9:9 in John 12:15 in particular, the Johannine verbal alteration in the Zechariah quotation from "mounting" to "sitting" (John 12:15) may serve to enhance the royal-messianic identification of Jesus, who is simultaneously the "king" in Zech 9:9 and the "Branch" in Zech 3:8–10 and 6:12–13. If this judgment is at least partly accurate, the portrayal of Jesus sitting on a donkey probably functions as a parabolic assertion of his kingship, though Jesus is not a nationalistic liberator as the gloated crowd supposes.

In evoking Zechariah's hopes concerning the end-time king, this Christological portrayal not only avows the identity of Jesus as Israel's king but also clarifies the nature of his kingship. Brunson claims that this portrayal presents Jesus as a warrior, by reason of the supposition that the Zechariah quotation in John 12:15 conjures up the combat overtones in the whole context of Zechariah 9. In response, it is true that the motif of Yahweh as a mighty warrior destroying Israel's foes holds a crucial place in Zechariah 9, especially verses 1–8. Yet there is no mention in this chapter that the king's function is martial or bellicose. On the contrary, the king is described as "humble" (Zech 9:9) and "speaking peace" (Zech 9:10; cf. in Mic 5:4 [5:5 Eng.]) to all nations. While royal figures might ride on donkeys in the ancient Near East, this kind of animal rarely relates to the notion of military power.[50] The king's profile in the setting of Zech 9:9–10 insinuates that Jesus, who fulfills this prophetic oracle, is a peaceful and universal savior (cf. John 12:20, 32, 47). In the Johannine context, the fact that Jesus rides on a donkey, instead of a warhorse (cf. 1 Kgs 4:26; Isa 31:1–3; Jer 17:19–25),[51] suggests that John's Christological interest in the

49. Tan, *The Zion Traditions and the Aims of Jesus*, 150.

50. Duguid, "Messianic Themes in Zechariah 9—14," 268; cf. Meyers and Meyers, *Zechariah 9—14*, 130; Peterson, *Zechariah 9—14 and Malachi*, 58.

51. Beasley-Murray, *John*, 210. In *Pss. Sol.* 17:33, the Davidic Messiah is described as relying not on "horse and rider and bow" but on God.

entry episode does not primarily lie in the warrior-king motif. The combat theme will come to the fore in John 12:31, which asserts that Jesus' death will lead to the defeat of the devil. However, the Christological depiction of John 12:14–15 shines the spotlight on Jesus as a peaceful king, who will bring salvation to the whole world.[52]

The action of Jesus mounting a donkey is simultaneously an "affirmation" and a "critique" of the people's honorific welcome of him into Jerusalem.[53] As the people joyfully cheer, Jesus comes in his Father's name and is indeed the awaited messianic king.[54] Yet against their wish, his mission is not to liberate the Jewish people from Rome and reinstate Israel's political fortunes. This interpretation that the crowd's conception of Jesus' kingship requires rectification is espoused by the evangelist's aside (John 12:17–18) that the crowd's enthusiasm towards Jesus is chiefly incited by a miracle, i.e., Lazarus' resurrection. In John's Gospel, this kind of "sign-based" faith is deemed as valid but inadequate to lead one to salvation (cf. John 2:23–24; 3:2–3; 6:30). Since the account of Jesus' entry into Jerusalem is tied to the Lazarus story, the fact that Martha does not seem to understand her messianic confession of Jesus as ὁ εἰς τὸν κόσμον ἐρχόμενος (John 11:27) suggests that the euphoric crowd's understanding of ὁ ἐρχόμενος ἐν ὀνόματι κυρίου (John 12:13) is most probably flawed. While some scholars consider Martha's faith paradigmatic, her address to Jesus simply as διδάσκαλος (John 11:28; cf. 11:8) and her interference of Jesus' act of raising Lazarus (John 11:39–40) are telling of her incomplete belief.[55] Thus the crowd in John 12:12–19, like other narrative characters who utter lofty Christological statements but do not fully apprehend their meaning, rightly recognizes Jesus' royal status but misconstrues the nature of his kingship. As a matter of fact, the evangelist's remark of the disciples' failure to grasp the true significance of the entry event before Easter (John 12:16) implies that the crowd is also in view.[56]

52. Köstenberger, "John," 472–74; Witherington, John's Wisdom, 222–23.

53. Daly-Denton, "The Psalms in John's Gospel," 126.

54. The crowd's acclamation at Jesus' arrival in Jerusalem can be viewed as parallel to the people's nationalistic attempt to make Jesus king (John 6:15).

55. Zimmermann, "The Narrative Hermeneutics of John 11," 90–93; Moloney, "Can Everyone Be Wrong? A Reading of John 11.1—12.8," 513–15; contra Conway, Men and Women in the Fourth Gospel, 141–43.

56. Carson, The Gospel according to John, 434.

Scriptural Witness and the Glorification of Jesus (John 12:16)

For the purpose of our research, the evangelist's statement in John 12:16 concerning the revelatory effect of Jesus' glorification is critical. As this statement asserts, the glorification of Jesus marks the watershed between the disciples' incomprehension and their comprehension of the biblical significance of Jesus' royal entrance into Jerusalem. Based on three deictic indicators (τό πρῶτον in v. 16a, ὅτε in v. 16b, and τότε in v. 16c), which map out three temporal moments or periods, this verse can be divided into three parts: (1) the (pre-Easter) time when Jesus arrives in Jerusalem (12:16a), (2) the time when Jesus is glorified (12:16b), and (3) the (post-Easter) time upon Jesus' glorification (12:16c).

ταῦτα οὐκ ἔγνωσαν αὐτοῦ οἱ μαθηταὶ τὸ πρῶτον (v. 16a) [57]
ἀλλ' ὅτε ἐδοξάσθη Ἰησοῦς (v. 16b)
τότε ἐμνήσθησαν ὅτι ταῦτα ἦν ἐπ' αὐτῷ γεγραμμένα καὶ ταῦτα ἐποίησαν αὐτῷ (v. 16c)

These deictic markers reveal John's conscious efforts in separating the events that occur before and after Easter—at least with regard to Jesus' entrance into Jerusalem. The neuter, plural demonstrative pronoun ταῦτα occurs thrice in John 12:16. Since such reiteration of pronouns is rare in the Fourth Gospel, the threefold use of ταῦτα within a single verse may serve to add importance to its content.[58] In the grammatical construction, the third occurrence of this pronoun denotes the object of the aorist indicative verb ἐποίησαν (v. 16c), whose subject is unclear. The perpetrators could be the disciples, who are the subjects of the preceding ἔγνωσαν (v. 16a) and ἐμνήσθησαν (v. 16c), or the perpetrator could be the crowd.[59] In the former case, this pronoun (ταῦτα) probably points to the disciples' acquisition of a donkey for Jesus to ride on—a narrative detail present in the synoptic traditions but absent from John's account. Thus, the disciples at first lack the theological insight into the things that they have done

57. Brown thinks that the pronoun αὐτοῦ in John 12:16a is not original (*The Gospel according to John*, 1:458).

58. Abbott, *Johannine Grammar*, 292–93, 461–62, 587 (§2395–96, 2621–22, 2757); cf. Morris, *The Gospel according to John*, 521, n. 51.

59. Bultmann, *The Gospel of John*, 418, n. 5.

to Jesus.[60] If the crowd is in view, the pronoun harks back to the tribute that the gloated people pay to Jesus (v. 13). What the disciples fail to fathom, then, is the import of the crowd's laudatory actions and words.[61] Since John explicitly speaks of Jesus rather than the disciples finding the donkey (v. 14a), it is probably best to treat the pronoun ταῦτα near the end of John 12:16 as generally referring to the event of Jesus' advent in Jerusalem, and his act of riding on a donkey in particular. Therefore, the evangelist insists that only after Jesus' glorification do the disciples come to understand that the manner in which Jesus enters Jerusalem fulfills the scriptural prophecies, specifically Ps 118:26 and Zech 9:9. It is worth noting that no extant Jewish literature dated to pre-100 CE unambiguously bears witness to a messianic reading of Zech 9:9.[62] While Zech 9:9 is interpreted as a messianic prophecy in later Judaism (e.g., *Gen. Rab.* 56:2; 75:6; 98:9),[63] on one occasion rabbi Joshua ben Levi declares—if the Jews are worthy, the Messiah will come on the clouds of heaven; otherwise, he will appear as "meek and sitting on an ass" (*b. Sanh.* 98a).[64] Despite the late date of the Mishnah, this rabbinic reference suggests that some Jews in the first century CE probably did not expect the Messiah-King to come to Jerusalem sitting on a lowly animal such as a donkey. This may partly explain the disciples' failure to call to mind the royal prophecy of Zech 9:9 at Jesus' arrival in Jerusalem.

The statement in John 12:16 that upon Jesus' glorification the disciples "remember" (μιμνήσκομαι) certain things and associate them with the Scripture is reminiscent of the evangelist's aside in John 2:22 (cf. 20:9). According to this early aside, the disciples "remember" (μιμνήσκομαι) Jesus' saying at the temple and believe the "Scripture" (γραφή) and his words upon his resurrection. In both of these verses, the verb μιμνήσκομαι does not simply mean a recollection of the event but an attaining of a

---

60. Morris takes this position (*The Gospel according to John*, 521).

61. Abbott seems to hold this view (*Johannine Grammar*, 461 §2621).

62. Tan, *The Zion Traditions and the Aims of Jesus*, 139, but Köstenberger notes that a possible reference to Zech 9:9 is present in 1QM XII, 13 ("John," 473). Unlike *Tg.* Zech 3:8 and 6:12 ("Branch" = Messiah), the king in *Tg.* Zech 9:9–10 is not identified as the Messiah. Levey believes that the lack of a messianic reference in the latter passage indicates that "the humble, suffering, and dying Messiah was not acceptable to the Jewish mind" (*The Messiah*, 100).

63. Köstenberger, "John," 473.

64. Ibid.; Bruce, "The Book of Zechariah and the Passion Narrative," 347.

deeper level of insight into the event's significance and especially its scriptural pertinence. The disciples' acquirement of this theological acumen is hinged upon a "temporal factor," namely that it could only come about after Jesus' death and resurrection.[65] In Johannine conceptualization, the "hour" of Jesus' glorification points to his death (e.g., John 7:39; 12:16, 23; 13:31), which is inseparable from his resurrection, ascension, and departure to the Father.[66] The conceptual unity between crucifixion and resurrection undergirds the Fourth Gospel's twofold assertion that the capability of the disciples' spiritual discernment is temporally dependent upon Jesus' glorification (John 12:16) and resurrection (John 2:22; 20:9).

In John's theological mosaic, the disciples' pre-Easter incapability of discerning the scriptural testimony of certain incidents in Jesus' life (including his death and resurrection) is partly due to the fact that the Spirit has not yet been bestowed on them. In this Gospel, the Spirit of truth (John 14:17; 15:26; 16:13; cf. 1 John 4:6)—also called the Paraclete (John 14:16, 26; 15:26; 16:7)—will not come to the disciples to enlighten their knowledge of truth until Jesus "is glorified" (John 7:39).[67] The Spirit's illuminating function is elaborated in detail in the farewell discourses. When the Spirit-Paraclete comes, he will "teach" (διδάσκω) the disciples all things and "remind" (ὑπομιμνῄσκω) them the teaching of Jesus (John 14:26), which is tantamount to that of the Father (cf. John 7:16–17; 8:28). The Spirit-Paraclete will also "bear witness to" (μαρτυρέω) Jesus (John 15:26). According to John 16:13–15, the Spirit of truth will "guide" (ὁδηγέω) the disciples into all truth and "tells" (ἀναγγέλλω) them what is yet to come; further, the Spirit will take what is of Jesus and "tell" it to the disciples.[68] In enabling the disciples to understand the truth, the Spirit not only grants to them the theological acumen to correlate the Scripture and certain events surrounding Jesus, but also provides a fresh way of reading the biblical texts through the hermeneutical prism that the crucified Jesus is the promised Messiah. Because the time of the Spirit's coming is con-

---

65. Carson, "Understanding Misunderstandings in the Fourth Gospel," 80–81; cf. Stuhlmacher, "Spiritual Remembering," 63.

66. Smith, *The Theology of the Gospel of John*, 119–22.

67. Chibici-Revneanu underlines the connection between the "glory" motif in John 7:39 and that in John 12:16. See Chibici-Revneanu, *Die Herrlichkeit des Verherrlichten*, 166–67.

68. Hamid-Khani, *Revelation and Concealment of Christ*, 337–41.

tingent upon Jesus' glorification, his death is the prerequisite of the Spirit's enlightening and edifying activities in the believing community.[69]

The Spirit's function is not to add novel revelation in addition to the existing revelation in the Scripture and from Jesus, who is the true locus of God's revelation (John 1:51).[70] Rather, the Spirit of truth enlightens the disciples so that they may grasp the Scripture's deeper meaning concerning the Messiah and perceive the scriptural witness to Jesus accordingly. From the evangelist's perspective, this deeper meaning (albeit veiled before Easter) is not foreign to the thought of the Scripture but is there "in" it. For John, Moses and the prophets wrote of Jesus (John 1:45); the whole Scripture bears witness to him (John 5:39); Abraham rejoiced when he saw Jesus' day (John 8:56); Isaiah saw Jesus or his glory in the Solomonic temple (John 12:41). While the Scripture has foretold the life of Jesus, the Christological signification of the biblical texts remains "hidden" until the revelatory moment of Jesus' death and resurrection. In the occasion of Jesus' entry into Jerusalem, the disciples, with the Spirit's illuminating help, recognize in post-Easter times that the manner of Jesus' arrival in the city fulfills Zechariah's prophecy of the peaceful and universal king (Zech 9:9). In effecting the bestowal of the Spirit and the disclosure of the Scripture's deeper signification, Jesus' death and resurrection (which are a unified event in Johannine thinking) turn out to be a striking corroboration of the authenticity of his royal-messianic identity.

Conclusion

We have analyzed the kinship-cross interaction in the entry scene (John 12:12–19), where a jubilant crowd hails Jesus as "the king of Israel" (v. 13) at his arrival in Jerusalem. It was underlined that this royal title on the lips of the festal people carries primarily a messianic overtone. This construal received support from the Johannine special references to "palm branches" and "the coming one" with respect to the people's welcome of Jesus, references that intimate their (incorrect) royal-messianic perception of Jesus' identity. While examining the Johannine re-contextualization of the

---

69. Chibici-Revneanu, *Die Herrlichkeit des Verherrlichten*, 167–68.

70. Beasley-Murray, *John*, 261. Hamid-Khani notes that the verb ἀναγγέλλω, which is found three times in John 16:13–15 regarding the Spirit's enlightening work among the disciples, frequently occurs in Isaiah and Jeremiah and some Jewish apocalyptic writings to express "the interpretation or clarification of a previous revelation which had been either veiled or obscured" (*Revelation and Concealment of Christ*, 359).

prophecy of Zech 9:9, we noted that the evangelist has omitted or modified certain prophetic elements in order to highlight the Christological features that directly pertain to his interest of composition. Moreover, in light of certain (royal) traditions in the OT, the evangelist's depiction of Jesus "sitting" on a "donkey" most probably bears a royal significance. The remark in John 12:16 about the disciples' post-Easter understanding of the entry event's significance indicates that Jesus' death is the precondition of their perceptive apprehension of the Zechariah oracle and Ps 118:26. We have attempted to read this Johannine notion about the disciples' post-Easter insight in the Scripture's "veiled" thrust in connection with the other notion regarding the Spirit's enlightening activity within the believing community. Our conclusion is that the cross motif in the entry episode serves to buttress the crucified Jesus' royal-messianic authenticity by articulating Jesus' death (and resurrection) as effectuating the scriptural witness to his royal messiahship.

8

Conclusion

W E HAVE ADVANCED THE state of scholarship by providing a thorough investigation of the kingship-cross interactions that take place in John's narrative prior to the passion account. The findings of our study have indicated that the cross motif in the Fourth Gospel serves the apologetic function of corroborating the royal-messianic legitimacy of the crucified Jesus. This function is seen in the Johannine correlation of the cross's achievement or result with certain royal-messianic expectations in the biblical and post-biblical Jewish traditions. Moreover, the cross motif buttresses the royal messiahship of Jesus by presenting his death as having the revelatory outcome of unveiling the Scripture's deeper meaning regarding the royal-messianic hope. The following paragraphs summarize the basic results of the foregoing discussion.

Summary

Chapter 1 called attention to the dearth of systematic research on the theological entailments of the kingship-cross link outside the passion account in John's Gospel. As noted in the survey of previous research on the kingship theme, several scholars play down the royal-messianic aspect of Johannine Christology on the ground that this Gospel shows minimal interest in Jesus' Davidic ancestry. By contrast, we have taken seriously into consideration John's stated aim of demonstrating that Jesus is the Messiah (20:31). Regarding the topic of the death of Jesus, Johannine scholarship in the post-Bultmann-Käsemann era generally affirms the passion narrative's integral connection with the rest of the Fourth Gospel as well as the importance of Jesus' crucifixion in Johannine thinking. However, existing works have not adequately related the passion account's royal-messianic portrait of the crucified Jesus to other references to his death that can also be shown to pertain to royal messianism. In view of this lacuna in current scholarship regarding Jesus' kingship and death, we set out to investigate the significance and function of the cross in the Johannine portrayal of the crucified Jesus as the Messiah-King and to show that a backdrop of Jewish royal-messianic expectations must be invoked in order to understand it.

Chapter 2 established the basis for this investigation by demonstrating the organic connection between Jesus' kingship and messiahship in Johannine conceptualization. The brief analysis of Jewish royal-messianic phenomena during the late Second Temple age (ca. 200 BCE–100 CE) confirmed that the hope for a royal Messiah was not only alive but also gaining influence across various Jewish religious groups at this time. This circumstantial evidence significantly reinforced the probability that John's Gospel, which explicitly proclaims Jesus as Messiah and king, is very much interested in his identity as the Messiah-King. We also set forth internal evidence from this Gospel in order to demonstrate its concern with the royal-messianic identity of Jesus. Two observations proved helpful. First, we established a highly probable presence of a Davidic typology in John's narrative presentation of Jesus. Second, we noted the ways in which John's messianic intent (cf. 20:31) plays a determinative role in interpreting the kingship theme. That is to say, the messiahship of Jesus must be central to the Gospel's depiction of his kingship and so any view that relegates the former notion to the periphery of John's royal Christology is at the risk of interpretive fallacy.

Chapter 3 analyzed the kingship-cross interaction that takes place in the Nathanael account in John 1:43–51. This initial kingship-cross interplay in the Gospel story looks forward to the Messiah-King's death in the passion account and furthermore reveals John's attempt to reinterpret royal messianism in relation to the cross. To support the presence of royal-messianism in the Jesus-Nathanael dialogue, we examined a number of OT and post-biblical Jewish texts that bear witness to a royal-messianic use of the appellations "Son of God," "king of Israel," and "Son of Man." All of these three royal-messianic appellations are applied to Jesus in the Nathanael account in John 1. In particular, the epithet "king of Israel" in John 1:49 thematically links with the ensuing "Son of Man" vision (v. 51), which anticipates the revelation of divine glory in the cross. Thus the first occurrence of this royal epithet in the Fourth Gospel has the function of anticipating the Messiah-King's crucifixion, an event which will be unfolded in the passion narrative.

Chapter 4 dealt with the temple pericope in John 2:13–22, where the evangelist propounds the Christological redefinition of the temple as the crucified and risen body of Jesus. By surveying the relevant OT and extra-canonical Jewish writings, we emphasized that the notions of kingship and temple building/restoration are intimately connected in Jewish thought. Against this Jewish background and in view of the Johannine assertion that Jesus' death is necessary for the eschatological restoration of the temple, the cross motif in the temple passage amounts to a powerful argument for the royal messiahship of the crucified Jesus. Moreover, the Johannine quotation of a line from the Davidic Psalm 68:10 LXX adds a Davidic tint to Jesus' ardor for the temple. Within the Christological scheme of John's Gospel, this Davidic tint has the effect of giving credence to the contention that the crucified Jesus is the royal Messiah promised in the Scripture.

Chapter 5 examined the kingship-cross connection in the Nicodemus account (John 3:1–21). There the death of Jesus is expressed in terms of the "lifting up" of the Son of Man and is related to the intertwined notions of the kingdom of God and eternal life. We argued that the Johannine idea of the dispensing of the life in God's kingdom resonates with the OT and post-biblical Jewish royal-messianic traditions concerning the Messiah-King's involvement in implementing God's kingly dominion. Among the royal-messianic figures in the OT, the exalted and glorified Servant in Isa 52:13 LXX and the man-like figure in Dan 7:13–14 exhibit obvious correspondences with the Johannine depiction of the "lifting up" of Jesus as "the Son of Man." In the Nicodemus passage, the notion of "begotten of water and the Spirit" in John 3:5 (cf. 3:3) points forward to the declaration in John 7:39 that Jesus' death will lead to the divine bestowal of the Spirit on the believers. This statement regarding the Spirit's life-giving activity looks forward to the crucifixion of Jesus as the Messiah-King, an event on which the coming of the Spirit hinges.

Chapter 6 investigated the shepherd discourse in John 10. Our discussion of the kingship-cross interplay focused on the relevant themes in John 10:14–18, where repeated allusions to Jesus' death (and resurrection) in verses 14–15 and 17–18 encircle the critical statement in verse 16

regarding the constitution of "one flock" under Jesus as "one shepherd."
We observed that the Johannine designation of Jesus as εἷς ποιμήν (v. 16)
shares the same nominative form with the title ποιμὴν εἷς for the new
David in Ezek 37:24 LXX. We also proposed that this lexical parallel between John 10 and Ezekiel 37 may point to the Johannine interest in the
good shepherd's royalty, as the eschatological Davidic shepherd is denoted
"one king" in Ezekiel 37 but not in Ezekiel 34. In Johannine understanding,
the death of the shepherd will bring about the gathering of "other sheep"
outside the present fold and their confederation with the sheep inside.
As a result, there will be "one flock" under Jesus as the royal-messianic
shepherd. Since the constitution of a unified flock is the consequence of
Jesus' death, the crucifixion does not subvert but rather validates the royal
messiahship of Jesus. After analyzing the kingship-cross interaction in the
shepherd discourse, we provided an excursus about three passages (John
6:1–15; 11:46–53; 12:30–36) that lack explicit shepherd terminology but
nevertheless link together the notions of Jesus' kingship/death and Israel's
unification/gathering.

Chapter 7 treated the kingship-cross interplay in the entry account
in John 12:12–19. We called attention to the allusion to the death of Jesus
in the evangelist's post-Easter remark (v. 16), which commented on the
disciples' failure in apprehending the significance of the entry event on
the scene but their subsequent understanding of this event's deeper meaning after the glorification of Jesus. We argued that the basic notion of the
crowd's royal reception of Jesus is messianic in the traditional sense and
that this reception hints at the crowd's perception of Jesus as a victorious
liberator. Further, the Johannine depiction of Jesus entering Jerusalem on
a donkey evokes the prophecy with regard to the arrival of an end-time
king in Zion in Zech 9:9 and identifies Jesus with this awaited king accordingly. We noted that the description of Jesus' posture as "sitting" on
the donkey diverges from Zechariah's description of the king "mounting"
it, and further proposed that this Johannine description may serve to
highlight the royal status of Jesus. In addition to sundry OT texts about
the "sitting" of a royal figure that scholars have observed, we suggested
that the prophetic vision of the royal-messianic Branch "sitting" on the
throne in Zech 6:13 may have increased the evangelist's interest in the
"sitting" gesture of Jesus at his advent in Jerusalem. In John 12:16, the
Johannine commentary indicates that only after Jesus' death do the disciples come to grips with the fact that the manner in which Jesus arrives

in Jerusalem fulfills the prophecies of Ps 118:26 and especially Zech 9:9. Since the cross-event (i.e., the crucifixion, resurrection, and ascension as a unified whole) is the precondition of the disclosure of these scriptural texts' "hidden" royal-messianic thrust, the death of Jesus turns out to be critical for effectuating the scriptural witness to his royal messiahship.

Implications for Johannine Research

John's Royal Christology as (Davidic) Messianic

The results of our research carry implications regarding the place of messianism in the royal Christology of the Fourth Gospel. As noted in previous chapters, there has been a recent tendency in Johannine scholarship to divorce the notion of Jesus' kingship from that of his messiahship and to downplay the messianic dimension of John's royal Christology. Against the currents of this tendency, we have put forward arguments for holding together these notions in our scrutiny of the cross motif's literary-theological contribution to the Johannine assertion that the crucified Jesus is Israel's Messiah-King. Seen in light of the stated intent of John's Gospel (cf. 20:31), the messianic notion should be central to Johannine royal Christology. The findings of our investigation have confirmed that the evangelist is very much concerned with the royal-messianic identity of Jesus and has woven together the royal and the messianic notions in a dramatic presentation of his death.

It must be emphasized that we are not against the view that discerns a presence of the divine or prophetic aspect in John's portrait of Jesus as king. Nevertheless, the burden of proof remains on those who sever or undermine the linkage between the messianic and royal notions in the Christology of the Fourth Gospel. In particular, the results of our research call into question the proposals of Meeks and Lierman, which tend to overstate the influences of the Mosaic traditions to Johannine royal Christology. Both Meeks and Lierman set forth two basic arguments in support of their proposals, namely the dearth of explicit Davidic references in John's Gospel and the association of Moses with kingship in certain Jewish writings. In response to the first argument, we have underscored that a Davidic presence can be evoked by not only a mention of the name "David" (John 7:42) but also the intertextual references to the biblical traditions about him. In this respect, Daly-Denton has observed a number of Davidic allusions in this Gospel that are subtly at work through multiple references to the Psalms.[1] As for the Johannine lack of a mention of Jesus' Davidic ancestry, we have suggested that the Johannine emphasis on Jesus' heavenly provenance and the nationalistic connotations associated with traditional Davidic messianism are two highly probable reasons.

In response to the second argument, it should be noted that the examples of Moses's kingship given by Meeks that are roughly contemporary with the Fourth Gospel are primarily from the writings of Philo.[2] These examples do not directly pertain to the subject of royal messianism under our examination. Although Meeks puts forward some examples from the Samaritan and the rabbinic documents,[3] all of them are dated to the post-NT era and so their relevance for interpreting Johannine royal Christology is questionable. Lierman provides additional evidence from *Sib. Or.* 11:38–40, which speak of a "king" from Egypt. However, this passage does not mention Moses by name and the sibyl's reference to Moses's royalty is most likely based on his adoption by Pharaoh's daughter (cf. Exod 2:10). In the other few examples given by Lierman (e.g., Justus of Tiberias and Heb 3:1–6), the kingship of Moses is only implied and never directly stated. Therefore, without substantial evidence Lierman's claim that the basic parameters of John's royal Christology "rest . . . on Jewish traditions of Moses as king" remains an overstatement.[4] More probable, Johannine royal Christology centers on the messianic status of Jesus and strengthens this Christological presentation by subtly building up a Jesus-David typological correspondence.

Johannine Royal Messianism and Judaism

There are both similarities and differences between Johannine royal messianism and Jewish royal messianism. Both John and the Jews of his time looked forward to the arrival of the royal Messiah and associated him with the realization of certain Jewish hopes including the restoration of the temple, the inauguration of God's kingdom, and the unification of his people. In formulating his royal-messianic beliefs, it is notable that the evangelist has reinterpreted the contents of the traditional hopes in light of the cross-event. For instance, the eschatological temple of God is not

---

1. Daly-Denton, *David in the Fourth Gospel*.
2. Meeks, *The Prophet-King*, 100–130.
3. Ibid., 176–257.
4. Lierman, "The Mosaic Pattern of John's Christology," 217.

a magnificent edifice that stands at the top of Mount Zion but rather is the crucified and resurrected body of Jesus (John 2:21). Also diverging from the traditional hope about the reconstitution of the Davidic dynasty on earth, the kingdom that Jesus the Messiah-King will inaugurate is not of this world (John 18:36). Instead of fighting against the Romans and overthrowing their regime, Jesus the Messiah-King enters Jerusalem in a humble manner and the ruler that he will dethrone is "the prince of this world," i.e., Satan (cf. John 12:31). Unlike the contemporary Jews that held fast to a nationalistic hope, Jesus as the royal-messianic shepherd will establish "one flock" of God that transcends racial boundaries in encompassing both Jewish and Gentile believers. All these indicate that there is a certain degree of discontinuity between Johannine and Jewish royal messianisms.

Above all, the notion of a crucified Messiah-King is the most critical issue that sets apart Johannine royal messianism from its contemporary royal-messianic hopes. This can be seen in a succinct episode in John 12:32–34, where some Jews of Jesus' (and John's) day found this notion inconceivable. As this episode unfolds, a Jewish multitude is greatly puzzled upon hearing Jesus' statement of the Son of Man being "lifted up" from the earth and they cannot reconcile this statement with the belief about the Messiah's eternality. For John, the Messiah-King reigns from the cross and it is through crucifixion (and resurrection) that he accomplishes the royal-messianic tasks including the restoration of the temple, the bestowal of eternal life, and the unification of God's people. So while ascribing a royal-messianic significance to the cross, the evangelist has at the same time redefined royal messianism in relation to the death of Jesus. The corollary is that the royal messiahship of Jesus is inseparable from his crucifixion.

The Passion Narrative as an Integral Part of John's Gospel

As noted in chapter 1, Käsemann undermined the Johannine passion narrative's literary-theological connection with the remainder of the Fourth Gospel by alleging that this narrative is "a mere postscript which had to be included because John could not ignore this tradition nor yet could he fit it organically into his work."[5] Several scholars have responded to this claim of Käsemann and emphasized various ways in which the passion narra-

---

5. Käsemann, *The Testament of Jesus*, 7.

tive is related to the prior episodes. For example, Matera observes that the presentation of the crucified Jesus in the passion narrative resonates with three themes relating to Jesus' death (i.e., "on behalf of others," "cleansing," and "return") that surface in the first half of the Gospel.[6] Frey stresses that the repeated references to the "hour" of Jesus before the passion account (John 2:4; 4:21, 23; 7:30; 8:20; 12:23, 27; 13:1; 17:1) look forward to the arrival of this "hour," when Jesus is nailed to the cross.[7]

Few interpreters, however, have approached the passion narrative's relationship with other parts of John's Gospel from the viewpoint of the kingship theme. It is widely observed that the Johannine trial and crucifixion accounts (18:28–19:16a and 19:16b–37) contain a high concentration of kingship terms.[8] Twelve of the 21 occurrences of the terms βασιλεύς and βασιλεία in this Gospel reside in these accounts (18:33, 36 [3x], 37 [2x], 39; 19:3, 12, 14, 15 [2x], 19, 21 [2x]). The title "king of the Jews" occurs five times in 18:33, 39; 19:3, 19, 21 in John 18—19. In addition to explicit kingship vocabulary, several features of the Johannine portrayal of the crucified Jesus are suggestive of his royal status. These include the ironic coronation of Jesus by the Roman soldiers, who put a thorny crown and a purple robe on him (John 19:2). The soldiers also place a multilingual inscription (with the words "king of the Jews" on it) on the cross (John 19:19).

In view of the strong accent on the kingship of Jesus in the passion account, our analysis of the kingship-cross interactions that take place prior to this account has made a unique contribution to the ongoing debate regarding the Johannine passion narrative's relationship to the remainder of the Fourth Gospel. One of the observations in this study is that the cross motif occurs in close proximity and is linked with the kingship motif in a number of places in the first half of this Gospel (John 1:43–51; 2:13–22; 3:1–21; 10:14–18; 12:12–19). These kingship-cross interplays not only anticipate but also add weight to the graphic presentation of Jesus' death as the Messiah-King in the crucifixion episode. Undermining Käsemann's allegation that the Johannine passion narrative is inconsequential and a "mere postscript," the evidence that we have marshaled points in the di-

---

6. Matera, "'On Behalf of Others,' 'Cleansing,' and 'Return': Johannine Images for Jesus' Death," 161–78 (esp. 178).

7. Frey, "Die ,theologia crucifixi' des Johannesevangeliums," 197.

8. For the kingship-cross interplay in John's passion narrative, see Leung, "The Roman Empire and the Johannine Passion Narrative in Light of Jewish Royal Messianism."

rection that this narrative marks the zenith of the Johannine plot of the Messiah-King's death. Consequently, the findings of this study affirm the view that discerns an integral connection of the passion narrative with the rest of John's Gospel.

The Cross's Royal-Messianic Consequences and Apologetic Function

For the Jews of John's day, the crucifixion of Jesus was the greatest obstacle that had to be removed in order for their coming to believe in him as the royal Messiah. Facing this theological challenge, the evangelist contends that the crucifixion does not nullify the royal-messianic legitimacy of Jesus but rather paradoxically validates it. As McGrath says, "John was able to present the crucifixion of Jesus not merely as a scandal foreordained in Scripture, but as the expected victory of the Son of Man."[9]

Certain *consequences* of the death of Jesus are reminiscent of the Jewish hope concerning the works or the advent of the royal Messiah. With regard to the Jewish royal-messianic hope connected with the eschatological temple, John asserts that the body of the crucified and risen Jesus is the new temple (John 2:1–22). The implication of this assertion is that the realization of this restoration hope hinges on the cross-event and in fact results from it. With regard to the Jewish royal-messianic hope connected with the kingdom of God, John underlines that the "lifting up" of the Son of Man is the necessary means by which the "life" in this kingdom is bestowed on everyone who believes (John 3:14–15). Thus Jesus the Messiah-King goes on the cross in order to make eternal life available to all people belonging to God's kingdom. With regard to the Jewish royal-messianic hope connected with the unification of Israel, the evangelist stresses that by dying Jesus as the royal-messianic shepherd would gather all of his sheep and establish a unified flock under him (John 10:14–18). In this light, the constitution of "one" people of God is an achievement of the cross.

In addition to the three consequences of the cross above, we have observed that the death of Jesus has the revelatory effect of making known the "deeper" thrust of certain scriptural passages that is concerned about the Messiah-King (e.g., Zech 9:9 in John 12:15). From the Johannine perspective, this royal-messianic thrust lies in the scriptural

9. McGrath, *John's Apologetic Christology*, 215.

text but remains veiled until the crucifixion, resurrection, and exaltation of Jesus—incidents that are conceived of as a unified whole in Johannine thinking. Therefore, the significance of Jesus' death is related to the role and function of the Scripture as a witness to his royal messiahship. For John, the crucifixion of the Messiah-King is not a novel idea foreign to the Scripture. Rather, Jesus the Messiah-King dies according to the divine will and his death has been foretold in the Scripture.

Our study of the cross motif's contribution to the Johannine royal-messianic aim supports the view that the Johannine portrayal of Jesus' death (specifically, the portrayal of the cross's consequences or results) has an apologetic function. Dennis briefly addresses this subject in a section of his work that is entitled "Jesus' Death as an Issue of Apology and Legitimation."[10] His analysis is inspiring but touches primarily on the sociological dimension of the evangelist's apology within the presumable context of the religious conflicts between John's community and the Diaspora synagogue. Our research has obtained insights from Dennis's work but differs from it in that we have sought to give due notice to John's stated messianic objective and to the passion narrative's heavy stress on the kingship of Jesus. Given our specific focus on royal messianism, we have only briefly addressed three passages that are not of direct pertinence to our investigation but nevertheless can be related to the notion of Israel's unification as an outcome of the cross (see the excursus of chapter 6). In this respect, the cross's apologetic function in the Gospel of John as a whole is an area that merits further investigation. Such investigation may explore other probable consequences (or what Dennis calls the "effects") of Jesus' death that have not received attention in this study due to our specific interest in royal messianism.[11] It is hoped that this study and similar ones on the topic of the cross will lead to a better understanding of its significance in Johannine thinking and to a greater appreciation of what Jesus the Messiah-King has achieved through his death.

---

10. Dennis, *Jesus' Death and the Gathering of True Israel*, 324–31 (see p. 328 for the apologetic function of the "effects" of Jesus' death).

11. For Dennis's observation about the "effects" of Jesus' death, see ibid., 328.

Bibliography

Abbott, Edwin A. *Johannine Grammar*. London: Adam and Charles Black, 1906.

———. *Johannine Vocabulary: A Comparison of the Words of the Fourth Gospel with Those of the Three*. London: Adam & Charles Black, 1902.

Ahearne-Kroll, Stephen P. *The Psalms of Lament in Mark's Passion: Jesus' Davidic Suffering*. Cambridge: Cambridge University Press, 2007.

Allen, Leslie C. *Jeremiah: A Commentary*. Louisville: Westminster John Knox, 2008.

Allen, Ronald B. *Numbers*. Grand Rapids: Zondervan, 1990.

Anderson, Bernhard W. *Contours of Old Testament Theology*. Minneapolis: Fortress, 1999.

Anderson, Bernhard W., and Walter Harrelson, eds. *Israel's Prophetic Heritage: Essays in Honor of James Muilenburg*. New York: Harper & Brothers, 1962.

Anderson, Francis I., and David N. Freedman. *Micah: A New Translation with Introduction and Commentary*. New York: Doubleday, 2000.

Appold, Mark L. *The Oneness Motif in the Fourth Gospel: Motif Analysis and Exegetical Probe into the Theology of John*. Tübingen: J. C. B. Mohr, 1976.

Ashton, John. *Understanding the Fourth Gospel*. Oxford: Clarendon, 1993.

Atkinson, Kenneth. *I Cried to the Lord: A Study of the Psalms of Solomon's Historical Background and Social Setting*. Leiden/Boston: E. J. Brill, 2004.

———. *An Intertextual Study of the Psalms of Solomon*. Lewiston/Queenston/Lampeter: Edwin Mellen, 2000.

———. "On the Use of Scripture in the Development of Militant Davidic Messianism at Qumran: New Light from Psalm of Solomon 17." Pages 106–23 in *The Interpretation of Scripture in Early Judaism and Christianity: Studies in Language and Tradition*. Edited by Craig A. Evans. Sheffield: Sheffield Academic Press, 2000.

———. "On the Herodian Origin of Militant Davidic Messiah at Qumran: New Light from *Psalm of Solomon 17*." *Journal of Biblical Literature* 118 (1999): 435–60.

———. "Toward a Redating of the *Psalms of Solomon*: Implications for Understanding the *Sitz im Leben* of an Unknown Jewish Sect." *Journal for the Study of Pseudepigrapha* 17 (1998): 95–112.

———. "Herod the Great, Sosius, and the Siege of Jerusalem (37 B.C.E.) in Psalm of Solomon 17." *Novum Testamentum* 38 (1996): 313–22.

Aune, David E. "From the Idealized Past to the Imaginary Future: Eschatological Restoration in Jewish Apocalyptic Literature." Pages 147–77 in *Restoration: Old Testament, Jewish, and Christian Perspectives*. Edited by James M. Scott. Leiden/New York/Köln: E. J. Brill, 2001.

Aune, David E., Torrey Seland, and Jarl H. Ulrichsen, eds. *Neotestamentica et Philonica: Studies in Honor of Peder Borgen*. Leiden/Boston: E. J. Brill, 2003.

Ådna, Jostein. *Jesu Stellung zum Tempel: Die Tempelaktion und das Tempelwort als Ausdruck seiner messianischen Sendung.* Tübingen: J. C. B. Mohr, 2000.

Ball, David M. *"I Am" in John's Gospel.* Sheffield: Sheffield Academic Press, 1996.

Bammel, Ernst. "Φίλος τοῦ Καίσαρος." *Theologische Literaturzeitung* 77 (1952): 205–10.

Barker, Kenneth L., and Waylon Bailer. *Micah, Nahum, Habakkuk, and Zephaniah.* Nashville: Broadman & Holman, 1998.

Barrett, C. K., *The Gospel according to St. John: An Introduction with Commentary and Notes on the Greek Text.* Philadelphia: Westminster, 1978.

Bauckham, Richard, and Carl Mosser, eds. *The Gospel of John and Christian Theology.* Grand Rapids: Eerdmans, 2007.

Bauckham, Richard. *Jesus and the God of Israel: God Crucified and Other Studies on the New Testament's Christology of Divine Identity.* Grand Rapids: Eerdmans, 2008.

———. "Messianism according to the Gospel of John." Pages 34–68 *Challenging Perspectives on the Gospel of John.* Edited by John Lierman. Tübingen: J. C. B. Mohr, 2006.

———. *Gospel Women: Studies of the Named Women in the Gospels.* Grand Rapids: Eerdmans, 2002.

———. "Life, Death, and the Afterlife in Second Temple Judaism." Pages 80–95 in *Life in the Face of Death: The Resurrection Message of the New Testament.* Edited by Richard N. Longenecker. Grand Rapids: Eerdmans, 1998.

———. "Jesus' Demonstration in the Temple." Pages 72–89 in *Law and Religion: Essays on the Place of the Law in Israel and Early Christianity.* Edited by Barnabas Lindars. Cambridge: James Clarke & Co., 1988.

Bauer, Walter, Frederick W. Danker, W. F. Arndt, and F. W. Gingrich. *A Greek-English Lexicon of the New Testament and Other Early Christian Literature.* 3d ed. Chicago: The University of Chicago Press, 2000.

Beale, Gregory K., and D. A. Carson, eds. *Commentary on the New Testament Use of the Old Testament.* Grand Rapids: Baker Academic, 2007.

Beale, Gregory K. "The Problem of the Man from the Sea in IV Ezra 13 and Its Relation to the Messianic Concept in John's Apocalypse." *Novum Testamentum* 25 (1983): 182–88.

Beasley-Murray, George R. *John.* 2d ed. Nashville: Thomas Nelson, 1999.

———. *Jesus and the Kingdom of God.* Grand Rapids: Eerdmans, 1986.

Becker, Joachim. *Messianic Expectation in the Old Testament.* Translated by David E. Green. Philadelphia: Fortress, 1980.

Belle, Gilbert, van, ed. *The Death of Jesus in the Fourth Gospel.* Leuven: Leuven University Press, 2007.

Belle, Gilbert van, J. G. van der Watt, and P. Maritz, eds. *Theology and Christology in the Fourth Gospel: Essays by the Members of the SNTS Johannine Writings Seminar.* Leuven: Leuven University Press, 2005.

Belleville, Linda. "Born of Water and Spirit: John 3:5." *Trinity Journal* 1 (1980): 125–41.

Beuken, Wim, Seán Freyne, and Anton Weiler, eds. *Messianism Through History.* London: SCM; New York: Orbis, 1993.

Beutler, Johannes. "The Use of 'Scripture' in the Gospel of John." Pages 147–62 in *Exploring the Gospel of John: In Honor of D. Moody Smith.* Edited by R. Alan Culpepper and C. Clifton Black. Louisville: Westminster John Knox, 1996.

———. "Two Ways of Gathering: The Plot to Kill Jesus in John 11.47–53." *New Testament Studies* 40 (1994): 399–406.

————. "Der Alttestamentlich-Jüdische Hintergrund der Hirtenrede in Johannes 10." Pages 18–32 in *The Shepherd Discourse of John and Its Context*. Edited by Johannes Beutler and Robert T. Fortna. Cambridge: Cambridge University Press, 1991.

Beutler, Johannes, and Robert T. Fortna, eds. *The Shepherd Discourse of John and Its Context*. Cambridge: Cambridge University Press, 1991.

Bieringer, Reimund, Didier Pollefeyt, and Frederique Vandecasteele-Vanneuville, eds. *Anti-Judaism and the Fourth Gospel*. Louisville: Westminster John Knox, 2001.

Blass, F., and A. Debrunner. *A Greek Grammar of the New Testament and Other Early Christian Literature*. Translated and edited by Robert W. Funk. Rev. ed. Chicago: The University of Chicago Press, 1961.

Blenkinsopp, Joseph. *Isaiah 40—55: A New Translation with Introduction and Commentary*. New York: Doubleday, 2002.

Block, Daniel I. "Bring Back David: Ezekiel's Messianic Hope." Pages 167–88 in *The Lord's Anointed: Interpretation of Old Testament Messianic Texts*. Edited by Philip E. Satterthwaite, Richard S. Hess, and Gordon J. Wenham. Grand Rapids: Baker, 1995.

Boccaccini, Gabriele, ed. *Enoch and the Messiah Son of Man: Revisiting the Book of Parables*. Grand Rapids: Eerdmans, 2007.

Bock, Darrell L. "Blasphemy and the Jewish Examination of Jesus." Pages 589–67 in *Key Events in the Life of the Historical Jesus: A Collaborative Exploration of Context and Coherence*. Edited by Darrell L Bock and Robert L. Webb. Grand Rapids: Eerdmans, 2010.

Bockmuehl, Markus. "A 'Slain Messiah' in 4Q Serekh Milḥamah (4Q285)?" *Tyndale Bulletin* 43 (1992): 155–69.

————. "Why Did Jesus Predict the Destruction of the Temple?" *Crux* 25 (1989): 11–18.

Boer, Martinus C. de. *Johannine Perspectives on the Death of Jesus*. Kampen, the Netherlands: Kok Pharos, 1996.

————, ed. *From Jesus to John: Essays on Jesus and New Testament Christology in Honor of Marinus de Jonge*. Sheffield: Sheffield Academic Press, 1993.

Boismard, M. -É. *Moses or Jesus: An Essay in Johannine Christology*. Translated by B. T. Viviano. Minneapolis: Fortress, 1993.

————. "Le titre de 'fils de Dieu' dans les évangiles: Sa portée salvifique." *Biblical Interpretation* 72 (1991): 442–50.

Bordreuil, Pierre. "Les 'Graces de David' et 1 Maccabees II 57." *Vetus Testamentum* 31 (1981): 73–75.

Bracke, John M. *Jeremiah 30—52 and Lamentations*. Louisville: Westminster John Knox, 2000.

Braude, William G. *The Midrash on Psalms*. 2 volumes. New Haven: Yale University Press, 1959.

Brooke, George J. "Kingship and Messianism in the Dead Sea Scrolls." Pages 434–55 in *King and Messiah in Israel and Ancient Near East: Proceedings of the Oxford Old Testament Seminar*. Edited by John Day. Sheffield: Sheffield Academic Press, 1998.

————. *Exegesis at Qumran: 4QFlorilegum in Its Jewish Context*. Sheffield: JSOT Press, 1985.

Brown, Raymond E. *The Death of the Messiah: From Gethsemane to the Grave: A Commentary on the Passion Narratives in the Four Gospels*. 2 volumes. New York: Doubleday, 1994.

————. *The Community of the Beloved Disciple*. New York: Paulist Press, 1979.

———. *The Gospel according to John*. 2 volumes. New York: Doubleday, 1966.

Bruce, F. F. *The Gospel of John: Introduction, Exposition and Notes*. Grand Rapids: Eerdmans, 1983.

———. "The Book of Zechariah and the Passion Narrative." *Bulletin of the John Rylands University Library of Manchester* 43 (1961): 336–53.

Brunson, Andrew C. *Psalm 118 in the Gospel of John: An Intertextual Study on the New Exodus Pattern in the Theology of John*. Tübingen: J. C. B. Mohr, 2003.

Bryan, Steven M. *Jesus and Israel's Traditions of Judgment and Restoration*. Cambridge: Cambridge University Press, 2002.

Buitenwerf, Rieuwerd. *Book III of the Sibylline Oracles and Its Social Setting: With Introduction, Translation, and Commentary*. Leiden/Boston: E. J. Brill, 2003.

Bultmann, Rudolf. *Theology of the New Testament*. 2 volumes. Translated by Kendrick Grobel. New York: Scribner, 1951–1955. Repr., Waco: Baylor University Press, 2007.

———. *The Gospel of John: A Commentary*. Translated by George R. Beasley-Murray. Oxford: Basil Blackwell, 1971.

Burge, Gary M. *John*. Grand Rapids: Zondervan, 2000.

———. *The Anointed Community: The Holy Spirit in the Johannine Tradition*. Grand Rapids: Eerdmans, 1987.

Burger, Christoph. *Jesus als Davidssohn: Eine traditionsgeschichtliche Untersuchung*. Göttingen: Vandenhoeck & Ruprecht, 1970.

Burkett, Delbert. *The Son of Man in the Gospel of John*. Sheffield: Sheffield Academic Press, 1991.

Burridge, Richard A. *What Are the Gospels? A Comparison with Graeco-Roman Biography*. 2d ed. Grand Rapids: Eerdmans, 2004.

Busse, Ulrich. "Metaphorik und Rhetorik im Johannesevangelium: Das Bildfeld vom König." Pages 279–317 in *Imagery in the Gospel of John: Terms, Forms, Themes, and Theology of Johannine Figurative Language*. Edited by Jörg Frey, Jan G. van der Watt, and Ruben Zimmermann. Tübingen: J. C. B. Mohr, 2006.

———. "Open Questions on John 10." Pages 6–17 in *The Shepherd Discourse of John 10 and Its Context*. Edited by Johannes Beutler and Robert T. Fortna. Cambridge: Cambridge University Press, 1991.

Calvin, John. *Commentary on the Gospel according to John*. 2 volumes. Translated by William Pringle. Edinburg: Calvin Translation Society, 1847.

Carroll, John T., and Joel B. Green. *The Death of Jesus in Early Christianity*. Peabody: Hendrickson, 1995.

Carson, D. A. *The Gospel according to John*. Grand Rapids: Eerdmans, 1991.

———. "Understanding Misunderstandings in the Fourth Gospel." *Tyndale Bulletin* 33 (1982): 59–91.

Carson, D. A., and H. G. M. Williamson, eds. *It Is Written: Scripture Citing Scripture: Essays in Honour of Barnabas Lindars, SSF*. Cambridge: Cambridge University Press, 1988.

Carter, Warren. *John and Empire: Initial Explorations*. New York/London: T&T Clark International, 2008.

———. *Pontius Pilate: Portraits of a Roman Governor*. Collegeville: The Liturgical Press, 2003.

Casey, Maurice. *Son of Man: The Interpretation and Influence of Daniel 7*. London: SPCK, 1979.

Cassidy, Richard J. *John's Gospel in New Perspective: Christology and the Realities of Roman Power*. New York: Orbis Books, 1992.

Cathcart, Kevin J., and Robert P. Gordon. *The Targum of the Minor Prophets: Translated, with a Critical Introduction, Apparatus, and Notes*. Volume 14 of *The Aramaic Bible*. Wilmington: Michael Glazier, 1989.

Chae, Young S. *Jesus as the Eschatological Davidic Shepherd: Studies in the Old Testament, Second Temple Judaism, and in the Gospel of Matthew*. Tübingen: J. C. B. Mohr, 2006.

Charles, R. H. *The Apocrypha and Pseudepigrapha of the Old Testament*. 2 volumes. Oxford: Oxford University Press, 1913.

Charlesworth, James H., ed. *Jesus and Archaeology*. Grand Rapids: Eerdmans, 2006.

————, ed. *The Messiah: Developments in Earliest Judaism and Christianity*. Minneapolis: Fortress, 1992.

————. "From Messianology to Christology: Problems and Prospects." Pages 3–35 in *The Messiah: Developments in Earliest Judaism and Christianity*. Edited by James H. Charlesworth. Minneapolis: Fortress, 1992.

————, ed. *Old Testament Pseudepigrapha*. 2 volumes. New York: Doubleday, 1983–1985.

Charlesworth, James H., Hermann Lichtenberger, and Gerbern S. Oegema, eds., *Qumran-Messianism: Studies on the Messianic Expectations in the Dead Sea Scrolls*. Tübingen: J. C. B. Mohr, 1998.

Chazon, Esther G., David Satran, and Ruth A. Clements, eds. *Things Revealed: Studies in Early Jewish and Christian Literature in Honor of Michael E. Stone*. Leiden/Boston: E. J. Brill, 2004.

Chester, Andrew. *Messiah and Exaltation: Jewish Messianic and Visionary Traditions and New Testament Christology*. Tübingen: J. C. B. Mohr, 2007.

Chibici-Revneanu, Nicole. *Die Herrlichkeit des Verherrlichten: Das Verständnis der δόξα im Johannesevangelium*. Tübingen: J. C. B. Mohr, 2007.

Childs, Brevard S. *Isaiah*. Louisville: Westminster John Knox, 2001.

Chilton, Bruce D. "Salvific Exile in the Isaiah Targum." Pages 239–47 in *Exile: Old Testament, Jewish, and Christian Conceptions*. Edited by James M. Scott. Leiden/New York/Köln: E. J. Brill, 1997.

————. "The Temple in the Isaiah Targum." Pages 251–62 in *Jesus in Context: Temple, Purity, and Restoration*. Edited by Bruce D. Chilton and Craig A. Evans. Leiden/New York/Köln: E. J. Brill, 1997.

————. *The Isaiah Targum: Introduction, Translation, Apparatus and Notes*. Wilmington: Michael Glazier, 1987.

————. *The Glory of Israel: The Theology and Provenience of the Isaiah Targum*. Sheffield: JSOT Press, 1982.

Chilton, Bruce D., and Craig A. Evans. *Jesus in Context: Temple, Purity, and Restoration*. Leiden/New York/Köln: E. J. Brill, 1997.

Cho, Sukmin. *Jesus as Prophet in the Fourth Gospel*. Sheffield: Sheffield Phoenix Press, 2006.

Churgin, Pinkhos. *Targum Jonathan to the Prophets*. New Haven: Yale University Press, 1927. Repr., New York/Baltimore: KTAV Publishing House and the Baltimore Hebrew College, 1983.

Clarke, Ernst G. "Jacob's Dream at Bethel as Interpreted in the Targums and the New Testament." *Studies in Religion* 4 (1974–1975): 367–77.

Coakley, J. F. "Jesus' Messianic Entry into Jerusalem (John 12:12–19 Par.)." *Journal of Theological Studies* 46 (1995): 461–82.

Cole, R. Dennis. *Numbers*. Nashville: Broadman & Holman, 2000.

Collins, Adela Yarbro, and John J. Collins. *King and Messiah as Son of God: Divine, Human, and Angelic Messianic Figures in Biblical and Related Literature*. Grand Rapids: Eerdmans, 2008.

Collins, Adela Yarbro. "The Apocalyptic Son of Man Sayings." Pages 220–28 in *The Future of Early Christianity: Essays in Honor of Helmut Koester*. Edited by Birger A. Pearson. Minneapolis: Fortress, 1991.

Collins, John J. "Enoch and the Son of Man: A Response to Sabino Chialà and Helge Kvanvig." Pages 216–27 in *Enoch and the Messiah Son of Man: Revisiting the Book of Parables*. Edited by Gabriele Boccaccini. Grand Rapids: Eerdmans, 2007.

———. "The Third Sybil Revisited." Pages 3–19 in *Things Revealed: Studies in Early Jewish and Christian Literature in Honor of Michael E. Stone*. Edited by Esther G. Chazon, David Satran, and Ruth A. Clements. Leiden/Boston: E. J. Brill, 2004.

———. "Messianism in the Maccabean Period." Pages 97–109 in *Judaisms and Their Messiahs at the Turn of the Christian Era*. Edited by Jacob Neusner, William S. Green, and Ernest Frerichs. Cambridge: Cambridge University Press, 1987. Repr., 2003.

———. *The Apocalyptic Imagination: An Introduction to Jewish Apocalyptic Literature*. 2d ed. Grand Rapids: Eerdmans, 1998.

———. *The Scepter and the Star: The Messiahs of the Dead Sea Scrolls and Other Ancient Literature*. New York: Doubleday, 1995.

———. *Daniel: A Commentary on the Book of Daniel*. Minneapolis: Fortress, 1993.

———. "The Son of God Text from Qumran." Pages 65–82 in *From Jesus to John: Essays on Jesus and New Testament Christology in Honor of Marinus de Jonge*. Edited by Martinus de Boer. Sheffield: Sheffield Academic Press, 1993.

———. "The Kingdom of God in the Apocrypha and Pseudepigrapha." Pages 81–95 in *The Kingdom of God in 20th-Century Interpretation*. Edited by Wendell Willis. Peabody: Hendrickson, 1987.

———. *The Sibylline Oracles of Egyptian Judaism*. Atlanta: Scholars Press, 1974.

Collins, John J., and George W. E. Nickelsburg, eds. *Ideal Figures in Ancient Judaism: Profiles and Paradigms*. Chico: Scholars Press, 1980.

Collins, Terry. "The Literary Contexts of Zechariah 9:9." Pages 29–40 in *The Book of Zechariah and Its Influence*. Edited by Christopher Tuckett. Hampshire, U.K./Burlington; Ashgate, 2003.

Coloe, Mary L. *Dwelling in the Household of God: Johannine Ecclesiology and Spirituality*. Collegeville: The Liturgical Press, 2007.

———. "The Nazarene King: Pilate's Title as the Key to John's Crucifixion." Pages 839–48 in *The Death of Jesus in the Fourth Gospel*. Edited by Gilbert van Belle. Leuven: Leuven University Press, 2006.

———. *God Dwells with Us: Temple Symbolism in the Fourth Gospel*. Collegeville: The Liturgical Press, 2001.

Concord, Edgar W. *Zechariah*. Sheffield: Sheffield Academic Press, 1999.

Condra, Ed. *Salvation for the Righteous Revealed: Jesus amid Covenantal and Messianic Expectations in Second Temple Judaism*. Leiden/Boston: E. J. Brill, 2002.

Conway, Colleen M. *Men and Women in the Fourth Gospel: Gender and Johannine Characterization*. Atlanta: Society of Biblical Literature, 1999.

Cooper, Lamar E. *Ezekiel*. Nashville: Broadman & Holman, 1994.

Culpepper, R. Alan, and C. Clifton Black, eds. *Exploring the Gospel of John: In Honor of D. Moody Smith*. Louisville: Westminster John Knox, 1996.

Culpepper, R. Alan. *Anatomy of the Fourth Gospel: A Study in Literary Design*. Philadelphia: Fortress, 1983.

Cuss, Dominique. *Imperial Cult and Honorable Terms in the New Testament*. Fribourg, Switzerland: The University Press, 1947.

Daly-Denton, Margaret. "The Psalms in John's Gospel." Pages 119–37 in *The Psalms in the New Testament*. Edited by Steve Moyise and Maarten J. J. Menken. London/New York: T&T Clark International, 2004.

———. *David in the Fourth Gospel*. Leiden/Boston/Köln: E. J. Brill, 2000.

Dauer, Anton. *Die Passionsgeschichte im Johannesevangelium: Eine traditionsgeschichtliche und theologische Untersuchung zu Joh 18.1—19.30*. München: Kösel, 1972.

Davenport, Gene L. "The 'Anointed of the Lord' in Psalms of Solomon 17." Pages 67–92 in *Ideal Figures in Ancient Judaism: Profiles and Paradigms*. Edited by John J. Collins and George W. E. Nickelsburg. Chico: Scholars Press, 1980.

Davis, Ellen F., and Richard B. Hays, eds. *The Art of Reading Scripture*. Grand Rapids: Eerdmans, 2003.

Davis, Michael T., and Brent A. Strawn, eds. *Qumran Studies: New Approaches, New Questions*. Grand Rapids: Eerdmans, 2007.

Day, John, ed. *King and Messiah in Israel and the Ancient Near East: Proceedings of the Oxford Old Testament Seminar*. Sheffield: Sheffield Academic Press, 1998.

Deeley, Mary K. "Ezekiel's Shepherd and John's Jesus: A Case Study in the Appropriation of Biblical Texts." Pages 252–64 in *Early Christian Interpretation of Scriptures of Israel: Investigation and Proposals*. Edited by Craig A. Evans and James A. Sanders. Sheffield: Sheffield Academic Press, 1997.

Denaux, Adelbert, ed. *John and the Synoptics*. Leuven: Leuven University Press, 1992.

Dennis, John A. Review of Brant Pitre, *Jesus, the Tribulation, and the End of the Exile: Restoration Eschatology and the Origin of the Atonement. Review of Biblical Literature*. http://www.bookreviews.org (2008).

———. "The 'Lifting Up of the Son of Man' and the Dethroning of the 'Ruler of This World': Jesus' Death as the Defeat of the Devil in John 12, 31–32." Pages 677–91 in *The Death of Jesus in the Fourth Gospel*. Edited by Gilbert van Belle. Leuven: Leuven University Press, 2007.

———. *Jesus' Death and the Gathering of True Israel: The Johannine Appropriation of Restoration Theology in the Light of John 11.47–52*. Tübingen: J. C. B. Mohr, 2006.

Dettwiler, Andreas, and Jean Zumstein, eds. *Kreuzestheologie im Neuen Testament*. Tübingen: J. C. B. Mohr, 2002.

Dodd, C. H. *The Interpretation of the Fourth Gospel*. Cambridge: Cambridge University Press, 1953. Repr., 2005.

Duguid, Iain M. *Ezekiel*. Grand Rapids: Zondervan, 1999.

———. "Messianic Themes in Zechariah 9—14." Pages 265–80 in *The Lord's Anointed: Interpretation of Old Testament Messianic Texts*. Edited by Philip E. Satterthwaite, Richard S. Hess, and Gordon J. Wenham. Grand Rapids: Baker, 1995.

Duke, Paul D. *Irony in the Fourth Gospel*. Atlanta: John Knox, 1985.

Dunn, James D. G. *Jesus Remembered*. Grand Rapids: Eerdmans, 2003.

———. "'Son of God' as 'Son of Man' in the Dead Sea Scrolls? A Response to John Collins on 4Q246." Pages 198–210 in *The Scrolls and the Scriptures: Qumran Fifty Years After*. Edited by Stanley E. Porter and Craig A. Evans. Sheffield: Sheffield Academic Press, 1997.

Durham, John I. "The King as 'Messiah' in the Psalms." *Review and Expositor* 8 (1984): 425–35.

Eaton, John H. *Kingship and the Psalms*. London: SCM, 1976.

Ego, Beate, Armin Lange, and Peter Pilhofer, eds. *Gemeinde ohne Tempel: Zur Substituierung und Transformation des Jerusalemer Tempels und seines Kults im Alten Testament, antiken Judentum und frühen Christentum*. Tübingen: J. C. B. Mohr, 1999.

Ehrman, Bart D, ed. and trans. *The Apostolic Fathers*. Volumes 24 and 25 of *The Loeb Classical Library*. Cambridge, Massachusetts/London: Harvard University Press, 2003. Repr., 2005.

Elliott, Mark A. *The Survivors of Israel: A Reconsideration of the Theology of Pre-Christian Judaism*. Grand Rapids: Eerdmans, 2000.

Embry, Bradley. "The *Psalms of Solomon* and the New Testament: Intertextuality and the Need for a Re-Evaluation." *Journal for the Study of the Pseudepigrapha* 13 (2002): 93–136.

Emil Schürer. *The History of the Jewish People in the Age of Jesus Christ, 175 B.C. –A.D. 135*. Rev. ed. 2 divisions. 5 volumes. Edinburgh: T&T Clark, 1979.

Evans, Craig A., ed. *From Prophecy to Testament: The Function of the Old Testament in the New*. Peabody: Hendrickson, 2004.

———, ed. *Of Scribes and Sages: Early Jewish Interpretation and Transmission of Scripture*. London/New York: T&T Clark International, 2004.

———. "Messianic Hopes and Messianic Figures in Late Antiquity." *Journal of Greco-Roman Christianity and Judaism* 3 (2006): 21–22.

———, ed. *The Interpretation of Scripture in Early Judaism and Christianity: Studies in Language and Tradition*. Sheffield: Sheffield Academic Press, 2000.

———. "Qumran's Messiah: How Important Is He?" Pages 135–49 in *Religion in the Dead Sea Scrolls*. Edited by John J. Collins and Robert A. Kugler. Grand Rapids: Eerdmans, 2000.

———. "Jesus and the Continuing Exile of Israel." Pages 77–100 in *Jesus and the Restoration of Israel: A Critical Assessment of N. T. Wright's Jesus and the Victory of God*. Edited by Carey C. Newman. Downers Grove: InterVarsity; Carlisle, UK: Paternoster, 1999.

———. "David in the Dead Sea Scrolls." Pages 183–97 in *The Scrolls and the Scriptures: Qumran Fifty Years After*. Edited by Stanley E. Porter and Craig A. Evans. Sheffield: Sheffield Academic Press, 1997.

———. *Jesus and His Contemporaries: Comparative Studies*. Leiden/New York: E. J. Brill, 1995.

———. *Word and Glory: On the Exegetical and Theological Background of John's Prologue*. Sheffield: Sheffield Academic Press, 1993.

———. "Jesus' Action in the Temple: Cleansing or Portent of Destruction?" *Catholic Biblical Quarterly* 51 (1989): 237–70.

Evans, Craig A., and Stanley E. Porter, eds. *Dictionary of New Testament Background*. Downers Grove: InterVarsity, 2000.

Evans, Craig A., and James A. Sanders, eds. *Early Christian Interpretation of the Scriptures of Israel: Investigations and Proposals*. Sheffield: Sheffield Academic Press, 1997.

———, eds. *Paul and the Scriptures of Israel*. Sheffield: Sheffield Academic Press, 1993.

Evans, Craig A., and W. Richard Stegner, eds. *The Gospels and the Scriptures of Israel*. Sheffield: Sheffield Academic Press, 1994.

Fabry, Heinz-Josef. "Messianism in the Septuagint." Pages 193–205 in *Septuagint Research: Issues and Challenges in the Study of the Greek Jewish Scriptures*. Edited by Wolfang Kraus and R. Glenn Wooden. Atlanta: Society of Biblical Literature, 2006.

Farmer, William G. "The Palm Branches in John 12, 13." *Journal of Theological Studies* 3 (1952): 62–66.

Fee, Gordon D., and Douglas Stuart. *How to Read the Bible for All Its Worth*. 3d ed. Grand Rapids: Zondervan, 2003.

Felder, Stephen. "What Is the Fifth Sibylline Oracle?" *Journal for the Study of Judaism in the Persian, Hellenistic, and Roman Periods* 33 (2002): 363–85.

Feldmeier, Reinhard, Ulrich Heckel, and Martin Hengel, eds. *Die Heiden: Juden, Christen und das Problem des Fremden*. Tübingen: J. C. B. Mohr, 1994.

Fewell, Danna N., ed. *Reading between Texts: Intertextuality and the Hebrew Bible*. Louisville: Westminster John Knox, 1992.

Fishbane, Michael. "Inner Biblical Exegesis: Types and Strategies of Interpretation in Ancient Israel." Pages 19–37 in *Midrash and Literature*. Edited by G. H. Hartmann and G. Budick. New Haven: Yale University Press, 1986.

Fitzmyer, Joseph A. *The One Who Is to Come*. Grand Rapids: Eerdmans, 2007.

———. *The Dead Sea Scrolls and Christian Origins*. Grand Rapids: Eerdmans, 2000.

———. *The Semitic Background of the New Testament*. Grand Rapids: Eerdmans, 1997.

———. "4Q246: The 'Son of God' Document from Qumran." *Biblica* 74 (1993): 153–74.

———. "Aramaic Evidence Affecting the Interpretation of *Hosanna* in the New Testament." Pages 110–118 in *Tradition and Interpretation in the New Testament: Essays in Honor of E. Earle Ellis*. Edited by Gerald F. Hawthorne and Otto Betz. Grand Rapids: Eerdmans; Tübingen: J. C. B. Mohr, 1987.

Flint, Peter W. *The Dead Sea Scrolls and the Book of Psalms*. London/New York/Köln: E. J. Brill, 1997.

Flint, Peter W., and Patrick D. Miller, eds. *The Book of Psalms: Composition and Reception*. Leiden/Boston: E. J. Brill, 2005.

Flusser, David. *Judaism and the Origins of Christianity*. Jerusalem: Magnes, 1988.

Forestell, J. Terence. *The Word of the Cross: Salvation as Revelation in the Fourth Gospel*. Rome: Biblical Institute Press, 1974.

Fortna, Robert T. *The Fourth Gospel and Its Predecessor*. Philadelphia: Fortress, 1988.

———. *The Gospel of Signs: A Reconstruction of the Narrative Source Underlying the Fourth Gospel*. Cambridge: Cambridge University Press, 1970.

Freed, Edwin D. *Old Testament Quotations in the Gospel of John*. Leiden: E. J. Brill, 1965.

Freedman, David N., ed. *The Anchor Bible Dictionary*. 6 volumes. New York: Doubleday, 1992.

Freund, Richard A. "From Kings to Archons: Jewish Political Ethics and Kingship Passages in the LXX." *Scandinavian Journal of the Old Testament* 2 (1990): 58–72.

Frey, Jörg. "Edler Tod–wirksamer Tod–stellvertrender Tod–heilschaffender Tod: Zur narrativen und theologischen Deutung des Todes Jesu im Johannesevangelium." Pages 65–94 in *The Death of Jesus in the Fourth Gospel*. Edited by Gilbert van Belle. Leuven: Leuven University Press, 2007.

———. "Die ,theologia crucifixi' des Johannesevangeliums." Pages 169–238 in *Kreuzestheologie im Neuen Testament*. Edited by Andreas Dettwiler and Jean Zumstein. Tübingen: J. C. B. Mohr, 2002.

————. "Zur johanneischen Deutung des Todes Jesu." *Theologische Bücherei* 32 (2001): 346–62.

————. *Die eschatologische Verkündigung in den johanneischen Texten.* Volume 3 of *Die johanneische Eschatologie.* Tübingen: J. C. B. Mohr, 2000.

————. *Das johanneische Zeitverständnis.* Volume 2 of *Die johanneische Eschatologie.* Tübingen: J. C. B. Mohr, 1998.

————. "Heiden-Greichen-Gooteskinder: Zu Gestalt und Funktion der Rede von den im 4. Evamgelium." Pages 249–64 in *Die Heiden: Juden, Christen und das Problem des Fremden.* Edited by R. Feldmeier and U. Heckel. Tübingen: J. C. B. Mohr, 1994.

Frey, Jörg, Jan G. van der Watt, and Ruben Zimmermann, eds. *Imagery in the Gospel of John.* Tübingen: J. C. B. Mohr, 2006.

Frey, Jörg, and Udo Schnelle, eds. *Kontexte des Johannesevangeliums: Das vierte Evangelium in religions-und traditionsgeschichtlicher Perspektive.* Tübingen: J. C. B. Mohr, 2004.

Fuller, Michael E. *The Restoration of Israel: Israel's Re-Gathering and the Fate of the Nations in Early Jewish Literature and Luke-Acts.* Berlin/New York: Walter de Gruyter, 2006.

Gaston, Lloyd. *No Stone on Another: Studies in the Significance of the Fall of Jerusalem in the Synoptic Gospels.* Leiden: E. J. Brill, 1970.

Geffcken, Johannes. *Die Oracula Sibyllina.* Leipzig: J. C. Hinrichs, 1902.

Gentry, Peter J. "Rethinking the 'Sure Mercies of David' in Isaiah 55:3." *Westminster Theological Journal* 69 (2007): 279–304.

Glasson, T. Francis. "Davidic Links with the Betrayal of Jesus." *Expository Times* 85 (1973–1974): 118–19.

Goldingay, John. *Psalms.* 3 volumes. Grand Rapids: Eerdmans, 2006–2008.

Goldingay, John, and David Payne. *Isaiah 40—55.* 2 volumes. London/New York: T&T Clark International, 2006.

Goppelt, Leonhard. *Typos: The Typological Interpretation of the Old Testament in the New.* Translated by Donald H. Madvig. Grand Rapids: Eerdmans, 1982. Repr., Eugene: Wipf & Stock, 2002.

Green, Joel B. *The Death of Jesus: Tradition and Interpretation in the Passion Narrative.* Tübingen: J. C. B. Mohr, 1988.

Green, Joel B., Scot McKnight, and I. Howard Marshall, eds. *Dictionary of Jesus and the Gospels.* Downers Grove: InterVarsity, 1992.

Greenberg, Moshe. *Ezekiel 21—37: A New Translation with Introduction and Commentary.* New York: Doubleday, 1997.

Gruen, Erich S. *Heritage and Hellenism: The Reinvention of Jewish Tradition.* Berkeley/Los Angeles/London: University of California Press, 1998.

Hamid-Khani, Saeed. *Revelation and Concealment of Christ: A Theological Inquiry into the Elusive Language of the Fourth Gospel.* Tübingen: J. C. B. Mohr, 2000.

Hann, Robert R. "Christos Kyrios in PsSOL 17.32: 'The Lord's Anointed' Reconsidered." *New Testament Studies* 31 (1985): 620–27.

Hartmann, Geoffrey H., and Sanford Budick, eds. *Midrash and Literature.* New Haven: Yale University Press, 1986.

Harvey, A. E. *Jesus on Trial: A Study in the Fourth Gospel.* London: SPCK, 1976.

Hasel, Gerhard F. *New Testament Theology: Basic Issues in the Current Debate.* Grand Rapids: Eerdmans, 1978. Repr., 1990.

Hawthorne, Gerald F. and Otto Betz, eds. *Tradition and Interpretation in the New Testament: Essays in Honor of E. Earle Ellis.* Grand Rapids: Eerdmans; Tübingen: J. C. B. Mohr, 1987.

Hayes, John H., and Stuart A. Irvine. *Isaiah: The Eighth-Century Prophet.* Nashville: Abingdon, 1987.

Hayman, A. Peter. "The Man from the Sea." *Journal of Jewish Studies* 49 (1998): 1–16.

Hays, Richard B. *The Conversion of the Imagination: Paul as Interpreter of Israel's Scripture.* Grand Rapids: Eerdmans, 2005.

———. *Echoes of Scripture in the Letters of Paul.* New Haven: Yale University Press, 1989.

Heil, John P. *Blood and Water: The Death and Resurrection of Jesus in John 18-21.* Washington, D.C.: The Catholic Biblical Association of America, 1995.

Hempel, Charlotte, and Judith M. Lieu, eds. *Biblical Traditions in Transmission: Essays in Honour of Michael A. Knibb.* Leiden/Boston: E. J. Brill, 2006.

Hengel, Martin. *Studies in Early Christology.* Edinburgh: T&T Clark, 1995.

———. "The Old Testament in the Fourth Gospel." Pages 380–95 in *The Gospels and the Scriptures of Israel.* Edited by Craig A. Evans and W. Richard Stegner. Sheffield: Sheffield Academic Press, 1994.

———. *The Zealots: Investigations into the Jewish Freedom Movement in the Period from Herod I Until 70 A.D.* Translated by David Smith. Edinburgh: T&T Clark, 1989.

Hengel, Martin, and Anna M. Schwemer, eds. *Königsherrschaft Gottes und himmlischer Kult im Judentum, Urchristentum und in der hellenistischen Welt.* Tübingen: J. C. B. Mohr, 1991.

Hess, Richard S., and Carroll R., eds. *Israel's Messiah in the Bible and the Dead Sea Scrolls.* Grand Rapids: Baker Academic, 2003.

Hiers, Richard H. "Purification of the Temple: Purification for the Kingdom of God." *Journal of Biblical Literature* 90 (1971): 82–90.

Hill, John S. "τὰ βαΐα τῶν φοινίκων (John 12:13): Pleonasm or Prolepsis." *Journal of Biblical Literature* 101 (1982): 133–35.

Hogan, Karina M. *Theologies in Conflict in 4 Ezra: Wisdom Debate and Apocalyptic Solution.* Leiden/Boston: E. J. Brill, 2008.

Hollander, Harm W., and Marinus de Jonge. *The Testaments of the Twelve Patriarchs: A Commentary.* Leiden: E. J. Brill, 1985.

Horbury, William. *Messianism among Jews and Christians: Twelve Biblical and Historical Studies.* London/New York: T&T Clark, 2003.

———. *Jewish Messianism and the Cult of Christ.* London: SCM, 1998.

Horsley, Richard. "Palestinian Jewish Groups and Their Messiahs in Late Second Temple Times." Pages 14–29 in *Messianism Through History.* Edited by Wim Beuken, Seán Freyne, and Anton Weiler. London: SCM; New York: Orbis; 1993.

Horsley, Richard A., and John S. Hanson. *Bandits, Prophets, and Messiahs: Popular Movements at the Time of Jesus.* San Francisco: Harper & Row, 1985.

Hoskins, Paul M. *Jesus as the Fulfillment of the Temple in the Gospel of John.* Paternoster, 2006.

Hoskyns, Edwyn C. *The Fourth Gospel.* London: Faber and Faber, 1947.

Hossfeld, Frank-Lothar, and Erich Zenger. *Psalms 2: A Commentary on Psalms 51—100.* Minneapolis: Fortress, 2005.

Hultgård, Anders. "The Ideal 'Levite,' the Davidic Messiah and the Savior Figure in the Testaments of the Twelve Patriarchs." Pages 93–110 in *Ideal Figures in Ancient*

Judaism: Profiles and Paradigms. Edited by George W. E. Nickelsburg and John J. Collins. Chico: Scholars Press, 1980.

Hurowitz, Victor. *"I Have Built You an Exalted House": Temple Building in the Bible in Light of Mesopotamian and Northwest Semitic Writings.* Sheffield: JSOT Press, 1992.

Janowski, Bernd, and Peter Stuhlmacher, eds. *The Suffering Servant: Isaiah 53 in Jewish and Christian Sources.* Translated by David P. Bailey. Grand Rapids: Eerdmans, 2004.

Jarick, John. "The Temple of David in the Book of Chronicles." Pages 365–81 in *Temple and Worship in Biblical Israel: Proceedings of the Oxford Old Testament Seminar.* Edited by John Day. London/New York: T&T Clark, 2005.

Jervell, Jacob, and Wayne A. Meeks, eds. *God's Christ and His People: Studies in Honour of Nils Alstrup Dahl.* Oslo/Bergen/Tromsö: Universitets Forlaget, 1977.

Jobes, Karen H., and Moisés Silva. *Invitation to the Septuagint.* Grand Rapids: Baker Academic, 2000.

Jones, Larry P. *The Symbol of Water in the Gospel of John.* Sheffield: Sheffield Academic Press, 1997.

Jonge, Marinus de. *Jewish Eschatology, Early Christian Christology and the Testaments of the Twelve Patriarchs.* Leiden/New York/København/Köln: E. J. Brill, 1991.

———. "The Future of Israel in the Testaments of the Twelve Patriarchs." *Journal for the Study of Judaism in the Persian, Hellenistic, and Roman Periods* 17 (1986): 196–211.

———. *Jesus: Stranger from Heaven and Son of God.* Translated by John E. Steely. Missoula: Scholars Press, 1977.

———. "Nicodemus and Jesus: Some Observations on Misunderstanding and Understanding in the Fourth Gospel." *Bulletin of the John Rylands University Library of Manchester* 53 (1971): 337–59.

Juel, Donald. *Messianic Exegesis: Christological Interpretation of the Old Testament in Early Christianity.* Philadelphia: Fortress, 1988.

———. *Messiah and Temple: The Trial of Jesus in the Gospel of Mark.* Missoula: Scholars Press, 1977.

Kazen, Thomas. "Son of Man as Kingdom Imagery: Jesus between Corporate Symbol and Individual Redeemer Figure." Pages 87–108 in *Jesus from Judaism to Christianity: Continuum Approaches to the Historical Jesus.* Edited by Tom Holmén. London/New York: T&T Clark, 2007.

Kasemann, Ernst. *The Testament of Jesus according to John 17.* Translated by Gerhard Krodel. Philadelphia: Fortress, 1968.

Keener, Craig S. *The Gospel of John: A Commentary.* 2 volumes. Peabody: Hendrickson, 2003.

Kerr, Alan R. *The Temple of Jesus' Body: The Temple Theme in the Gospel of John.* Sheffield: Sheffield Academic Press, 2002.

Kiefer, Odo. *Die Hirtenrede: Analyse und Deutung von Joh 10,1–18.* Stuttgart: Verlag Katholisches Bibelwerk, 1967.

Kim, Seyoon. *Christ and Caesar: The Gospel and the Roman Empire in the Writings of Paul and Luke.* Grand Rapids: Eerdmans, 2008.

———. *The Son of Man as the Son of God.* Grand Rapids: Eerdmans, 1985.

Kindt, Tom, and Hans-Harald Müller. *The Implied Author: Concept and Controversy.* Berlin/New York: Walter de Gruyter, 2006.

Kinman, Brent. *Jesus' Entry into Jerusalem: In the Context of Lukan Theology and the Politics of His Day*. Leiden/New York/Köln: E. J. Brill, 1995.

Kittel, Gerhard, and Gerhard Friedrich, eds. *Theological Dictionary of the New Testament*. Translated by G. W. Bromiley. 10 volumes. Grand Rapids: Eerdmans, 1976.

Klausner, Joseph. *The Messianic Idea in Israel: From Its Beginning to the Completion of the Mishnah*. Translated by W. F. Stinespring. New York: Macmillan, 1955.

Klawans, Jonathan. "Moral and Ritual Purity." Pages 266–84 in *The Historical Jesus in Context*. Edited by Amy-Jill Levine, Dale C. Allison Jr., and John D. Crossan. Princeton: Princeton University Press, 2006.

———. *Impurity and Sin in Ancient Judaism*. Oxford: Oxford University Press, 2000.

Klink III, Edward W. *The Sheep of the Fold: The Audience and Origin of the Gospel of John*. Cambridge: Cambridge University Press, 2007.

Knobel, Peter. "Hallel." Page 296 in *The Oxford Dictionary of the Jewish Religion*. Edited by R. J. Zwi Werblowsky and Geoffrey Wigoder. New York/Oxford: Oxford University Press, 1997.

Knöppler, Thomas. *Sühne im Neuen Testament: Studien zum urchristlichen Verständnis der Heilshedeutung des Todes Jesu*. Neukirchen-Vluyn: Neukirchener Verlag, 2001.

———. *Die theologia crucis des Johannesevangeltums. Das Verständnis des Todes Jesu im Rahmen der johanneischen Inkarnations- und Erhöhungschristologie*. Neukirchen-Vluyn: Neukirchener Verlag, 1994.

Koester, Craig R. *The Word of Life: A Theology of John's Gospel*. Grand Rapids/Cambridge, U.K.: Eerdmans, 2008.

———. "Jesus' Resurrection, the Signs, and the Dynamics of Faith in the Gospel of John." Pages 47–7 in *The Resurrection of Jesus in the Gospel of John*. Edited by Craig R. Koester and Reimund Bieringer. Tübingen: J. C. B. Mohr, 2008.

———. "Messianic Exegesis and the Call of Nathanael (John 1:45–51)." *Journal for the Study of the New Testament* 39 (1990): 23–34.

———. "The Savior of the World (John 4.42)." *Journal of Biblical Literature* 109 (1990): 665–80.

———. *The Dwelling of God: The Tabernacle in the Old Testament, Intertestamental Jewish Literature, and the New Testament*. Washington, D.C.: The Catholic Biblical Association of America, 1989.

Koester, Craig R., and Reimund Bieringer, eds. *The Resurrection of Jesus in the Gospel of John*. Tübingen: J. C. B. Mohr, 2008.

Kooij, Arie van der. "The Septuagint of Zechariah as Witness to an Early Interpretation of the Book." Pages 53–64 in *The Book of Zechariah and Its Influence*. Edited by Christopher Tuckett. Hampshire, U.K./Burlington; Ashgate, 2003.

Köstenberger, Andreas J. *A Theology of John's Gospel and Letters*. Grand Rapids: Zondervan, 2009.

———. "John." Pages 415–512 in *Commentary on the New Testament Use of the Old Testament*. Edited by G. K. Beale and D. A. Carson. Grand Rapids: Baker Academic, 2007.

———. *John*. Grand Rapids: Baker Academic, 2004.

———. *The Missions of Jesus and the Disciples according to the Fourth Gospel*. Grand Rapids: Eerdmans, 1998.

———. "Jesus the Good Shepherd Who Will Also Bring Other Sheep (John 10:16): The Old Testament Background of a Familiar Metaphor." *Bulletin for Biblical Research* 12 (2002): 67–96.

Köstenberger, Andreas J., and Peter T. O'Brien. *Salvation to the Ends of the Earth: A Biblical Theology of Mission*. Downers Grove: InterVarsity; Nottingham, England: Apollos, 2001.

Kovacs, Judith L. "'Now Shall the Ruler of This World Be Driven Out': Jesus' Death as Cosmic Battle in John 12:20–36." *Journal of Biblical Literature* 114 (1995): 227–47.

Kraus, Hans-Joachim. *Theology of the Psalms*. Translated by Keith Crim. Minneapolis: Augsburg, 1986.

Kraus, Wolfgang, and R. Glenn Wooden, eds. *Septuagint Research: Issues and Challenges in the Study of the Greek Jewish Scriptures*. Atlanta: Society of Biblical Literature, 2006.

Kuhn, Karl A. "The 'One Like a Son of Man' Becomes the 'Son of God'" *Catholic Biblical Quarterly* 69 (2007): 22–42.

Kügler, Joachim. *Der andere König: Religionsgeschichtliche Perspektiven auf die Christologie des Johannesevangeliums*. Stuttgart: Verlag Katholisches Bibelwerk, 1999.

———. "Der andere König: Religionsgeschichtliche Anmerkungen zum Jesusbild des Johannesevangeliums." *Zeitschrift für die neutestamentliche Wissenschaft und die Kunde der älteren Kirche* 88 (1997): 223–41.

Kysar, Robert. *Voyages with John: Charting the Fourth Gospel*. Waco: Baylor University Press, 2005.

La Potterie, Ignace de. *The Hour of Jesus: The Passion and the Resurrection of Jesus according to John*. Translated by Dom G. Murray. New York: Alba House, 1989.

La Potterie, Ignace de, and Stanislas Lyonnet. *The Christian Lives by the Spirit*. Translated by John Morris. New York: Alba House, 1971.

Ladd, George E. *A Theology of the New Testament*. Rev. ed. Grand Rapids: Eerdmans, 1993.

Lang, Manfred. *Johannes und die Synoptiker: Eine redaktionsgeschichtliche Analyse von Joh 18—20 vor dem markinischen und lukanischen Hintergrund*. Göttingen: Vandenhoeck & Ruprecht, 1999.

Laniak, Timothy S. *Shepherds After My Own Heart: Pastoral Traditions and Leadership in the Bible*. Downers Grove: InterVaristy, 2006.

Laurin, Robert B. "The Question of Immortality in the Qumran 'Hodayot.'" *Journal of Semitic Studies* 3 (1958): 344–55.

Leung, Mavis M. "The Roman Empire and the Johannine Passion Narrative in Light of Jewish Royal Messianism." *Bibliotheca Sacra* (forthcoming).

———. "The Narrative Function and Verbal Aspect of the Historical Present in the Fourth Gospel." *Journal of the Evangelical Theological Society* 51 (2008): 703–20.

Levey, Samson H. *The Messiah: An Aramaic Interpretation. The Messianic Exegesis of the Targum*. Cincinnati/New York/Los Angeles/Jerusalem: Hebrew Union College Press, 1974.

Levine, Amy-Jill, Dale C. Allison Jr., and John Dominic Crossan, eds. *The Historical Jesus in Context*. Princeton: Princeton University Press, 2006.

Levine, Baruch A. *Numbers 21—36*. New York: Doubleday, 2000.

Levinson, Jerrold. *The Pleasures of Aesthetics: Philosophical Essays*. Ithaca/London: Cornell University Press, 1996.

Lierman, John, ed. *Challenges Perspectives on the Gospel of John*. Tübingen: J. C. B. Mohr, 2006.

———. "The Mosaic Pattern of John's Christology." Pages 210–34 in *Challenging Perspectives on the Gospel of John*. Edited by John Lierman. Tübingen: J. C. B. Mohr, 2006.

Lincoln, Andrew T. *The Gospel according to Saint John.* London: Continuum/New York: Hendrickson, 2005.

———. *Truth on Trial: The Lawsuit Motif in the Fourth Gospel.* Peabody: Hendrickson, 2000.

———. "'I am the Resurrection and the Life': The Resurrection Message of the Fourth Gospel." Pages 122–44 in *Life in the Face of Death: The Resurrection Message in the New Testament.* Edited by Richard N. Longenecker; Grand Rapids: Eerdmans, 1998.

Lindars, Barnabas, ed. *Law and Religion: Essays on the Place of the Law in Israel and Early Christianity.* Cambridge: James Clarke & Co.: 1988.

———. "The Son of Man in the Johannine Christology." Pages 43–60 in *Christ and Spirit in the New Testament: In Honour of C. F. D. Moule.* Edited by Barnabas Lindars and Stephen S. Smalley. Cambridge: Cambridge University Press, 1973.

———. *The Gospel of John.* London: Marshall, Morgan & Scott; Grand Rapids: Eerdmans, 1972.

Lindars, Barnabas, and Stephen S. Smalley, eds. *Christ and Spirit in the New Testament: In Honour of C. F. D. Moule.* Cambridge: Cambridge University Press, 1973.

Loader, William. *The Christology of the Fourth Gospel: Structure and Issues.* Bern/New York/Paris: Peter Lang, 1989.

Litwak, Kenneth D. "Echoes of Scripture?" *Currents in Research: Biblical Studies* 6 (1998): 260–88.

Loisy, Alfred. *Le Quatrième Évangile.* 2d ed. Paris: Émile Nourry, 1921.

Longenecker, Richard N., ed. *Life in the Face of Death: The Resurrection Message in the New Testament.* Grand Rapids: Eerdmans, 1998.

Longman III, Tremper. "The Messiah: Explorations in the Law and Writings." Pages 13–34 in *The Messiah in the Old and New Testaments.* Edited by Stanley E. Porter. Grand Rapids: Eerdmans, 2007.

Lozada, Francisco, and Tom Thatcher, eds. *New Currents Through John: A Global Perspective.* Leiden/Boston: E. J. Brill, 2006.

Lundbom, Jack R. *Jeremiah 21—36.* New York: Doubleday, 2004.

Lust, Johan. *Messianism and the Septuagint: Collected Essays by J. Lust.* Edited by K. Hauspie. Leuven: Leuven University Press, 2004.

McKane, William. *The Book of Micah: Introduction and Commentary.* Edinburgh, Scotland: T&T Clark, 1998.

McKelvey, R. J. *The New Temple: The Church in the New Testament.* Oxford: Oxford University Press, 1969.

McKnight, Scot. *Jesus and His Death: Historiography, the Historical Jesus, and Atonement Theory.* Waco: Baylor University Press, 2005.

McKnight, Scot, and Grant R. Osborne, eds. *The Face of New Testament Studies: A Survey of Recent Research.* Grand Rapids: Baker Academic, 2004.

McWhirter, Jocelyn. *The Bridegroom Messiah and the People of God.* Cambridge: Cambridge University Press, 2006.

Malina, Bruce J., and Richard L. Rohrbaugh. *Social Science Commentary on the Gospel of John.* Minneapolis: Fortress, 1998.

Manns, Frédéric. "Traditions targumiques en Jean 10, 1–30." *Revue des sciences religieuses* 60 (1986): 135–57.

Marcus, Joel. *The Way of the Lord: Christological Exegesis of the Old Testament in the Gospel of Mark.* Louisville: Westminster John Knox, 1992.

Martínez, Florentino G. "Divine Sonship at Qumran: Between the Old and the New Testament." Pages 109–32 in *Biblical Traditions in Transmission: Essays in Honour of Michael A. Knibb*. Edited by Charlotte Hempel and Judith M. Lieu. Leiden/Boston: E. J. Brill, 2006.

———. *Qumran and Apocalyptic: Studies on the Aramaic Texts from Qumran*. Leiden/New York/Köln: E. J. Brill, 1992.

Martínez, Florentino G., and Eibert J. C. Tigchelaar. *The Dead Sea Scrolls: Study Edition*. 2 volumes. Leiden/New York/Köln: E. J. Brill, 1997–1998.

Martyn, J. Louis. "A Gentile Mission that Replaced an Earlier Jewish Mission?" Pages 122–44 in *Exploring the Gospel of John: In Honor of D. Moody Smith*. Edited by R. Alan Culpepper and C. Clifton Black. Louisville: Westminster John Knox, 1996.

———. *History and Theology in the Fourth Gospel*. 2d ed. Nashville: Abingdon, 1979.

Matera, Frank. "'On Behalf of Others,' 'Cleansing,' and 'Return': Johannine Images for Jesus' Death." *Louvain Studies* 13 (1988): 161–78.

McGrath, James F. *John's Apologetic Christology: Legitimation and Development in Johannine Christology*. Cambridge: Cambridge University Press, 2001.

McWhirter, Jocelyn. *The Bridegroom Messiah and the People of God: Marriage in the Fourth Gospel*. Cambridge: Cambridge University Press, 2007.

Meeks, Wayne A. *The Prophet-King: Moses Tradition and the Johannine Christology*. Leiden: E. J. Brill, 1967.

Mendner, Siegfreid. "Nikodemus." *Journal of Biblical Literature* 77 (1958): 293–323.

Menken, Maarten J. J. *Old Testament Quotations in the Fourth Gospel: Studies in Textual Form*. Kampen, the Netherlands: Kok Pharos, 1996.

Metzger, Bruce M. *A Textual Commentary on the Greek New Testament*. 2d ed. Stuttgart: German Bible Society, 1994. Repr., 2002.

Meyers, Carol L., and Eric M. Meyers. *Zechariah 9—14: A New Translation with Introduction and Commentary*. New York: Doubleday, 1993.

Michaels, J. Ramsey. "Nathanael under the Fig Tree." *Expository Times* 78 (1966–1967): 182–83.

Midrash Rabbah: Leviticus. Translated by J. Israelstam and Judah J. Slotki. London: Soncino, 1939. Repr., 1961.

Mitchell, David C. *The Message of the Psalter: An Eschatological Programme in the Book of Psalms*. Sheffield: Sheffield Academic Press, 1997.

Miura, Yuzuru. *David in Luke-Acts: His Portrayal in the Light of Early Judaism*. Tübingen: J. C. B. Mohr, 2007.

Moloney, Francis J. "The Johannine Son of Man Revisited." Pages 177–202 in *Theology and Christology in the Fourth Gospel: Essays by the Members of the SNTS Johannine Writings Seminar*. Leuven: Leuven Unviersity Press, 2005.

———. "The Gospel of John as Scripture." *Catholic Biblical Quarterly* 67 (2005): 454–68.

———. "Can Everyone Be Wrong? A Reading of John 11.1—12.8." *New Testament Studies* 49 (2003): 505–27.

———. *The Gospel of John*. Collegeville: The Liturgical Press, 1998.

———. *The Johannine Son of Man*. 2d ed. Rome: LAS, 1978.

Moo, Douglas J. *The Old Testament in the Gospel Passion Narratives*. Sheffield, England: Almond Press, 1983.

Moo, Jonathan. "A Messiah 'Whom the Many Do not Know'? Reading 4 Ezra 5:6–7." *Journal of Theological Studies* 58 (2007): 525–36.

Morgan, Michèle. "La Promesse de Jésus à Nathanaël (Jn 1, 51)." *Revue des sciences religieuses* 67 (1993): 3–21.

Morris, Leon. *The Gospel according to John*. Rev. ed. Grand Rapids: Eerdmans, 1995.

Mowinckel, Sigmund. *He That Cometh*. Translated by G. W. Anderson. New York/ Nashville: Abingdon, 1956. Repr., Grand Rapids: Eerdmans, 2005.

Moyise, Steve, and Maarten Menken, J. J., eds. *Isaiah in the New Testament*. London/New York: T&T Clark International, 2005.

———, eds. *The Psalms in the New Testament*. Steve Moyise and Maarten J. J. Menken. London/New York: T&T Clark International, 2004.

Murphy, Frederick J. "The Temple in the Syriac Apocalypse of Baruch." *Journal of Biblical Literature* 106 (1987): 671–83.

———. *The Structure and Meaning of Second Baruch*. Atlanta: Scholars Press, 1985.

Müller, Ulrich B. "Zur Eigentümlichkeit des Johannesevangeliums. Das Problem des Todes Jesu." *Zeitschrift für die neutestamentliche Wissenschaft und die Kunde der älteren Kirche* 88 (1997): 24–55.

———. "Der Bedeutung des Kreuzestodes Jesu im Johannesevangelium." *Kerygma und Dogma* 21 (1975): 49–71.

Neusner, Jacob, William S. Green, and Ernest Frerichs, eds. *Judaisms and Their Messiahs at the Turn of the Christian Era*. Cambridge: Cambridge University Press, 1987. Repr., 2003.

Neusner, Jacob. *Genesis Rabbah: The Judaic Commentary to the Book of Genesis. A New American Translation*. 3 volumes. Atlanta: Scholars Press, 1985.

———. *Leviticus Rabbah*. 4 volumes. Lanham/New York/Oxford: University Press of America, 2001.

Newman, Carey C., ed. *Jesus and the Restoration of Israel: A Critical Assessment of N. T. Wright's Jesus and the Victory of God*. Downers Grove: InterVarsity; Carlisle, UK: Paternoster, 1999.

Nicholson, Godfrey C. *Death as Departure: The Johannine Descent-Ascent Schema*. Chico: Scholars Press, 1983.

Nickelsburg, George W. E. *Resurrection, Immorality, and Eternal Life in Intertestamental Judaism and Early Christianity*. Expanded ed. Boston: Harvard University Press, 2006.

———. *Jewish Literature Between the Bible and the Mishnah: A History and Literary Introduction*. 2d ed. Minneapolis: Fortress, 2005.

Nickelsburg, George W. E., and James C. VanderKam. *1 Enoch: A New Translation* Minneapolis: Fortress, 2004.

Nickelsburg, George W. E., and John J. Collins, eds. *Ideal Figures in Ancient Judaism: Profiles and Paradigms*. Chico: Scholars Press, 1980.

Nielsen, Helge K. "John's Understanding of the Death of Jesus." Pages 232–54 in *New Readings in John: Literary and Theological Perspectives*. Edited by Johannes Nissen and Sigfred Pedersen. Sheffield: Sheffield Academic Press, 1999.

Nissen, Johannes, and Sigfred Pedersen, eds. *New Readings in John: Literary and Theological Perspectives*. Sheffield: Sheffield Academic Press, 1997.

Nolland, John. "Sib. Or. III. 265–94: An Early Maccabean Messianic Oracle." *Journal of Theological Studies* 30 (1979): 158–67.

Obielosi, Dominic C. *Servant of God in John*. Frankurt: Peter Lang, 2008.

Oegema, Gerbern S. *The Anointed and His People: Messianic Expectations from the Maccabees to Bar Kochba*. Sheffield: Sheffield Academic Press, 1998.

O'Grady, John. "Good Shepherd and the Vine and the Branches." *Biblical Theology Bulletin* 8 (1978): 86–89.

O'Neill, J. C. "Son of Man, Stone of Blood (John 1:51)." *Novum Testamentum* 45 (2003): 374–81.

Orchard, Helen C. *Courting Betrayal: Jesus as Victim in the Gospel of John.* Sheffield: Sheffield Academic Press, 1998.

Osborne, Grant R. *The Hermeneutical Spiral: A Comprehensive Introduction to Biblical Interpretation.* 2d ed. Downers Grove: InterVarsity, 2006.

Painter, John. "Sacrifice and Atonement in the Gospel of John." Pages 287–311 in *Israel und seine Heilstraditionen im Johannesevangelium: Festgabe für Johannes Beutler SJ zum 70. Geburtstag.* Edited by Michael Labahn, Klaus Scholtissek, and Angelika Strotmann. Paderborn/München/Wien/Zürich: Ferdinand Schöningh, 2004.

———. *The Quest for the Messiah: The History, Literature, and Theology of the Johannine Community.* 2nd ed. Nashville: Abingdon/Edinburgh: T&T Clark, 1993.

Pearson, Birger A., ed. *The Future of Early Christianity: Essays in Honor of Helmut Koester.* Minneapolis: Fortress, 1991.

Peterson, David L. *Zechariah 9—14 and Malachi.* Louisville: Westminster John Knox, 1995.

Pietersma, Albert. "David in the Greek Psalter." *Vetus Testamentum* 30 (1980): 213–26.

Pitre, Brant. *Jesus, the Tribulation, and the End of the Exile.* Tübingen: J. C. B. Mohr, 2005.

Pomykala, Kenneth E. "Images of David in Early Judaism." Pages 33–46 in volume 1 of *Of Scribes and Sages: Early Jewish Interpretation and Transmission of Scripture.* Edited by Craig A. Evans. London/New York: T&T Clark International, 2004.

———. *The Davidic Dynasty Tradition in Early Judaism: Its History and Significance for Messianism.* Atlanta: Scholars Press, 1995.

Porter, Stanley E., ed. *The Messiah in the Old and New Testaments.* Grand Rapids: Eerdmans, 2007.

———, ed. *Hearing the Old Testament in the New Testament.* Grand Rapids: Eerdmans, 2006.

———. "The Use of the Old Testament in the New Testament: A Brief Comment on Method and Terminology." Pages 79–96 in *Early Christian Interpretation of the Scriptures of Israel: Investigation and Proposals.* Edited by Craig A. Evans and James A. Sanders. Sheffield: Sheffield Academic Press, 1997.

———. *Verbal Aspect in the Greek of the New Testament with Reference to Tense and Mood.* New York: Peter Lang, 1989.

Porter, Stanley E., and Craig A. Evans, eds. *The Scrolls and the Scriptures: Qumran Fifty Years After.* Sheffield: Sheffield Academic Press, 1997.

Poulssen, Niek. *König und Tempel im Glaubenszeugnis des Alten Testamentes.* Stuttgart: Verlag Katholisches Bibelwerk, 1967.

Powell, Mark A. *What Is Narrative Criticism?* Minneapolis: Fortress, 1990.

Puech, Émile. "Messianism, Resurrection, and Eschatology at Qumran and in the New Testament." Pages 235–56 in *The Community of the Renewed Covenant: The Notre Dame Symposium on the Dead Sea Scrolls.* Edited by Eugene Ulrich and James C. VanderKam. Notre Dame: The University of Notre Dame Press, 1994.

Pyle, William T. "Understanding the Misunderstanding Sequences in the Gospel of John." *Faith and Mission* 11 (1994): 26–47.

Rabinowitz, Peter J. *Before Reading: Narrative Conventions and the Politics of Interpretation.* Columbus: Ohio State University Press, 1987. Repr., 1998.

————. "What Readers Do When They Read/What Authors Do When They Write." Pages 48–72 in *Authorizing Readers: Resistance and Respect in the Teaching of Literature*. Edited by Peter J. Rabinowitz and Michael W. Smith. New York/London: Teachers College, 1998.

————. "Truth in Fiction: A Reexamination of Audiences." *Critical Inquiry* 4 (1977): 121–41.

Rand, Jan A. du. "A Syntactical and Narratological Reading of John 10 in Coherence with Chapter 9." Pages 94–115 in *The Shepherd Discourse of John 10 and Its Context*. Edited by Johannes Beutler and Robert T. Fortna. Cambridge: Cambridge University Press, 1991.

Reim, Günter. *Studien zum alttestamentlichen Hintergrund des Johannesevangeliums*. Cambridge: The University Press, 1974.

Rensberger, David. *Johannine Faith and Liberating Community*. Philadelphia: The Westminster Press, 1988.

Renz, Thomas. *The Rhetorical Function of the Book of Ezekiel*. Boston/Leiden: E. J. Brill, 1999. Repr., 2002.

Reynolds, Benjamin E. *The Apocalyptic Son of Man in the Gospel of John*. Tübingen: J. C. B. Mohr, 2008.

————. "The 'One Like a Son of Man' According to the Old Greek of Daniel 7, 13–14." *Biblica* 89 (2008): 70–80.

Richey, Lance B. *Roman Imperial Ideology and the Gospel of John*. Washington, D.C.: The Catholic Biblical Association of America, 2007.

Ridderbos, Herman N. *The Gospel according to John: A Theological Commentary*. Translated by John Vriend. Grand Rapids: Eerdmans, 1997.

Roberts, J. J. "The Old Testament's Contribution to Messianic Expectations." Pages 39–51 in *The Messiah: Developments in Earliest Judaism and Christianity*. Edited by James H. Charlesworth. Minneapolis: Fortress, 1992.

Robinson, John A. T. *Twelve New Testament Studies*. London: SCM, 1962.

Rose, Martin, ed. *Johannes-Studien: Interdisziplinäre Zugänge zum Johannes-Evangelium*. Zürich: Theologischer Verlag, 1991.

Rose, Wolter H. *Zemah and Zerubbabel: Messianic Expectations in the Early Postexilic Period*. Sheffield: Sheffield Academic Press, 2000.

Rowe, Robert D. *God's Kingdom and God's Son: The Background to Mark's Christology from Concepts of Kingship in the Psalms*. Leiden/Boston/Köln: E. J. Brill, 2002.

Rowland, Christopher. *The Open Heaven: A Study of Apocalyptic in Judaism and Early Christianity*. Eugene: Wipf and Stock, 1982.

Ryle, Herbert E., and Montague R. James. ΨΑΛΜΟΙ ΣΟΛΟΜΩΝΤΟΣ. *Psalms of the Pharisees, Commonly Called the Psalms of Solomon*. Cambridge: Cambridge University Press, 1891.

Sailer, Bill. "Jesus, the Emperor, and the Gospel according to John." Pages 284–301 in *Challenging Perspectives on the Gospel of John*. Edited by John Lierman. Tübingen: J. C. B. Mohr, 2006.

Salier, Willis H. *The Rhetorical Impact of the Sēmeia in the Gospel of John*. Tübingen: J. C. B. Mohr, 2004.

Sanders, E. P. *Judaism: Practice and Belief, 63 BCE–66 CE*. London: SCM/Philadelphia: Trinity Press International, 1992. Repr., 1998.

————. *Jesus and Judaism*. London: SCM; Philadelphia: Fortress, 1985.

Satterthwaite, Philip E., Richard S. Hess, and Gordon J. Wenham, eds. *The Lord's Anointed: Interpretation of Old Testament Messianic Texts*. Grand Rapids: Baker, 1995.

Sayler, Gwendolyn B. *Have the Promises Failed? A Literary Analysis of 2 Baruch.* Chico: Scholars Press, 1984.

Schaefer, Konrad. *Psalms.* Collegeville: The Liturgical Press, 2001.

Schiffman, Lawrence H., and James C. VanderKam, eds. *Encyclopedia of the Dead Sea Scrolls.* 2 volumes. Oxford/New York: Oxford University Press, 2000.

Schnackenburg, Rudolf. *The Gospel according to St. John.* Translated by David Smith and G. A. Kon. 3 volumes. New York: Crossroad, 1987.

———. *God's Rule and God's Kingdom.* 2d enlarged ed. Translated by John Murray. New York: Herder and Herder, 1968.

Schnelle, Udo. "Cross and Resurrection in the Gospel of John." Pages 127–51 in *The Resurrection of Jesus in the Gospel of John.* Edited by Craig R. Koester and Reimund Bieringer. Tübingen: J. C. B. Mohr, 2008.

———. "Die Tempelreinigung und die Christologie des Johannesevangeliums." *New Testament Studies* 42 (1996): 359–73.

Scholtissek, Klaus. "Johannine Studies: A Survey of Recent Research with Special Regard to German Contributions II." *Currents in Rsearch: Biblical Studies* 9 (2001): 277–305.

Schreiber, Stefan. *Gesalbter und König: Titel und Konzeptionen der königlichen Gesalbtenerwartung in frühjüdischen und urchristlichen Schriften.* Berlin/New York: Walter de Gruyter, 2000.

Schuchard, Bruce G. *Scripture Within Scripture: The Interpretation of Form and Function in the Explicit Old Testament Citations in the Gospel of John.* Atlanta: Scholars Press, 1992.

Schüpphaus, Joachim. *Die Psalmen Salomos: Ein Zeugnis Jerusalemer Theologie und Frömmigkeit in der Mitte des vorchristlichen Jahrhunderts.* Leiden: E. J. Brill, 1977.

Schürer, Emil. *A History of the Jewish People in the Age of Jesus Christ.* Translated by Sophia Taylor and Peter Christie. Rev. ed. 2 divisions. 5 volumes. Edinburgh: T&T Clark, 1979.

Scott, James M., ed. *Restoration: Old Testament, Jewish, and Christian Perspectives.* Leiden/New York/Köln: E. J. Brill, 2001.

———, ed. *Exile: Old Testament, Jewish, and Christian Conceptions.* Leiden/New York/Köln: E. J. Brill, 1997.

Scrutton, Anastasia. "'The Truth Will Set You Free': Salvation as Revelation." Pages 359–68 in *The Gospel of John and Christian Theology.* Edited by Richard Bauckham and Carl Mosser. Grand Rapids: Eerdmans, 2008.

Segroeck, F. van, C. M. Tuckett, G. van Belle, and J. Verheyden, eds. *The Four Gospels: Festschrift Frans Neirynck.* Leuven: Leuven University Press, 1992.

Senior, Donald. *The Passion of Jesus in the Gospel of John.* Collegeville: The Liturgical Press, 1991.

Shepherd, Michael B. "Targums, the New Testament, and Biblical Theology of the Messiah." *Journal of the Evangelical Theological Society* 51 (2008): 45–58.

Smith, D. Moody. *John Among the Gospels.* 2d ed. Columbia: University of South Carolina Press, 2001.

———. *The Theology of the Gospel of John.* Cambridge: Cambridge University Press, 1995.

Smith, Gary V. *Isaiah 1—39.* Nashville: Broadman & Holman, 2007.

Stanton, Graham N., Bruce W. Longenecker, Stephen C. Barton, eds. *The Holy Spirit and Christian Origins: Essays in Honor of James D. G. Dunn.* Grand Rapids/Cambridge, U.K.: Eerdmans, 2004.

Stibbe, Mark W. G., ed. *The Gospel of John as Literature: An Anthology of Twentieth-Century Perspectives.* Leiden/New York/Köln: E. J. Brill, 1993.

———. *John as Storyteller: Narrative Criticism and the Fourth Gospel.* Cambridge: Cambridge University Press, 1992.

Stone, Michael E. *Fourth Ezra: A Commentary on the Book of Fourth Ezra.* Minneapolis: Fortress, 1990.

———. "The Question of the Messiah in 4 Ezra." Pages 209–24 in *Judaisms and Their Messiahs at the Turn of The Christian Era.* Edited by Jacob Neusner, William S. Green, and Ernest Frerichs. Cambridge: Cambridge University Press, 1987. Repr., 2003.

Strauss, Mark L. *The Davidic Messiah in Luke-Acts: The Promise and Its Fulfillment in Lukan Christology.* Sheffield: Sheffield Academic Press, 1995.

Stuckenbruck, Loren T. "Messianic Ideas in the Apocalyptic and Related Literature of Early Judaism." Pages 90–116 in *The Messiah in the Old and New Testaments.* Edited by Stanley E. Porter. Grand Rapids: Eerdmans, 2007.

Stuhlmacher, Peter. "Spiritual Remembering: John 14:26." Pages 55–68 in *The Holy Spirit and Christian Origins: Essays in Honor of James D. G. Dunn.* Edited by Graham N. Stanton, Bruce W. Longenecker, and Stephen C. Barton. Grand Rapids: Eerdmans, 2004.

Subramanian, Samuel. *The Synoptic Gospels and the Psalms as Prophecy.* London/New York: T&T Clark International, 2007.

Tan, Kim Huat. *The Zion Traditions and the Aims of Jesus.* Cambridge: Cambridge University Press, 1997.

Tate, Marvin E. *Psalms 51—100.* Dallas: Word, 1990.

Thatcher, Tom, and Stephen D. Moore, eds. *Anatomies of Narrative Criticism: The Past, Present, and Futures of the Fourth Gospel as Literature.* Leiden/Boston: E. J. Brill, 2008.

Thatcher, Tom, ed. *What We Have Heard from the Beginning: The Past, Present, and Future of Johannine Studies.* Waco: Baylor University Press, 2007.

Thettayil, Benny. *In Spirit and Truth: An Exegetical Study of John 4:19–26 and A Theological Investigation of the Replacement Theme in the Fourth Gospel.* Leuven/Paris/Dudley: Peeters, 2007.

Thiselton, Anthony C. *New Horizons in Hermeneutics.* Grand Rapids: Zondervan, 1992.

Thompson, Marianne M. "The Breath of Life: John 20:22–23 Once More." Pages 69–78 in *The Holy Spirit and Christian Origins: Essays in Honor of James D. G. Dunn.* Edited by Graham N. Stanton, Bruce W. Longenecker, and Stephen C. Barton. Grand Rapids: Eerdmans, 2004.

———. *The Humanity of Jesus in the Fourth Gospel.* Philadelphia: Fortress, 1988.

Tilborg, Sjef van. *Reading John in Ephesus.* Leiden: Brill, 1996.

Tournay, Raymond J. *Seeing and Hearing God with the Psalms: The Prophetic Liturgy of the Second Temple in Jerusalem.* Translated by J. Edward Crowley. Sheffield: Sheffield Academic Press, 1991.

Trafton, Joseph L. "The *Psalms of Solomon* in Recent Research." *Journal for the Study of Pseudepigrapha* 12 (1994): 3–19.

Troxel, Ronald L. *LXX-Isaiah as Translation and Interpretation: The Strategies of the Translator of the Septuagint of Isaiah.* Leiden/Boston: E. J. Brill, 2008.

Tuckett, Christopher, ed. *The Book of Zechariah and Its Influence.* Hampshire, U.K.; Burlington: Ashgate, 2003.

Turner, Max. "Atonement and the Death of Jesus in John—Some Questions to Bultmann and Forestell." *Evangelical Quarterly* 62 (1990): 99–122.

Ulrich, Eugene, and James VanderKam, eds. *The Community of the Renewed Covenant: The Notre Dame Symposium on the Dead Sea Scrolls.* Notre Dame: University of Notre Dame Press, 1994.

Urban, Christina. *Das Menschenbild nach dem Johannesevangelium: Grundlagen johanneischer Anthropologie.* Tübingen: J. C. B. Mohr, 2001.

VanderKam, James C. "Daniel 7 in the Similitudes of Enoch (1 Enoch 37—71)." Pages 291–304 in *Biblical Traditions in Transmission: Essays in Honour of Michael A. Knibb.* Edited by Charlotte Hempel and Judith M. Lieu. Leiden/Boston: E. J. Brill, 2006.

———. "Exile in Jewish Apocalyptic Literature." Pages 89–100 in *Exile: Old Testament, Jewish, and Christian Conceptions.* Edited by James M. Scott. Leiden/New York/ Köln: E. J. Brill, 1997.

———. "Messianism in the Scrolls." Pages 211–34 in *The Community of the Renewed Covenant: The Notre Dame Symposium on the Dead Sea Scrolls.* Edited by Ulrich Eugene and James C. VanderKam. Notre Dame: University of Notre Dame Press, 1994.

———. "Righteous One, Messiah, Chosen One, and Son of Man in 1 Enoch 37—71." Pages 169–91 in *The Messiah: Developments in Earliest Judaism and Christianity.* Edited by James H. Charlesworth. Minneapolis: Fortress, 1992.

VanGemeren, Willem A., ed. *New International Dictionary of Old Testament Theology and Exegesis.* Grand Rapids: Zondervan, 1997.

Vermes, Geza. *The Complete Dead Sea Scrolls in English.* Rev. ed. New York: Penguin Books, 2004.

———. *Jesus in His Jewish Context.* London: SCM, 1983. Philadelphia: Fortress, 1984. Repr., Minneapolis: Fortress, 2003.

———. "The Oxford Forum for Qumran Research Seminar on the Rule of War from Cave 4 (4Q285)." *Journal of Jewish Studies* 43 (1992): 85–90.

Wahlde, Urban C. von. "Archaeology and John's Gospel." Pages 523–86 in *Jesus and Archaeology.* Edited by James H. Charlesworth. Grand Rapids: Eerdmans, 2006.

Wallace, Daniel B. *Greek Grammar Beyond the Basics.* Grand Rapids: Zondervan, 1996.

Watkins, H. W. *The Gospel according to John: With Commentary.* Edited by Charles J. Ellicott. Grand Rapids: Zondervan, 1957.

Watt, Jan G. van der. *Family of the King: Dynamics of Metaphor in the Gospel According to John.* Leiden: E. J. Brill, 2000.

———, ed. *Salvation in the New Testament: Perspectives on Soteriology.* Leiden/Boston: E. J. Brill, 2005.

Watts, John D. W. *Isaiah 34—66.* Waco: Word, 1987.

———. *Isaiah 1—33.* Waco: Word, 1985.

Watts, Rikk E. "The Lord's House and David's Lord: The Psalms and Mark's Perspective on Jesus and the Temple." *Biblical Interpretation* 15 (2007): 307–22.

Wead, D. W. *The Literary Devices of John's Gospel.* Basel: Reinhardt, 1970.

Weidemann, Hans-Ulrich. *Der Tod Jesu im Johannesevangelium.* Berlin/New York: Walter de Gruyter, 2004.

Weissenrieder, Annette, Friederike Wendt, and Petra von Gemünden, eds. *Picturing the New Testament: Studies in Ancient Visual Images.* Tübingen: J. C. B. Mohr, 2005.

Wenham, Gordon J. *Genesis 16—50.* Dallas: Word, 1994.

———. *Numbers: An Introduction and Commentary.* Leicester, U.K.; Downers Grove: InterVarsity, 1981.

Westcott, Brooke F. *The Gospel according to St. John.* 2 volumes. London: John Murray, 1908.

Westermann, Claus. *Prophetic Oracles of Salvation in the Old Testament.* Translated by Keith Crim. Louisville: Westminster John Knox, 1991.

———. *Genesis 37—50: A Commentary.* Translated by John J. Scullion. Minneapolis: Augsburg, 1986.

Wikenhauser, Alfred. *Das Evangelium nach Johannes.* 2d ed. Regensburg: Verlag Friedrich Pustet, 1957.

Williams, Catrin H. "Isaiah in John's Gospel." Pages 101-16 in *Isaiah in the New Testament.* Edited by Steve Moyise and Maarten J. J. Menken. London/New York: T&T Clark International, 2005.

Willitts, Joel. *Matthew's Messianic Shepherd-King: In Search of "The Lost Sheep of the House of Israel."* Berlin/New York: Walter de Gruyter, 2007.

Wilson, Gerald H. "King, Messiah, and the Reign of God: The Royal Psalms and the Shape of the Psalter." Pages 391-409 in *The Book of Psalms: Composition and Reception.* Edited by Peter W. Flint and Patric D. Miller. Leiden: E. J Brill, 2005.

Winninge, Mikael. *Sinners and the Righteous: A Comparative Study of the Psalms of Solomon and Paul's Letters.* Stockholm: Almqvist & Wiksell, 1995.

Winsor, Ann R. *A King is Bound in the Tresses: Allusions to the Song of Songs in the Fourth Gospel.* New York: Peter Lang, 1999.

Wirgin, Wolf, and Siegfried Mandel. *The History of Coins and Symbols in Ancient Israel.* New York: Exposition Press, 1958.

Witherington, Ben. *John's Wisdom: A Commentary on the Fourth Gospel.* Louisville: Westminster John Knox, 1995.

Wolff, Hans W. *Micah: A Commentary.* Translated by Gary Stansell. Minneapolis: Ausburg, 1990.

Wolters, Al. "The Messiah in the Qumran Documents." Pages 75–89 in *The Messiah in the Old and New Testaments.* Edited by Stanley E. Porter. Grand Rapids: Eerdmans, 2007.

Wright, N. T. *The Resurrection of the Son of God.* Minneapolis: Fortress, 2003.

———. *Jesus and the Victory of God.* Minneapolis: Fortress, 1996.

———. *The New Testament and the People of God.* Minneapolis: Fortress, 1992.

Wright, Robert B. *The Psalms of Solomon: A Critical Edition of the Greek Text.* New York: T&T Clark, 2007.

Xeravits, Géza G. *King, Priest, Prophet: Positive Eschatological Protagonists of the Qumran Library.* Leiden/Boston: E. J. Brill, 2003.

Young, Edward J. *The Book of Isaiah.* 3 volumes. Grand Rapids: Eerdmans, 1972. Repr., 2000.

Zenger, Erich, ed. *Der Septuaginta-Psalter: Sprachliche und Theologische Aspekte.* Freiburg: Herder, 2001.

Zimmerli, Walter. *Ezekiel 1: A Commentary on the Book of the Prophet Ezekiel Chapters 1—24.* Translated by Ronald E. Clements. Philadelphia: Fortress, 1979.

———. *Ezekiel 2: A Commentary on the Book of the Prophet Ezekiel Chapters 25—48.* Translated by James D. Martin. Philadelphia: Fortress, 1983.

Zimmermann, Frank. "The Language, the Date, and the Portrayal of the Messiah in IV Ezra." *Hebrew Studies* 26 (1985): 203-18.

Zimmermann, Jean. "Intratextuality and Intertextuality in the Gospel of John." Pages 121–35 in *Anatomies of Narrative Criticism: The Past, Present, and Futures of the Fourth Gospel as Literature.* Edited by Tom Thatcher and Stephen D. Moore. Leiden/Boston: E. J. Brill, 2008.

Zimmermann, Johannes. *Messianische Texte aus Qumran: Königliche, priesterliche und prophetische Messiasvorstellungen in den Schriftfunden von Qumran.* Tübingen: J. C. B. Mohr, 1998.

―――. "Observations on 4Q246—The 'Son of God.'" Pages 175–90 in *Qumran-Messianism: Studies on the Messianic Expectations in the Dead Sea Scrolls.* Edited by James H. Charlesworth, Hermann Lichtenberger, and Gerbern S. Oegema. Tübingen: J. C. B. Mohr, 1998.

Zimmermann, Ruben. "The Narrative Hermeneutics of John 11: Learning with Lazarus How to Understand Death, Life, and Resurrection." Pages 75–101 in *The Resurrection of Jesus in the Gospel of John.* Edited by Craig R. Koester and Reimund Bieringer. Tübingen: J. C. B. Mohr, 2008.

―――. *Christologie der Bilder im Johannesevangelium: Die Christopoetik des vierten Evangeliums unter besonderer Berücksichtigung von Joh 10.* Tübingen: J. C. B. Mohr, 2004.

―――. "Jesus im Bild Gottes: Anspielungen auf das Alte Testament im Johannesevangelium am Beispiel der Hirtenbildfelder in Joh 10." Pages 81–116 in *Kontexte des Johannesevangeliums: Das vierte Evangelium in religions-und traditionsgeschichtlicher Perspektive.* Edited by Jörg Frey and Udo Schnelle. Tübingen: J. C. B. Mohr, 2004.

Zumstein, Jean. "L'interprétation de la mort de Jésus dans les discours d'adieu." Pages 95–119 in *The Death of Jesus in the Fourth Gospel.* Edited by Gilbert van Belle. Leuven: Leuven University Press, 2007.

Zwi Werblowsky, R. J., and Geoffrey Wigoder, eds. *The Oxford Dictionary of the Jewish Religion.* New York/Oxford: Oxford University Press, 1997.

Index of Authors

Index of Scripture

Old Testament

Made in the USA
Columbia, SC
23 November 2017